Recruiting on the Web

Smart Strategies for Finding the Perfect Candidate

Recruiting on the Web

Smart Strategies for Finding the Perfect Candidate

Michael Foster

McGraw-Hill

New York Chicago San Francisco Lisbon London
Madrid Mexico City Milan New Delhi San Juan
Seoul Singapore Sydney Toronto

The *McGraw-Hill* Companies

5 6 7 8 9 0 FGR/FGR 0 9

ISBN 0-07-138485-5

Editorial, design, and production services provided by CWL Publishing Enterprises, Madison, Wisconsin, www.cwlpub.com.

This publication is designed to provide accurate and authoritative information in regard to the subject matter covered. It is sold with the understanding that neither the author nor the publisher is engaged in rendering legal, accounting, or other professional service. If legal advice or other expert assistance is required, the services of a competent professional person should be sought.

> —*From a Declaration of Principles jointly*
> *adopted by a Committee of the American Bar*
> *Association and a Committee of Publishers*

McGraw-Hill books are available at special quantity discounts to use as premiums and sales promotions, or for use in corporate training programs. For more information, please write to the Director of Special Sales, McGraw-Hill, Two Penn Plaza, New York, NY 10121. Or contact your local bookstore.

For My Father

Who by example, taught me to work hard
and love my family.

Contents

Introduction

Powerful Ways to Find Great People

I n less than a decade the Internet has thoroughly transformed the recruitment process for global corporations and small local companies alike. Today, employers can post job ads to career hubs that reach millions of people a day, or choose from a shopping mall of over 40,000 boutique niche boards targeted to specialized candidates. Even better, they can drive traffic to their own job boards, where it's free to post jobs—and where they can follow a visitor's clicks, learn about what they like, assess their skills, and sweep them into a community of candidates to tap when they need new hires.

The Web also enables instant, enterprise-wide employee referral. It can match a staff member being downsized in Chicago with an internal opening in L.A.; and keep departed workers close by in alumni communities, so they can be rehired later, turned into new clients, or can refer their friends back to the company.

Managers who need new people can go to Google, run a search, and instantly find thousands of Web resumes and home pages that match their needs. With a single password, they can log in and search hundreds of resume banks at once, send e-mails simultaneously to dozens of candidates, direct them to an online screening tool—and schedule interviews for the best candidates first.

Headhunters can reach inside their target companies, rummage around, and find the right candidates without having to ruse their way past the gatekeepers at the front desk. They can find candidates with precise skills in Web forums, discussion groups, and mail lists; listen in for a while to see how smart they really are; and then make contact. Researchers can find employee directories, contact lists, membership and alumni rosters, attendee lists, and many more powerful resources inside publicly accessible servers scattered all over the Web.

Before job boards hit the Web, employers were paying thousands of dollars every Sunday for small ads in local newspapers. Recruiters were trying to reach candidates one at a time by telephone, and battling their way past receptionists, departmental assistants, and voice mail. Resumes were arriving in the mail, to be opened and routed to a stack, reviewed by someone in HR, routed to another stack, reviewed by the hiring manager, routed to more stacks and more hiring managers, and finally, stuffed into a file cabinet, or tossed into a dusty pile in a corner, into an archive box, or into the dumpster, never to be seen again.

Today, advertising is cheaper and searching for candidates is faster; the process of making contact, screening, assessing, and interviewing applicants has become more efficient; and resumes have become a ubiquitous digital asset—no more piles, just good clean electronic data that can be moved around, stored, and retrieved by any desktop with a link to the Web.

So, recruiting on the Web is terrific! What's not to like? Well, for starters, all this change can be a bit tough to get your arms around—and new solutions often produce new kinds of problems.

Web Recruiting: The Freeway and the Cow Path

Rapid change is always painful. Building a freeway may be the fastest way between two points, but it means bulldozing structures that have been stable and familiar for decades—and until the trees grow up next to it, it can be really ugly. But just paving over the old cow path won't buy you much. It's a little better to drive on, but doesn't make a lot of difference in getting somewhere.

The Web can be a freeway or a cow path. You can use it to create a whole new recruiting system—to collapse recruiting time, slash costs, streamline your hiring process and attract better talent—or you can post jobs on job boards and call it a day. Job boards are well-paved cow paths. They offer lower prices and better turn-around time, and they clean up the paper resume piles around the office. They are faster, cheaper, better newspapers that have moved online, and that's not a bad thing. But recruiting on the Web can be much more powerful and offer better ways to get to better candidates. It's more complex than just using the job boards—it's like building a freeway—but the payoffs can be huge. This book describes both approaches to recruiting on the Web: how to get the most out of job boards, and how to create a whole recruiting strategy and system using the most that the Web has to offer.

With different kinds of recruiting roads being built all over the Web, there are bound to be some messy traffic jams and missed signals. Here are just a few:

1. In a 2001 Society of Human Resource Managers (SHRM) survey, members overwhelmingly agree that employee referrals produce the most cost effective, highest quality hires, yet fewer than 15 percent of major companies surveyed by AIRS News in 2002 are using their intranets or the Web to offer enterprise-wide referral programs.

2. According to iLogos Research, over 90 percent of Global 500 corporations have a career center and routinely post jobs on their own Web site—yet they will spend millions of dollars this year to post them again on third-party job boards, while budgeting a fraction of that amount to drive traffic to their own sites.

3. Job boards have been so successful at attracting job seekers that they are now flooding their clients with a tidal wave of unwanted, unqualified applicants. As a result, employers spend huge amounts of time reviewing resumes and entering them into applicant tracking systems and resume banks, only to discover that marketing managers are applying for computer programming positions and college students for Vice President of Finance. To make matters worse, over 50 percent of resumes being reviewed and entered by many companies are duplicates.

4. At the same time they're swimming in unqualified job seekers, employers are still paying search firms and headhunters to find the tough candidates. Though this is good news for the third-party recruitment industry, the missed opportunity is that most large

employers have their corporate recruiters sorting through bad resumes, when they could easily train them to headhunt, using the same Internet resources their third-party vendors do.

The Web is a very powerful young medium and there's a big learning curve here for recruiters and employers alike. In the beginning, recruiting on the Web simply meant posting jobs to job boards. Today, the Web is part of every step in the recruiting cycle, and being able to use it effectively to find, screen, and hire the best talent is a baseline professional skill for executives, HR professionals, corporate recruiters, and hiring managers, as it is for third-party recruitment, staffing, and executive search firms.

How to Use This Book

Recruiting on the Web is a sprawling subject, with lots of twists, turns, and cul-de-sacs. In a market this young and moving this quickly it's impossible to know which big boards, niche boards, communities, or various flavors of applicant tracking systems will be standing, even three years from now. Some great ideas have come and gone since the first job boards hit the Web in 1995, but many important recruiting techniques, such as "active searching for passive candidates" (which our company, AIRS, introduced in 1998), are here to stay.

So, this book describes the cutting edge of recruiting; it paints a picture of the best practices today and makes some best guesses as to where recruiting on the Web is heading in the coming years.

If you are a business owner, HR executive, or talent officer, this book is an aerial map of the battlefield. To compete successfully for the best talent, you and your organization must understand how to recruit on the Web. Use this book as a guide to the organization and strategies you'll need to win.

If you are an HR or recruiting manager, this book is a primer for understanding your arsenal and positioning your troops. It will help you put your priorities in order and allocate your resources more effectively as you build a strong employee referral engine, establish a powerful recruiting Web site, post jobs, and equip your Internet research team and recruiters with the tools they need to capture the right candidates— faster.

If you are a corporate recruiter, a manager, or in charge of staffing for a small business, you'll want to absorb the hands-on best practices and step-by-step instructions for using job boards, search engines, and other Web tools effectively. This book will teach you to fire up your browser and find exactly the candidates you're looking for—and all their friends—wherever they may be hiding on the Web.

If you are a third-party recruiter, staffing, or executive search professional, every line of this book is critical competitive knowledge. It is your business to find the very best talent for your clients, and to do it faster than your competitors. And increasingly, you are competing with your clients' own recruiting force and with the tools they're acquiring to streamline you right out of the process.

The bottom line for professional recruiters? No company with access to the same free Internet tools you have and a way to train salaried staff recruiters to use them is going to want to pay you 30 percent recruiting fees if they can help it. Just to keep up you'll need to recruit people your clients can't find—shaving every minute and every dime out of the process as you go. That means having some serious Internet research skills that can take you past job boards and right inside the companies, colleges, and communities to the passive candidates inside.

The Internet is a twisted interchange of fiber channels, Web sites, documents, and data. The good news is we have enough experience today to untangle and align these resources in new ways, ways that enable you to find the people you need—better, cheaper, and faster than ever before.

As you move through the process in this book, you'll find at each step new models and tools to evaluate, decisions to make, and opportunities to stay on the cow path or to build on-ramps to a new freeway.

Acknowledgments

This book is a product of the lessons we've learned at AIRS over the past five years, as we've helped shape a new human capital industry. AIRS is a great, creative company bursting with ideas and talent—and I'm grateful to every one of the people who've had a hand in it's making. Quite a few deserve special thanks.

AIRS couldn't have hoisted itself up into the market without the intellect and moxie of Melissa Young, nor survived its first winter without our training guru and friend Bill Craib.

The secret to AIRS brand success has always been the strength and commitment of our Training Force. In particular, Susan Oxford, Candace Wright, Archar Smith, Patrick Whelan, Otis Collier, Tracey McGinnis and Laura Stoker are each outstanding professionals, great teachers and self-less mentors to our AIRS Alumni. I'd like to especially thank Susan and Laura—and our new comrade-in-arms, Sharon Cook, for helping me stand on my number in the last weeks of this project.

The AIRS show couldn't go on without Tiffanie Ross working the levers backstage, or the perpetual motion machine that Nathan Acker built from spare parts into our powerful e-marketing engine. AIRS portals and tools wouldn't exist without the Web design and engineering A-team of Mark Florence, Chuck Officer, Jay Undercoffler and Matt Swett. And AIRS could not have grown so quickly into its leadership role without Nancy Maney, Chris McDonald, and Julie Wall, and so many others who have worked so hard to build a great company. Thanks, you guys.

I owe a personal debt of gratitude to Chris Forman and Elizabeth Lundberg for their steadfast allegiance, unflinching determination and leadership. And a special thank you to my friend Tim McKegney, for all he does, for all of us—as he stands his post late into the Vermont night, every night.

As we've grown AIRS, we are fortunate to have learned from the best—and we 're grateful for the thousands of clients and friends we've made. A very special thanks to Lou Adler, Jenna Adorno, De'Ann Anderson, Colleen Aylward, Shawn Banerji, Bill Bargas, Tracy Barry, Tim Beaumont, Mark Berger, Keira Blazer, Yves Lermusiaux, John Charboneau, Austin Cooke, Brian Cox, Jason Craft, Betsy Dey, Don Firth, Kate Froelich, Hilary Gallagher, Bill Gaul, Tracy Godfrey, Bill Gunn, Wade Haught, Steven Helmholz, Linda Holcomb, John Hughes, Marc Hutto, Eric Iverson, Mark Jennings, Kate Kennedy, Carl Kutsmode, Joni Lampl, Eric Lane, Koen Lockefeer, Suely Lohr, Andy Macklin, Madeline Krazit, Mike Marschke, Ronan McCann, Barry MacLaughlin, Michael McNeal, Derek Mercer, Kathy Meyers, Sarah Mino, Steve Morley, Stewart Morris, Dan Nikolic, John Nolitt, Karen Osofsky, Chemine Peters, Gabrielle Pineau, Steve Pollack, Paul Rowson, Donna Rutledge, David Sabol, Julian Sanchez, Ray Schreyer, Lavonne Sheets, Jim Sims, Alice Snell, Todd Stout, Judi Sugiyama,

Ernie Sullivan, Keith Vencel, Bill Warren, Christina Wilkinson, Steven Wood, and Arthur Young.

Most importantly, I owe my deepest thanks to those I adore most—my incredible wife Carol, our six children, and the crazy menagerie of friends and assorted animals that swirl through Feet First Farm. Thank you Carol, Maxwell, Harrison, Meron, O'Keefe, Tariku, and Sofia for being the best reasons in the world to be the best I can be.

Part One

First Steps in the Search

1

A Blueprint for Recruiting on the Web

Recruiting great people has never been more important-but there's never been a recruiting toolset like the Web.. Buried among 2 billion Web pages are more than 40,000 job boards and resume banks, 200 million HTML resumes and home pages, and more than 2 million company Web sites—along with hundreds of thousands of colleges, professional organizations, user groups, news and trade publications, and forums and other communities based on skills, industry, and other business connectors.

The 350 million people on the Internet today are scattered throughout those pages: looking for jobs, reading the news, playing games, discussing their projects, learning new skills, working, playing, and collaborating at all hours of the day. It's a recruiter's dream and a time management nightmare.

To complicate matters further, for almost a decade now vendors everywhere have been scurrying to build better mousetraps for attracting, evaluating, and hiring candidates. So, besides 40,000 job boards, we now have thousands of Internet ad agencies, job posting companies, Web-based employee referral systems, corporate alumni centers, search engines, meta-search engines, and spiders that find candidates, as well as

3

several hundred applicant-tracking systems with screening and assessment options.

In 2000, Forrester Research and other analysts predicted that proprietary end-to-end recruiting systems would soon emerge to make order out of the chaos and save the day. But in 2001, the floor fell out of the market, the big contenders flamed out, and the one-stop Web recruiting business plans joined the other walking dead of the Internet.

We're left with a complicated, balkanized marketplace, filled with solutions that promise to be a global e-recruiting answer but only solve their own sliver of the puzzle. The experts, analysts, and consultants haven't helped much either. They're like the Indian parable of the three blind men and the elephant: one feels the tusk, one the foot, and one the tail. The man who feels the tusk is sure the elephant is a ploughshare. The one who feels the foot is sure the elephant is a tree, and the one who feels the tail insists that the elephant is a brush. The big thinkers that big corporations tend to look to in times of big change just haven't been able to see the whole elephant, either.

So, for the foreseeable future, the 2 billion Web pages, tens of millions of candidates, and thousands of Web-based recruiting vendors will remain a swirling soup. The promise of the Web is better, faster, cheaper recruiting. But how do you organize this confusing jumble to bring you higher-quality candidates, in less time, for less money?

First you need a clear understanding of the traditional recruitment process and the new options enabled by the Web—then you need a plan. In this chapter, we'll look at a blueprint for e-recruiting that transforms the important milestones along the old recruiting path into a new, sequential plan for recruiting on the Web. There are five stages to this new process:

1. **Recruit Your Friends:** Build employee referral and corporate alumni systems.
2. **Create or Enhance Your Organization's Recruiting Web Site:** Build and drive traffic to your own Web site—and build communities of candidates for just-in-time recruiting.
3. **Attract the Best Active Candidates:** Advertise to job seekers in career hubs, niche boards, and communities.
4. **Find Passive Candidates:** Use active search techniques to find candidates hidden inside companies, colleges, organizations, and other destinations.

5. **Assess Your Applicants:** Screen, test, and evaluate your pipeline with new Web-based tools.

At each stage there are opportunities to save money and time and to target better candidates by using the Web. Let's take a brief look at each in turn, and then at some ways to prepare the ground for a successful recruitment plan.

First: Recruit Your Friends

HR executives and recruitment professionals agree that an employee referral program is the best way to hire the best people. Yet most companies are more adept at managing search firms that charge 30 percent of the first year's salary than at administering programs that encourage employees to recruit their friends at a fraction of that cost.

At the same time, most companies have legions of ex-workers in the marketplace. Some have been recruited to companies that are potential customers; some may be working as consultants or have been hired by competitors. Wherever they've landed, these corporate alumni represent an asset that can be used to grow new business or be re-recruited as boomerang employees.

Your employees and alumni know your company, your culture, and your industry more intimately than anyone. They can sell candidates on your organization better than a third-party headhunter and can become a powerful recruiting force for your firm.

Today, relatively few companies are managing compelling, enterprise-wide employee referral systems. Most referral programs are locally managed, poorly conceived, and weakly promoted. Many are too restrictive, complicated, or stingy to be of much interest to employees. At the same time, they represent another set of forms to route and chase through the HR department, and so administrators tend to neglect, rather than nurture them.

But the Web offers a freeway-building solution. A Web-based referral system can automate the administrative and promotional activities required to run a powerful, company-wide referral system. A Web-based referral system can offer a one-stop, self-service interface, an internal job board; it can provide tracking tools for the employee, announce new programs, and keep all parties up to date.

Corporate alumni platforms are as easy to deploy as employee referral systems—most are a simple, moderated Web forum or mail list, with a calendar and networking bulletin board.

So, start close to home, with your resources at hand. Referrals and boomerang workers are among the lowest-cost, most reliable hires. Your first e-recruiting investment should be to deploy strong, Web-based employee and alumni referral systems.

Second: Create or Enhance Your Organization's Recruiting Web Site

It costs thousands of dollars for a big Sunday ad in a metropolitan newspaper and thousands more to post a bundle of jobs to the largest boards. But it only costs pennies to post jobs to your own job board.

Investing to build a comprehensive career center and job board on your own corporate site should be your next focus. Do to the monster job boards exactly what they've done to the newspapers: Step in front of their traffic, drive it to your own site, and lower your costs exponentially!

Job board postings and newspaper ads can only sell the job, whereas your own career center sells your company, culture, and opportunities for growth and advancement—a vision of what it will be like to contribute with a great team of people to grow a great company.

Your Web site has exactly the same reach as any job board: 350 million pairs of eyeballs at desktops all over the world. Until recently, the largest companies were spending millions of dollars every year to post jobs to job boards. Today, many are realizing they can get in front of job seekers and passive candidates where they work and play and attract them to a corporate Web site for a fraction of that cost.

Building your own media platform not only breaks the stranglehold of third-party media, it also increases market awareness and the quality of your candidates. Every kind of jobseeker in the world is surfing the big job boards; theoretically, only people who are interested in your industry, your company, or your opportunities will be visiting your site. This focused audience is self-profiling, and so of higher quality than any you can find at a job board.

Adding a career center to your corporate board takes some time, but very little capital. Most of the effort is in telling the story and organizing the information so that it is attractive and accessible. Job boards have become a low-cost, off-the-shelf commodity, so even this relatively complex component can be integrated very simply.

The cost justification is simple: Every single hire saves you money. You've saved the $350 job posting fee, the $1,000 newspaper ad, the $2,500 referral fee, or the $20,000 search fee.

But your career center does more than cut posting costs. It provides a focal point for your entire recruiting process, online and off. It is more than a source of candidates, it is your candidate funnel, the entry point to which you drive applicants, screen and assess them, then pass them into a resume bank or fast-track them to a hiring manager for an immediate interview.

To maximize its value, your team must understand where your targeted candidates gather, how to get ads in front of them, and how to attract, engage, profile, and capture them into communities once they arrive.

Community building is a powerful new paradigm that provides the key to a just-in-time supply chain of candidates. It closes the loop and keeps potential candidates close by, so you can tap them as you need them.

This career information center, job board, digital gateway, and community platform should be your second e-recruiting investment. You'll find much more information on these topics in Part II of this book.

Third: Attract the Best Active Candidates

Understanding the universe of job boards—how 40,000 boards can be organized into nine principal categories, how different business models attract different job seekers, and the kinds of candidates you'll find on each type of board—is the first step to lowering your Internet job posting costs and attracting better candidates.

By organizing the market, you'll be able to find the right boards faster. Understanding the various business models and the character of candidates you'll find on the big boards, niche boards, and in communities will help you better target and diversify your media campaign.

Your object is to post the fewest jobs necessary, in the least expensive job boards possible, yet reach the highest quality candidate pools. You'll find that the deeper you go into the Web and the farther you travel from the overcrowded big career hubs—in short, the more you reach into untapped reservoirs of passive candidates—the more successful you'll be in reaching the most experienced, most talented candidates at the lowest cost.

The trade-off is your time and learning curve. It is just plain simpler to post jobs on the big branded boards than learn to find, sort, and sample niche boards and communities. Like building an employee referral system or a career center, understanding how to go off the beaten path and use better resources to find better candidates takes effort and focus.

But it can be a powerful investment that delivers a high return. There is great competitive advantage in knowing where to go to find candidates who are happily employed and productively working away, hidden inside your competitor's companies, and how to reach them with a compelling message that drives them to your own opportunities. In fact, no other skill set is more central to recruiting.

Whether you are advertising, headhunting, or building communities, you need to be able to get away from the jostling competition, the inexperienced job seekers, and the swirling mass of data at the big job boards and figure out where your target candidates are gathering on the Web.

Once you know how to reach past the big boards and into niche communities, you can post ads to drive traffic to your own career center, post jobs to their job boards to find active, experienced candidates, and reach inside their Web sites to find links to resumes, home pages, member's names, directories, and contact lists.

So, understanding how to optimize your use of the big boards—while you learn to navigate the world beyond the career hubs—works on multiple levels to speed up your process, lower your costs, and help you recruit better candidates. It should be your third e-recruiting investment.

Fourth: Find Passive Candidates

The best candidates are working for your competitors today; they are not out shopping for a new job. That is the mantra of the executive search and recruitment industry, and it is absolutely true. Today, employers and recruiters are working with the same Internet toolset in a race to find these candidates.

Before the 1990s bubble-driven labor shortage hit, companies filled the vast majority of entry-level, mid-level, managerial, and even most executive positions through referral and newspaper ads. Only top executive placements and a fraction of the hardest-to-fill positions (most often technical or sales) were ever outsourced to headhunters.

Search firms and contingency recruiters were the shortest distance to candidates that employers simply could not reach otherwise, and they charged accordingly. The typical search fee ranged from 25 to 35 percent of a candidate's first year compensation, often including bonus and stock options. Because the typical position outsourced to search firms was an important manager, technical contributor, or executive, fees ranged from $25,000 to over $250,000.

Though quite a hurdle, companies willingly paid these fees for three reasons: First, they had neither the bandwidth nor desire to build their own Rolodexes of hard-to-find candidates. Second, there was a cultural taboo around directly calling into your competitors' offices to lure away their best workers. Third, and most importantly, the actual cost to recruit these few important workers represented a reasonable fraction of the annual corporate budgets.

But then the world changed, and the talent wars began. A roaring bull market, global expansion, hundreds of billions of dollars flowing to telecom infrastructure and Internet start-ups, and unbridled optimism sopped up every executive, manager, and knowledge worker in the marketplace.

To compete, companies had to grow, and fast. To grow, companies had to hire, and fast. To hire, companies had to headhunt, because the newspaper and job postings just didn't work fast enough and the best people were already working somewhere else. To headhunt, companies had to outsource, because they themselves did not have the tools, the mind-set, or the knowledge to headhunt.

In a year or two, companies looked up to find they weren't paying headhunting fees for a fraction of hard-to-find candidates; they were paying a 30 percent premium, on top of signing bonuses and perks, to headhunt everyone in sight. Companies were paying through the nose, recruiters were getting rich, and something had to give.

Traditional recruitment, like stock brokerage or real estate, is based on information brokerage. The delta between the actual cost to develop and store the information, and the fee charged is the arbitrage. So, if a recruiter has a database of hidden candidates they can pluck from, screen, and get hired, then the $25,000 or so average fee they charge has a lot of margin in it. As for the company—well, tough luck. If you don't have the database, you're stuck paying the fee.

But all of a sudden, companies did have the database. In fact, they had free desktop access to a larger database than any recruiter had ever assembled—and the majority of people in it were employed, passive candidates. In 1998, our company, AIRS, introduced the idea that recruiters and employers alike could go past the job boards and directly to companies, colleges, organizations, forums, publications, events, user groups, and other Internet communities to find candidates.

As the labor shortage deepened, and this new paradigm grew, decades old attitudes were challenged and changed. All of a sudden, corporations understood that labor was an imperative, strategic resource and that it was critical they learn to compete for candidates, as they've competed for customers all along.

Companies realized they could bypass the third-party recruiter by using Internet search tools and techniques to headhunt, thereby driving recruitment costs back down again. And recruiters woke up to find that e-recruiting knowledge and tools were absolutely vital to compete—not only with other recruiters, but with their own clients, as well.

In the most forward-looking organizations today, the taboo against headhunting competitors is long gone. In fact, more and more companies are realizing that recruitment is a competitive sales activity, not an administrative task. As a result, they are changing it from a general HR activity, to an independent focus, reporting to a Chief Talent Officer or other dedicated recruiting leader.

Knowing how to quickly and effectively reach into the Web to find and contact passive candidates is now baseline knowledge for HR professionals, corporate recruiters, hiring managers, small business owners, and search firms alike. The Web has leveled the playing field by giving everyone access to tools and a Rolodex that only headhunters could tap before.

Investing to understand the search techniques that take you to passive candidates will help you compete if you are a third-party recruiter and will save lots of time and money if you are an employer.

Fifth: Assess Your Applicants

In the old days, screening, testing, and evaluating candidates were expensive, time-consuming paper chores and, as a result, were often reserved for the few applicants who made it to the end of the process.

Today, the Web offers simple, low-cost tools to screen for criminal activities and drug use, to check credit history, employment, college credentials, and more, and to assess complex skills, aptitudes, and behaviors. There are even Web-based services that offer automated reference checking.

As a result, screening and testing are moving from the back end of the process to the front of the line. By funneling candidates through assessment tools as they travel through your site and apply for jobs, or as they play games with embedded skills tests or complete resume profiles with embedded personality indicators, you'll weed out ill-fitting candidates up front, before they consume recruiting, HR, and staff resources.

Many companies today put candidates through a gauntlet of team interviewing that can require a dozen people to take time from their day to meet and chat. This quickly becomes a discouraging time sink if candidates simply don't fit. In short, the better you screen and evaluate candidates up front, the more of everybody's time, money, and sanity you'll save.

Make Sure You're Attracting the Right Candidates

Before you venture out onto the Web, it's a good idea to create a strong recruitment message—and hone it as you go.

Whether you have 10 employees or 10,000, your company has a distinctive culture that reflects your values. Successful companies are built on shared priorities and teamwork, and the smartest headhunters know that a good cultural fit is an important predictor of success.

Building a recruiting process aimed at the wrong candidates is a waste of time, and hiring people who are liable to become unhappy can be a painful and costly mistake. It's important to understand what constitutes success in your organization and ensure that those traits are clearly and consistently projected in your ads and search activities.

The medium for this message is your recruitment brand. Branding is a simple but powerful baseline recruiting tool—and as important for small companies as it is for global corporations. A strong brand will attract more of the right candidates and discourage those with inconsistent values, and it will make your company more attractive overall.

Let's take a fast look at how any company, even a small one with a limited budget, can create a recruiting brand to make the hiring process more efficient and more effective.

Your Recruiting Brand

R ecruitment is a sales activity. First, you are selling candidates on an opportunity, then selling your best nominees back into your organization or client. Efficient sales are built on marketing campaigns that position the product or services for the consumer, and brands play an important part in the process.

Employment brands were born to help the largest global corporations attract the tens of thousands of people they needed to hire every year. In a booming bull market with an increasing labor shortage, these brands were designed to attract a mass of candidates—much like consumer brands are aimed at selling to as many undifferentiated customers as possible.

Today, recruiting brands have entered the mainstream, and are used by recruiters and companies of all sizes to project specific values, appeal to targeted candidates, and create a public vision of the workplace that serves to further their corporate mission as well.

Brands cut through the mass of information consumers are bombarded with daily. Their job is to reduce a complex buying decision to a simple default purchase. They do this through repetition and imagery, sending a consistent value message until it becomes familiar, and so trusted. The branded item becomes the customer's safest alternative.

This sequence works as well for prospective employees as it does for customers. By developing an attractive brand, you are positioning yourself to become the employer or recruiter of choice in your market space and becoming a magnet for the right candidates. A strong brand can be one of your most powerful recruitment tools.

But why worry about selling your company to candidates? Shouldn't they be selling themselves to you, instead? Sure, you're their customer, and a good candidate will sell you on the value he or she will add to your organization. But to attract the best candidates, you need to be prepared to sell your message first.

Sell Your Opportunities

Monster.com's advertising campaign summed it up pretty well: "Job Good. Life Good". Where people work, whom they work with, the kind of work they do—and how they describe their work to others—are important contributors to satisfaction and self-esteem. People are looking for opportunities to contribute, grow, achieve, and earn respect. Your recruitment brand's job is to promise they will find those opportunities with your company.

Recruitment brands are built on top of your corporate brand message, which should convey values like strength, success, and market leadership. Recruitment brands sell all that—plus opportunity. This message promises friendship, interesting work, and opportunities to contribute, grow, and advance. The formula is:

Successful Company + The Right Team
+ Opportunities = A Great Place to Work

Of course, these are subjective concepts, and can produce many different images. Which is precisely the reason a recruitment brand can be such a powerful hiring tool. A carefully crafted opportunity message not only attracts candidates, it attracts the *right* candidates—those people whose values and personal objectives are consistent with your own organizational goals.

Recruiters know that cultural fit is often a more powerful predictor of success than skills. Every company, every team has a set of personal values they consider essential to their success. A great recruitment brand conveys those values, and so attracts people with similar goals and aspirations.

Your recruiting message should articulate the skills and behaviors your organization considers key to its success. Surveys show that successful hiring and retention rely on this congruence. When workers feel secure in an environment that reflects their personal values, they are happiest. And when team members share a vision of success, they are much more likely to achieve their common objective.

Take a Snapshot of Your Culture

T he story of what it's like to work at your company is the cornerstone of your brand. It should communicate an exciting vision of your culture, work practices, management style, and growth opportunities.

Here's a checklist you can use to create a cultural message for your own organization. First, select the words that best describe how your company defines its corporate success. Next, select the words that describe the cultural attributes that are most valued. (Add your own, if these don't apply).

Corporate Success

- Largest
- Most established
- Fastest growing
- Entrepreneurial
- Traditional
- Highly respected
- Technology leader
- Most innovative
- Market-leading
- Service driven

Cultural Success

- Smart
- Diverse
- Hardworking
- Motivated
- Team player
- Friendly
- Loyal
- Happy
- Fun
- Flexible
- Serious
- Dedicated
- Ambitious
- Collaborative
- Independent

Use these words to craft a detailed message that describes the opportunities your company offers—and use them liberally as adjectives in job postings, banners ads, on your Web site, and in other forms of Internet advertising. The words you've chosen describe your organization's definition of success and the resulting brand message should excite and attract people who share your enthusiasm for it.

Remember, your brand needs to create an image that differentiates your company from a crowded field. Its job is to suggest an understanding and common bond with the people your company wants to attract and generate excitement around the opportunities your company has to offer. The image you create at the brand level becomes the baseline for all of your other recruitment marketing activities.

Let's Get Started

Okay, we have a plan and a brand! The next step is to invest in our own backyard to grow strong, Web-based employee referral and alumni systems.

2

Tap Your Employee Network

Your employees bring more than their skills to the table. They come with a network of friends and business associates who have graduated from the same colleges, worked with them at previous companies, or who belong to the same professional organizations. Because people tend to connect and form friendships with others who share common interests and values, these networks can instantly extend your recruiting reach to people with the right skills and cultural preferences.

Employees not only have access to great candidates, they tend to be very effective at screening them. Your employees understand the company's priorities and values more intimately than a third-party recruiter, and have a more complete view of the candidate than you can acquire through a round of job interviews. Most importantly, they have a personal stake in the success of both parties, their company and the people they refer. As a result, employee referrals virtually guarantee a better, more consistent match of job, company, and candidate.

Your employee referral system should not only deliver better candidates, it should provide a better return on investment than advertising or searching. Time is money, and referrals are faster because they bypass much of the traditional cycle of advertising, response, and review. (In most companies, the interval between ad and interview is measured in weeks, if not months.)

Also, by the time the referral candidate arrives for an interview, he or she has usually been briefed thoroughly on the opportunity, and is closer to a decision. As for hard costs, even after paying a substantial bonus, the savings in advertising and search fees make referrals the lowest cost-to-hire method, by far.

Surveys show that candidates who are hired through a colleague's referral feel like they are part of the team sooner and become productive more rapidly than candidates hired through other methods. In part, this is a result of a better fit at the time of hire—but also because the employees who referred them tend to serve as mentors, quickly acclimating them to the culture and strengthening their bonds to the company.

Referral programs can also be powerful retention tools. They foster morale and offer your employees an opportunity to participate—and be rewarded—for helping grow the company. In fact, many corporations consider their employee referral program to be part of their employee benefits package, and with good reason. Referral bonuses are a tangible incentive paid for a simple referral that most people would be happy to provide free of charge. But unlike other employee benefits, the more people who take advantage of this perk, the lower your costs.

Building an employee referral system is a relatively straightforward project. This chapter looks at referral strategies and the basic elements of rules and rewards. It also helps with ideas on sparking enthusiasm and participation and offers a structure for your Web-based program.

A Clear Competitive Advantage

By delivering lower costs, a faster hiring cycle, and better candidates, employee referrals are an important cornerstone of any recruiting strategy. Yet, a recent study shows that most companies allocate less than 5 percent of their recruiting budgets to building and administering their referral programs. This is astoundingly modest, given the benefits and potential return on investment.

In 2000, a survey conducted by the Society for Human Resource Management (SHRM) indicated that the average U.S. company hires 18 percent of its exempt employees and 22 percent of its non-exempt

> ### *Best in Class:* Employee Referral Software
>
> ***Applicant Tracking Systems with Employee Referral Modules***
> - **PeopleSoft:** www.peoplesoft.com
> - **PeopleClick:** www.peopleclick.com
> - **RecruitSoft:** www.recruitsoft.com
> - **RecruitMax:** www.recruitmax.com
>
> ***Web-Based Employee Referral Systems***
> - **Team Rewards:** www.careerrewards.com
> - **ERM Referral-Trac:** www.ereferralmarketing.com

employees through referrals. Over 70 percent of survey respondents also reported that they get *most* of their diversity hires through referral. This is quite a reward in itself for a budget investment of 5 percent.

Respondents who invested 10 percent of their budgets saw a corresponding increase to over 30 percent of hiring from referrals. This 30 percent quota seems to be the benchmark target for recruiters these days. Yet market-leading companies set targets well ahead of the norm. As a result, even in the most competitive job cycle of the last decade, companies like Cisco and PricewaterhouseCoopers achieved nearly half their hires through employee referral.

Have these companies become market leaders because they hire better people? Or can they hire better people because they're market leaders? Chances are it's a virtuous cycle. The data says that as companies recognize the value of employee referral programs and move to expand them, they reap the valuable reward of better hires. Those hires make a good company even better, enabling them to hire even better candidates. And so on.

Better, faster, cheaper. Employee referral programs offer the classic differentiators that create competitive business advantage.

Keep It Simple and Low Cost

There's no need to develop a complicated rewards structure for your employee referral system. In fact, studies show that the most successful programs are very simple. If an employee refers a friend, and that friend is hired, the employee receives a bonus or gift of some kind.

Most programs require that the friend stay with the company for some period of time before the referring party collects his or her bonus—90 to 120 days seems to be the rule, which corresponds to the traditional probationary period. This makes sense; in fact it is a model often used with third-party recruiters to make sure their placements are solid and successful.

An increasingly common practice is to pay half the bonus at the time of hire and the other half after 90 days of successful employment. Another is to simply absorb the cost of failed referrals (statistically a rare occurrence), but offer a more modest reward. The risk may be worth an increase in participation.

Today, the Employment Management Association (EMA) estimates that the average award for an employee referral is approximately $1,300. Measured against search fees that can range up to $20,000 for a mid-level contributor, that number can grow significantly and still be a great recruiting bargain.

Over 75 percent of companies surveyed in 2001 used cash as their referral reward. Most programs scale the incentive amount upwards, based on the importance of the hire and the effort required to fill the position. As a result, payments for managers are often double or triple the amount offered for line workers, and executive bounties can be five times great—or more.

A common starting point is 2 to 4 percent of the projected base salary. In most organizations this means rewards below $1,000 at the low end of the range, scaling up to $5,000 or so at the top. Larger rewards may make sense for truly critical positions, but take care to keep your priorities straight. The object of your rewards schedule is to attract attention and participation in the program, not to turn your employees into full-time headhunters.

Though participation invariably increases when you raise cash reward levels, there are lower-cost strategies that can be just as effective. Let's look at some of them.

Less Formal Is Sometimes More Effective

Many employees are happy to become ambassadors for their organizations and are less motivated by the cash value of a reward than by the fact that they are engaged and incentivized to help. As a result, companies of all sizes conduct very successful referral programs with creative, but inexpensive rewards. Theater tickets, a dinner for two, a nice bottle of wine, or a vacation day are all ways to show your appreciation without breaking the bank.

Other companies build the expectation of employee referral solidly into their culture. As new employees arrive, they make a point to explain that everyone is expected to help grow the company—and that identifying key players and recruiting them is part of everyone's job description.

The point is that there's no single model for building a referral program that works. Cash rewards may seem too cold and businesslike for your culture. Some companies use quarterly promotions, such as a weekend away at the beach or mountains for the employee who lands the most new referrals. Others enter each participant in a raffle or drawing.

These kinds of programs require more management focus and are more difficult to administer, but they can also be more fun—and are a less costly alternative to the automatic cash payment approach. The keys to these programs are a strong launch, constant promotion and some fanfare for the winner. The more fun you make it, the less the monetary value of the reward tends to matter.

Open the Throttle

Traditionally, referral programs have been restricted to current, full-time employees. Many programs also exclude hiring managers, company officers, and the entire HR department, on the grounds that they are stakeholders in the hiring process and may have a conflict of interest in forwarding candidates of their own.

There are many reasons your company might have adopted this policy—but you may want to determine if those reasons are still relevant; this policy may be a relic of times past. Bottom line, by restricting participation in your program you may miss out on some great referrals. As long as there's no direct conflict of interest (i.e., a manager nominating, then hiring the same candidate), why not broaden the network as far as possible?

Leap the Walls

S urveys show that fewer than 5 percent of employees in most companies actively participate in their referral programs today. This seems ridiculously low—particularly when it's known that referral is the fastest, cheapest route to better candidates. How does this statistic match up to the fact that market-leading companies are now hiring 30 percent and more of new employees through referral? And that some are predicting referral hire rates of more than 50 percent in the next decade?

One answer is that employee referral is a best practice of the best companies. It offers a strategic advantage that can be traced right through the organization to the bottom line. It seems that the most aggressive companies are rethinking how their referral programs work; they are not only opening the throttle internally but leaping the walls to the outside.

The logic is simple: The more people you engage, the more candidates you'll tap. Why not open your program to your employees' friends, your vendors, your customers—in fact, to anyone who can bring you a more qualified candidate than you'll find by advertising to job seekers on job boards?

It's a relatively simple project to fashion a specific referral program for associates, put it on the Web, and make it generally accessible outside your firewall. If you then invite a targeted group of familiar associates to participate, you've made the leap.

It's worth noting that a variety of companies were formed to take this idea to the mass market in the late 1990s. Among the contenders were Refer.com (an Idealab company) and HighCircle (a subsidiary of Priceline.com). These systems were designed so employers could offer a bounty on jobs they posted and pay rewards to anyone who assisted in bringing the right candidate to the table.

Every one of these ventures floundered in the perfect storm of 2000, when the markets crashed, capital vanished, and corporations began a cycle of massive layoffs. But the model was an innovative answer to that competitive and expensive candidate market, and it's a good bet that we'll see it again in the next decade.

A Model for Success

The most successful employee referral programs have a lot in common. Here are the Top Ten best practices they share:

1. **Leadership:** The best programs are grass roots campaigns—embraced, endorsed, and acknowledged frequently by the CEO and senior management. Too often, employee referral programs are perceived to be a mundane HR function, rather than a critical corporate mission. When the officers and top managers lead the charge, everyone understands the importance of participating.

2. **Cultural integration:** The company with the best talent wins! This is a familiar rallying cry for executives, HR professionals, and recruiters. But is it a part of your cultural DNA? Does every member of your team connect with the fact that business success is responsible for their career advancement, higher salaries, bonuses, and a more secure future? Market-leading companies make it clear that recruiting is a part of everyone's job description and that bringing great talent into the firm is a highly valued contribution.

3. **Fun and excitement:** Employee referral programs are an opportunity to build excitement and share success! Give your program a sense of humor and make it fun with games, contests, and events.

4. **Clear, simple rules:** Nothing takes the fun out of an incentive program faster than a set of Byzantine rules and regulations. Make your program as straightforward as possible and remove bureaucratic restrictions that discourage participation or make it hard to win.

5. **Strong promotion:** Constantly and creatively promote your program to underscore the importance of referral and to build "top of mind" awareness across the organization. Make sure your program is detailed in the company handbook and included in new employee orientation. Use posters, brochures, notes in e-mail, paycheck inserts, announcements in the company newsletter, and other internal publications. Try e-mailing a list of important positions to all employees once a month, with a hyperlink from each opening to your referral Web pages. Continual communication across your organization is vital to success.

6. **Variable rewards:** A good recruiting process differentiates and focuses harder on the most critical jobs first. This approach should

apply to your referral program as well. Prioritize your job openings according to their business impact, and vary your bonuses accordingly. Some companies do not attach a bonus to jobs that are readily filled by walk-in candidates—others pay a reward, no matter what position is filled. Either way, don't hesitate to scale the reward sharply up for key positions that create competitive advantage for your company.

7. **Ease of use:** Your referral program should be available 24/7 on the Web or accessible via your intranet menu. Participants should have ready access to your job openings, be able to push them to their friends with a click or two, and submit new candidates easily. Since it may be difficult for your participants to obtain a resume, provide a simple Web form they can use to get the process started with a name, contact information, and a brief profile.

8. **Recruiting tools:** Help your employees find more candidates by giving them the training and tools to pitch your company to friends and acquaintances. Your referral site should contain information on how to sell your opportunities, and it should include recruiting materials your employees can print out or forward via e-mail. Remember, fewer than 20 percent of referred hires come through close, lifelong friends. The vast majority are acquaintances made through the community, in church, sports, or other activities. Teach your people to turn their radar on and be ready to recruit as soon as they uncover a great candidate!

9. **Rapid response:** A common complaint about referral systems is that candidates are forwarded onto a slow conveyor belt, never to be heard from again. Speed and follow-up are both important, whether you make the hire or not. First, make sure that submissions are acknowledged and referral candidates are fast-tracked. Their resumes should go to the head of the line, and the candidates should be contacted, screened, and interviewed promptly. Next, provide all stakeholders with real time status via your Web site or by e-mail. Last but not least, never make your winners chase after their prize. Pay promptly on time, every time!

10. **Success stories:** Broadcast your progress and success stories loudly and often. Announce the jobs that have been filled, who helped, and what rewards have been paid on at least a monthly basis. Emphasize how easy it is to play and how happy the new workers

are to be there. Recognize your winners, their managers, and the teams that produce the most referrals.

Also, make sure your in-house recruiters are linked into your program. Anecdotally, many of the hires credited to referral systems are actually the result of an active staff recruiter working with the employee to surface their contacts. It's a great idea to have new employees debriefed by your recruiters soon after they arrive, and regularly contacted for help with positions similar to their own.

Put It on the Web

Your Employee Referral Program should be a self-service application hosted on a readily accessible Web site, linked across your organization. Depending on your hiring needs, it can be as simple as a page of rules, a page of job openings, and a simple submission form, or it can be a fully featured, automated referral system.

Today, most enterprise applicant tracking systems include some employee referral functionalities, and there are a number of turnkey ASP (applications service provider) programs in the market (see box, page 18). Whether you decide to buy or build, here are key features to consider:

- **Solid security:** You must provide access through your intranet only, or your system must include an administrative interface to store, update, and delete user names and passwords for all authorized users.
- **Linkage or integration:** Your referral system should connect to your job board, applicant tracking system, and resume database. Optimally, new job postings, edits, and deletions would flow simultaneously to your referral system. In turn, candidates surfaced through referral should be funneled through your applicant management system and into your resume database along with other applicants, so you can measure and report across the entire basket.
- **Flexible content:** Your program will change over time. Make sure you provide simple editing and graphic controls that allow users to amend program descriptions and rules and rewards and to add company information and new recruiting tools as they are developed.

- **Job routing:** Recruiters should be able to flag "hot" jobs to be routed automatically to employees via e-mail, instant messenger, or a desktop pop-up browser. Employees should be able to forward full job descriptions (as well as company marketing information) to prospects via e-mail.

- **Simple submission:** Your submission form should auto-record the referring party's identification, the date and time of submission, and capture the prospect's contact information and a paste-in resume. On submission, an acknowledgment e-mail should go to the referring party, and a notification to the recruiter assigned to the job opening and program administrator.

- **Resume routing:** Candidate profiles and resumes should be easily transferable to recruiters and hiring managers.

- **Real-time status:** Referral status should be available 24/7 to the referring party, recruiter, and program administrator, either through your referral or applicant tracking system. Employees should be able to query recruiters about their candidates from this screen. You may want parties to be notified automatically by e-mail as candidates move through each step in the process. Or consider an e-mail alarm that notifies stakeholders when a candidate is stuck in any active status too long.

- **Event tracking:** All status points from submission through hire or denial should be date-stamped, tracked, and stored by your referral or applicant tracking system.

- **Comprehensive reporting:** You'll want to be able to retrieve candidates and transactions by date, any party, job title, or other key fields you designate. Automatic alerts should go to HR and accounting at the point of hire, and at any milestone required to authorize payment (at the end of a 90-day probationary period, for example).

- **Program announcements:** Successful hires, the parties responsible, rewards paid, and other information can be collected into a standard format for automated announcements. The form should provide text areas for program changes, new contests, and messages from the administrator, and should be distributed company-wide at regular intervals.

Build Your Pipeline

A n easy-to-use, Web-based referral system is a key element in any e-recruiting strategy. Putting your program on an intranet or the Web not only takes the paperwork out of the process, it provides instant access, communications, status, and reporting across your enterprise, and around the world.

Employee referrals can be your single most successful recruitment channel. Before you invest in advertising your jobs or searching for candidates, make sure you have a strong and vital program in place—and a full pipeline of referrals moving through it.

3

Turn Your Alumni
into Recruiters

oday's talent market has become a revolving door. At the same
time companies are fighting to keep their best people and add
strategic hires to a growing division, they may be downsizing or
divesting another. It's a fact of life today that career cycles are brief and
that virtually everyone who walks in your door is liable to walk right back
out again within five years.

People leave for all sorts of reasons, and the best and brightest are
often the most difficult to retain. But forward-looking companies are now
realizing there are ways to keep the relationship alive, no matter the reasons for departure, and to keep those corporate alumni working for
them. In fact, many decide to return to the fold at some point, often to
become the most dedicated and committed workers in the organization.

In this new world, the objective is to create long-term relationships
with people who can help your organization grow, from the inside or out.
As a result, corporations are realizing their departed workers don't have
to turn into soon forgotten, ex-employees—they can become valuable
alumni instead.

This chapter looks first at some ways to plant the seeds for successful long-term relationships and then at strategies to nurture alumni and
turn them into clients, references, and recruiters.

Parting Is Such Sweet Sorrow

It is just business, after all. When an employee leaves to pursue another opportunity, it's always best to wish them well and help make their transition as pleasant as possible.

Admittedly, this can be pretty tough to do sometimes—particularly if it's a key player leaving to join your competitor. It can be equally tough from the other side, whether your employee is being cut out of the herd for performance or laid off for reasons beyond his or her control. But it's better for all, if passions can be set aside in favor of good business judgment.

When an employee departs, particularly a talented and valued contributor, it's important to view the event, not as the end of your association, but as the beginning of a new phase in your relationship. Let him or her know you want to stay in touch, and that the door will remain open for any future opportunity to return. Bottom line, stay friends if you can—and think in terms of lifetime relationships wherever possible.

The Business Case for Alumni Networks

For hundreds of years, colleges and universities have grown alumni networks that provide major economic and social value. Today, corporations are realizing their own alumni are an untapped source of new revenues, market opportunities, and talented employees.

Informal corporate alumni networks have always existed, and with the advent of the Web, many have moved online and grown quickly. Today, most communities are still launched and managed by interested individuals, as a way to stay in touch, network job leads, and share information. But market-leading companies are beginning to appreciate the power of these communities and are moving to build alumni networks of their own.

Here are the top five reasons why:

1. **New revenue:** Many departing workers stay in the industry, and often land with clients or potential customers. Once there, they can become powerful allies and ambassadors for your firm. Others may become consultants and develop new clients of their own, who in turn may be in need of your company's products or services.

2. **Boomerang employees:** Returning employees are low-cost hires that produce even more savings in training and time. In fact, surveys show that rehired workers require 50 percent less investment than new employees. Alumni communities keep you in touch with your best performers, even after they've transitioned through several new positions, and can help you bring them back without paying for advertising or headhunting fees.

3. **Recruitment and referral:** Your alumni know your company, its culture, and opportunities better than anyone. As they transition to their next company, they create access to entirely new personal networks that can be tapped for hires. Some companies are already extending their employee bonus programs to their alumni communities.

4. **Employment branding:** Alumni networks can be a powerful recruiting story. They demonstrate a long-term commitment to your business relationships, and a new kind of benefit for workers who choose to leave, or who are being downsized.

5. **Competitive intelligence:** Networks are a swirl of information—and alumni are liable to be sharing all kinds of news that can be useful in understanding current events or industry trends. Sponsoring companies also use their communities for market surveys, product testing, and other strategic group activities.

Alumni communities are a new, guerrilla recruiting resource that may soon become an important weapon system for the talent wars. Today, few companies understand them, and building communities is not a mainstream practice yet, so you have a near-term opportunity to create a significant competitive advantage.

Building the Network

The corporate alumni market is young, but there are already a series of important considerations and best practices at hand. Here are some thoughts on setting up and running an alumni network:

1. **Decide on the model:** Do you want the community to be a part of your company's activities, a prominently sponsored activity, or a hands-off enterprise? Some companies consider their corporate net-

work to be an important extension of their organization and take an active hand in building and helping the community grow. Others believe that alumni members should fully own and control their site.

2. **Assign ownership:** If your company runs or sponsors the site, make sure someone has clear responsibility for maintaining and growing it.

3. **Get members involved:** Regardless of the model you select, alumni should be active participants in managing the groups and making decisions. The most successful corporate-run programs offer global and local advisory boards that give members a clear voice and the power to steer the community.

4. **Contribute value:** If you run the community as if it is a recruiting and intelligence platform for your company, you will fail. Members must benefit from your participation, and it should be clear you are there to help, not to exploit them. Make sure you are providing value-added information, news, a current directory of members, career advice, and job openings. Be creative: Add value and you will create trust and loyalty.

5. **Move it on over:** Contact the private networks and make every attempt to incorporate them into your group.

6. **Make the sale:** It's worth doing some research, finding batches of alumni and selling them on joining up, maybe even offering a prize for bringing other members in. The faster you build a critical mass of participants, the better your chances of starting a vital campaign that will pull many more onboard with little further effort.

7. **Moderate the discussion:** Woe to the company that sponsors a non-moderated bulletin board or mail list. You will have unhappy people out there who may be waiting to take a cheap shot at you, their former boss, or each other. There should be a clear set of rules that keep the conversation courteous, positive, and helpful—and a way to intercept flames and derogatory messages before they hit the community.

8. **Involve senior management:** Some of the best companies today offer access to their CEOs and senior management teams through their alumni forums. This is not only a powerful recruiting strategy for potential boomerang hires, it's a great way to get your leaders out of the ivory tower and close to the market.

10. **Work the room:** Remember why you're doing this. Join the discussion and ask for business, while you're letting the community know about open jobs. Ask them to network with their friends and send the best ones your way.

You have invested lots of time, money, and effort in your employees—and a well-run community is a great way to realize a continuing return on that investment. Make sure it's managed in a professional, friendly manner that encourages your members to join and participate regularly.

Moving It to the Web

Your alumni community belongs on the Web, for the same reasons you are recruiting on the Web—it offers ubiquitous, 24/7 access from any point on the globe. Your community Web pages can be an extension of your corporate site, attached to your career center, or on a stand-alone site with its own URL.

Community features are powerful, and can be fairly low cost and relatively low tech. The most complex requirements will be your forums or mail lists, and job board; the rest of the site can be a series of HTML pages or run from a simple database.

Having said that, most companies today are choosing to outsource their community platform to a third-party vendor. There are a variety of low-cost ASPs (applications service providers) that offer robust, feature-rich alumni community software. This is a good route to take, as it will free you to focus on the strategic issues, rather than on specifications and programming.

Whether you decide to go with an existing ASP or develop your own, here are a set of key features to consider:

For Community Members:
- Secure access; passwords are a must
- Customizable home pages for different types of alumni—for example, former executives, retirees, or individuals targeted to be re-recruited
- A self-service membership directory with profiles and contact information

- A common calendar for corporate, alumni, career, and industry events
- A bulletin board for news and events
- A job board or forum for job opportunities
- Community forums and mail digest
- Links to career and educational resources
- Links to your employee referral system
- Links to help for COBRA, 401k rollover, and other post-employment issues
- Tools to form local chapters
- Tools to connect a friend

For Administrators:

- Simple interface, management tools, and reporting
- Search profiles
- Search threads
- Ability to monitor and moderate discussion
- Ability to post news, events, and jobs
- Ability to track job applications and referrals
- Individual and group messaging

Employees and alumni can be your most powerful recruiting assets. They often hold the key to better networks than your own recruiters or third-party partners, because they know lots more people with skills like theirs and with values that match yours.

Best in Class: Corporate Alumni Platforms

- **Corporate Alumni:** www.corporatealumni.com
- **SelectMinds:** www.selectminds.com
- **Aptium:** www.aptium.com
- **AIRS:** www.airscareerportal.com

Part Two

Your Recruiting Web Site

4

Develop Your Web-Based Career Center

Whether you're hiring 10 new employees a year or 10,000, you will save money, save time, and build more durable relationships by organizing your recruiting process around a strong Web site. The heart of your recruiting activities should be collected into a career center that includes:

- Comprehensive information about your company, culture, and opportunities
- A list of jobs or searchable job board
- A resume submission interface linked to your e-mail folders, resume bank or applicant tracking system
- A set of interactive, community-building features that help you profile and stay in touch with your prospects

In this chapter we'll look at a series of best practices in design, navigation, and content for this career center, and discuss how you can most effectively present your recruiting message.

In the following chapters, we'll take a detailed look at how to integrate your job board and resume bank applications, attract visitors to your site, and then profile and build relationships with them.

35

A Powerful, Low-Cost Tool

If your business was located in a busy shopping mall, you'd likely put a 79-cent help wanted sign in your window before you spent $1,000 on a newspaper ad. Well, the Internet is the ultimate high-traffic mall—and 350 million people are passing by, a mere mouse click away. Some of those people may be coming into your shop already—as friends, customers, vendors, and prospects. Because they are already interested in your business, they may in fact be the perfect candidates for your jobs.

Your Web site can be the most powerful, low-cost tool in your recruiting arsenal. Adding information and job ads to an existing corporate Web site is simple, and almost free. Mix in some imagination and elbow grease, and you can quickly build a powerful career center filled with comprehensive, attractive content, and an easy-to-shop storefront of compelling job opportunities.

Just like a commercial job board, your Web site is open and available 24/7, and it's accessible from hundreds of millions of desktops all over the globe. Before you spend your budget on posting jobs to third-party sites, take time to consider the low cost of driving traffic to your own career center. To the extent you can drive candidates around the intermediary job boards and straight to your site, the result will be better, faster, cheaper recruiting. This is a project that takes time and focus, but the benefits are enormous.

Market-leading employers and recruiters are moving quickly to lower their media costs by stepping in front of the third-party job boards. But advertising isn't the only function of a robust recruiting site. Your site can also enable instant, two-way communication with job seekers; it can screen and profile applicants and funnel digital resumes directly into your resume database and on to your applicant tracking system.

Deciding What to Build

Global corporations may hire tens of thousands of workers every year. These companies are in a perpetual hiring mode, regardless of the economy; and in an economic upturn they need to process huge numbers of candidates into workers at a rapid clip. That means using every resource available—advertising, recruiters, in-house search teams—

and the most advanced productivity tools in the market.

But smaller companies and most third-party search firms have very different needs, and it's important to avoid overinvesting in technology that may be cool, but irrelevant. So, where is your organization on the features-versus-cost curve? Here are a few simple guidelines and ideas that can help you decide:

Small Employer

If you are a small or stable company with modest hiring needs, append a simple career section to your existing Web site. Focus on describing your company clearly and attractively, and publish a static page of your jobs. "Static" means a simple HTML page listing job openings with brief descriptions, as opposed to a database-driven job board with sophisticated features.

Remember, people who visit your site are interested in *you*, and are much more valuable prospects than casual visitors to a third-party job board. They may be from the same industry, have skills that fit your company, or be a customer or client. Wherever they come from, their interest counts as a strong pre-qualification factor.

All companies, regardless of size or growth velocity, should be constantly trolling for these interested, qualified contributors. Even if you don't have current openings, it's a good idea to post a list of jobs you may have to fill in the next year or so, or of key positions you'd like to have backups for.

Once you are rotating more than a dozen new job openings every month, it's time to begin the transition to a formal job board and resume bank and to revisit the depth of content that describes your objectives, culture, and workplace. If you are planning significant growth, become familiar with the technology options and strategies offered in the next few chapters, and scale them into your site according to your needs and budget.

Recruiters and IT Consultants

If you are a third-party recruiter, search firm, or IT consulting organization, your living depends on attracting as many of the right candidates as you can, as fast as possible. Your entire corporate site should be focused on recruiting—and it should be powered by the most sophisticated job board and resume bank you can afford.

Increasingly, recruiters are in a race with their own clients. In an effort to reduce third-party recruiting fees, many corporations are building their own search teams. These in-house recruiters are attracting job seekers to their own corporate Web sites, posting jobs, and scouring the Internet for the same passive candidates recruiters are looking for.

Recruiters must acquire at least the same knowledge and tools their most advanced colleagues and clients possess to avoid being marginalized. To stay ahead, recruiters will need many of the same cutting-edge tools that large corporations are assembling today.

Large Companies

Global corporations have intense hiring needs that require supply chain management as well as recruiting expertise. For companies with hundreds or thousands of open jobs, it's important to deploy a recruiting Web site with deep, comprehensive information, a fully featured job board and resume bank (or profiling system), and real-time communications and community-building tools. In this section and the following chapters, we'll look at each of these tool sets in turn.

Your Development Team

Virtually anyone with some time and basic computer skills can build and launch a Web site these days. There are dozens of free and low-cost community sites that provide turnkey hosting and simple point-and-click publishing tools. From a standing start, most people can have a page built and on the Web inside of an hour.

But a complete career center, with a job board, resume bank, and some interactive bells and whistles can be a much more difficult project. There are low-cost, shrink-wrapped tools for simple do-it-yourself sites, but the more complex your feature set, the more likely you will need a software architect or developer to help.

Smaller companies often choose to outsource their Web development to a local IT consultant, or award the job to their most tech-savvy employee. These are fine practices—as long as there is strong guidance and strategic input from a knowledgeable recruiter or manager. There are too many great advantages to an active recruiting Web site, to have someone slap the text from your brochure on a Web page and call it a day.

In larger organizations, an internal IT group usually owns the technical side, a marketing group will produce general and product content, and an HR or recruiting manager is in charge of the career section. It's important to select a manager with the leadership skills to articulate the company's vision and cultural imperatives, and—because the site must serve internal customers from virtually every part of the company—the strength to coordinate the requirements of a wide group of stakeholders.

In most organizations, the responsibilities of this team leader include overall design, functionality, and content. Specific tasks the team might perform include:

- Strategy development
- Researching "best practices"
- Identifying successful features on similar sites
- Providing functional specifications to the IT group
- Testing the interactive features
- Gathering content from HR and other sources
- Developing original content
- Internal training

A small company or recruitment office can develop a site with simple but compelling features for well under $10,000. Larger companies will usually spend anywhere from $50,000 to $250,000 depending on the underlying platform, sophistication of the software tools, applicant tracking functionality, and how costs are allocated between technology, design and content.

Funding for career content and overall functionality is usually drawn from the staffing or HR budget, but specific applications that might run the job board and store resumes are typically a technology purchase. Whenever this is the case, both teams should work very closely on vendor selection, specifications, and integration.

Important Design Principles

Many of the concepts that will make your career section user-friendly are applicable throughout your Web site. Clean, simple page structure and good navigation are key to educating prospects and selling products of all types, including your job opportunities. Here are a handful of the most important design considerations:

1. **Fast download:** Time is money for everyone, and patience wears thin quickly on the Web. Most experts agree that pages must download in seven seconds or less, to keep readers engaged.
2. **Lots of white space:** Eye-tracking studies show that 78 percent of reader's interest is focused on text areas, and that white space is critical for separation and contrast.
3. **Spare graphics:** Pictures and other graphics should be used sparingly, as they can distract readers and severely impact download time. In particular, studies show that users are annoyed by flashing or blinking images.
4. **Standard text:** Steer away from using graphic images to convey text. Though the fancy fonts are attractive, it's a real problem when headlines or key text blocks are missing because the graphic file didn't download properly. HTML text may not be as interesting, but you can count on it to appear on the page every time.
5. **No flash video:** Flash introductions and slideshows are cool, but tend to backfire on the Web. You'll find that some visitors won't have the required plug-in and so can't participate; while others resent the fact that you make them sit through it. Basically, they are a bad idea because they stop users to tell a story, instead of letting users click around and learn by themselves.
6. **Persistent tabs:** Tabs or links to important site areas (including "jobs" or "careers") should run along the top or side of every interior page.
7. **Lots of links:** The more they click the longer they stay. The longer they stay, the more they learn. The more they learn, the more they trust. When they trust enough, they buy—or in this case, buy in. Links are your friends, because they keep your visitors engaged and interested. Look at the top Internet shopping sites. There are links to different kinds of content (especially products) everywhere and a link to the shopping cart and checkout stand from every page. This is a good model for your corporate and recruiting Web sites.
8. **Drill downs:** Usability studies show that people like to scan and click on the Web. Make sure your content is presented in bite-sized nuggets, with drill-down links to related topics. This lets your prospect browse their way through the fresh material they're interested in, without getting stuck halfway down a long page on any one topic.

9. **Breadcrumb trails:** This is a basic navigation device that allows users to see where they are, and where they've come from, in a linear fashion. A breadcrumb trail to your resume submittal form might look like this: Home > Careers > Job Board > Submit Your Resume. This structure also allows the user to click immediately back to any point in the trail.

10. **Site map:** This is a good idea for your entire site, or just for the career section. This can be a page or drop down menu that lists major topic areas, for fast reference and linking.

Bottom line, your design goals are simple. Keep your visitors clicking, scanning, and moving towards your job board and resume submission form.

Best in Class: Web Design Gurus and Resources
- **Jacob Nielsen:** www.useit.com
- **About Web Design:** http://webdesign.about.com
- **Internet.com:** www.internet.com
- **Web Monkey:** http://hotwired.lycos.com/webmonkey

Lessons from the Front Lines

Whether you are adding a brief career section to your corporate site, or building an enterprise-recruiting portal, the basics of good Web design apply. Attractive pages, effective navigation and clear, comprehensive information are all key. But at the end of the day what really matters is how well it sells your opportunities!

Recruitment is *sales*—and shopping for jobs is the second most common reason people visit company Web sites. Yet most companies stash their career sections in the back room. Links to jobs are often tiny, or hidden on interior pages in the "About the Company" section. Home pages sell the latest products and services, but don't advertise the hottest jobs. Given that we are on the verge of a generational labor shortage, and that a majority of American CEOs considers staffing to be a key strategic issue, this doesn't seem to make a lot of sense.

Your initial recruiting objectives are similar to Amazon's book-selling objectives: Attract the right people, help them make a purchase decision—and separate them from their credit cards (or resumes) as quickly and efficiently as possible.

In a decade of doing business over the Web, the smartest companies in the world (as well as some of the dumbest) have been experimenting with the best ways to sell products and services. The results are an important body of new knowledge about how people behave on the Web, how they prefer to be sold to, and what and how they will buy.

The lessons they've learned are a great model for your recruiting site. Web-based vendors have become experts at attracting the right customers, serving them the right information, moving them efficiently through their site to the storefront—and making it easy to buy. On a good e-commerce site, all roads lead to the shopping cart.

There are five principal design strategies that we can infer from evaluating successful e-commerce sites. Each helps the shopper engage, move to the products, and buy. Keep these points in mind as you design your site:

- **Easy to find:** There should be thousands of pathways from the Web to your home page, and from every page on your site to the career and jobs sections.
- **Easy to browse:** Simple, fast pages with spare graphics, but lots of links keep the prospects engaged and interested, provide access to important information from every page, and move them efficiently to the storefront.
- **Drill-down content:** The best sites have all the information any customer needs to make a purchase decision, presented in bite-sized snippets and organized in a way that encourages the customer to stop reading and *buy* whenever he or she is ready.
- **Specialty content areas:** All sites have diverse audiences. The more targeted the content, the more trusted the message—and the faster the sale.
- **Easy to buy:** Over 90 percent of customers leave an e-commerce site without purchasing. Chances are a similar number of job seekers surf your job openings and leave without submitting a resume. A fast, easy checkout process can improve those numbers dramatically.

Think of your content area as a sales brochure, your job board as a storefront, and your jobs as your products. You must educate your customer, sell your jobs, and compel your customer to "purchase" by submitting his or her resume. That means navigating candidates to and between your sales brochure and storefront—from the Web, from your home page, and throughout your site.

Linking Prospects from the Web

S teering prospects from the Web directly to your career center starts with a simple, intuitive URL. Studies show that an abutting extension to your corporate URL is the most easily memorable.

Example: **www.yourcompany.com/jobs**

The extension word /jobs is by far the best, as it is a more common keyword than /careers, /employment, or other opportunity words.

This is important for two reasons: First, it is an intuitive and well-known convention. Second, search engines always index the URL and page titles. By embedding the most commonly used search terms in your URL and titles, your pages will come up as a match more frequently, which is crucial for job seekers.

Most companies are content to navigate visitors to their corporate home page, and link them from there to the career center. But your objective is to separate the job seekers from the general traffic at the earliest possible point—even before they arrive—and get them to your career center, fast. Here are several ways you can take candidates past the home page and directly to your sales brochures and job openings:

1. Have your career center URL printed on your business cards and recruiting materials.
2. Put a link to your career center in your e-mail signature line.
3. Put a link to your career center in any auto-responders that go from your Web site to vendors, customers, or prospects.
4. Make sure your newspaper advertisements contain your career center URL.
5. Make sure all jobs posted on job boards link back to your own job board or career center URL.

Bottom line, stay alert to ways you can publish your recruiting URL—on the Web and off—in places that prompt potential job seekers (who may be customers, vendors, partners, or competitors today) to go right to your career center.

Linking Visitors from Your Corporate Pages

No matter how well you brand or link your recruiting pages, the corporate home page is likely to remain the starting point for most visitors. Here are some tips to optimize this valuable real estate:

1. Make sure your *jobs* link is prominent and well placed on the home page. It should be large enough to read and as close to the main text areas on the page as possible.

2. Whenever possible, display *hot jobs* on your home page. In a large corporation it may take quite a battle to win this valuable spot, but it will definitely be worth it. If you are a recruitment firm, this is a no-brainer. Your livelihood depends on interesting the right candidates in specific opportunities. This is a very compelling way to link them directly to your job board.

3. Another *hot jobs* idea is to link job titles (no description necessary) on related interior pages. For example, if you are a technology company that builds Java products, a link that reads *Hot Java Programmers Go Here* is a great ad for customers who are coming to your support and product pages. Or if you're a bank, you might put a link for *Great Loan Officers Wanted* on the pages where you list your interest rates. After all, isn't that where great loan officers from your competitors' companies are most liable to be looking?

4. Of course, links to *hot jobs* should appear on pages inside the content areas of the career center, too.

5. Optimally, your career center will be linked to each interior page, and every page of your career section will link to your job board (i.e., your storefront, where all your products are). Never forget the two-click rule: No page on your site should be more than two clicks from your job opportunities.

Describing Your Culture and Opportunities

Your career content should be a candid, powerful presentation of your company, culture, and opportunities. What you say to your prospects, how you say it, and how the information is organized are all critical to your sale.

It's important for your copy to be attractive to your target customer. It must contain *all* the information they need to make a "buy" decision, but be presented in bite-sized chunks that encourage them to stop reading and move to the purchase as soon as they are ready.

Fresh content counts on the Web. Make sure your message is not only compelling, but also current. And remember, you only have one chance to make a first impression. You are aiming to recruit top talent, so take care to present an attractive, professional image. Your page layout, the images your text conveys, the photographs you use, and your style all send a message.

Whether you dress up or dress down, work late or leave early, it's important to paint a true picture of the company, so that you will attract people who will be comfortable with your culture. Your content should convince the right pool of candidates that your organization provides the right fit for them. And who are these candidates? Let's review: Regardless of the skills you're hunting for, your best candidates are always those people who share your worldview and values—and who are excited by your opportunities. These are the very people you've created a recruiting brand to attract.

Career content is much more powerful when it is created for a specific audience. If you understand the people you're writing for, you can create a vivid picture that excites and attracts them. So revisit your branding message: How does your company define success? What aspects of your culture do you consider most important? What kind of contributors do you want to add to your team? The answers to those questions should determine what topics you focus on, what words you use, and how you link content areas together.

Your second objective is to make sure you've covered the information landscape. As experienced sales professionals know, even prospects with similar profiles and objectives are likely to have different "hot buttons." So, it's important that you provide as much information as possible across the entire range of topics a prospect may be interested in learning about. In keeping with the "scan and click" usability guidelines, treat each topic as a capsule of information, and link each capsule to as many others as may be relevant. Let's take a look at the major content areas and topics you may want to include.

Describe Your Company

What attributes will most attract your target candidates? Is it strength and security, or the excitement of a start-up, or the entrepreneurial environment? What makes your company unique, different, and yes, better? The quality of your management team? Industry leadership? Inventive, cutting-edge technology? Friendly service?

Many of the positive features you'll use to sell candidates are likely to be highlighted in your corporate folio, so you can link to those areas instead of creating each topic from scratch. But don't hesitate to build on what's there, or spin them in a different way if you need to. Here are some ideas for company topics and links that might help you sell, depending on the story you want to weave for your audience:

Topics

History	Clients	Products
Management	Market	Services
Board	Mission	Locations
Investors	Technology	Awards
Partners		

Link to

Annual report	Stock performance	News coverage

Describe Your Culture

Is it buttoned up? Buttoned down? Fast and lively or steady and deliberate? Does your company celebrate teamwork or individual achievement? Intellectual or visceral decision making? Is it messy, orderly, or sterile? Bottom line, what is it like to work there, and what constitutes success in your culture?

Some of the best ways to convey a cultural message are through workplace images, employee stories and interviews. The key is to make sure your presentation is honest, truly representative of your work environment, and attractive to candidates who will flourish in your organization. Cultural topics and links might include:

Topics

Values	Mentoring	Work/life balance
Work ethic	Management style	Career track
Objectives	Teamwork	Training and education

Expectations	Collaboration	Lateral opportunities
Rewards	Projects	Growth/Development
Quality	Diversity issues	Success stories
Workspace	Lifestyle concerns	Your community
Communication	Humorous perspectives	

Link to

Employee profiles	Schools	Churches
Employee interviews	Community events	Civic attractions
Employee events	Charities and sponsorships	

Describe Your People

Job seekers are examining your career content, photographs, and tone for answers to these very important questions: Will I fit in? Are there friends to be made there? Are there people like me?

We all hope to find people to connect with in our workplace. They might be people from the same college, the same home town, people who like to play softball, people at the beginning or end of their careers, MBAs, working mothers, bikers, hikers, bird watchers—in short, people with similar backgrounds and interests.

Intel has a great recruiting site that includes a section called "Careers and Profiles". Visitors can click through a series of sample career paths and see where they would work, the kinds of projects they might tackle, and the actual people they would be working with. There are brief profiles for each team member that includes personal interests and activities. In one step, this feature attracts the right candidates to the workplace, the job, and the team.

It's always a good idea to convey a sense of your spirit and the activities your people enjoy. Do you play volleyball after work? Have a bowling team? An annual golf tournament? Sponsor the Special Olympics or United Way? Many of the best recruiting sites offer links to photos and stories about their team members having fun or contributing to the community.

Discrete pools of important candidates require special attention, too. There are very specific recruiting strategies to attract, capture, and convince foreign, ethnically diverse, college, and executive candidates that your workplace is right for their needs. Because these groups have unique questions and concerns, it is important to create specialty content areas and images for each. (We'll take a detailed look at each in Part 4, Searching for Passive Candidates.)

Compensation, Benefits and Incentives

Salaries, medical, dental, and other insurance plans, pension benefits, stock options, commissions and bonuses, profit sharing, team incentives and special perquisites are all very important, and should be covered in detail.

Salaries, benefits, and incentives follow market cycles. In the candidate-hungry boom years of the late 1990s, companies were competing to invent new ways to attract workers, as well as boost productivity. The concepts of the corporate campus, and "always-connected" workers began to gain traction. Many companies invested heavily in concierge services, laundry pickups, company cafeterias with take-home prepared meals, and other labor-saving perks designed to give workers more hours to devote to their jobs.

Others made sure they were "cool" by providing gymnasiums, break rooms, foosball tables, pinball machines, free snacks, and nap areas. Many of these lavish perks vanished (at least temporarily), as the stock market collapsed and the United States slipped into recession in 2001. In a market with lower profits and crowded with downsized candidates, companies are less motivated to invest in expensive employee services.

But competitive salaries, incentives, and insurance plans, along with unique benefits that fit a company's culture, are as important today as ever. The compensation section of your career site should be as comprehensive as possible. Many companies are moving towards "self-service" HR portals that offer deep information about the complexities of each benefit program. The objective is to lower HR costs by reducing the time required to answer repetitive questions by phone or e-mail. The idea here is the same. Take the time up-front to completely describe your programs and perks, in detail. This is a powerful way to engage your candidates, answer their questions, and get them several steps closer to their purchase decision.

If you're uncertain about whether your salaries and benefits programs are competitive today, there are a number of reference sites on the Web that can help. Here is a checklist of the principal compensation features you should consider for your site—and some ideas for low-cost, but uniquely effective benefits you might want to offer.

Compensation

- Salaries
- Commissions
- Bonuses
- Stock options

Insurance

- Medical
- Dental
- Vision
- Life
- Disability
- Key man

Retirement

- 401k
- Matching programs
- Profit sharing
- Pension

Time Benefits

- Vacation
- Sick leave
- Flex time
- Leave of absence

Workspace

- Relocation
- Telecommute
- Campus facilities
- Parking

Educational

- Training
- Tuition
- Books and materials

Family

- Child care
- Adoption assistance

- Life partner benefits

Wellness

- Health club
- Athletic teams
- Fitness classes

Community

- Charitable match
- Community service
- Sponsorships

Best in Class: What to Offer

Salary Sites
- **Salary.com:** www.salary.com
- **Salary Expert:** www.salaryexpert.com
- **World at Work:** www.worldatwork.org

Company Benefits
- **Benefit News:** www.benefitnews.com
- **Benefits Alerts:** www.benefitsalerts.com
- **Employee Benefit Research Institute:** www.ebri.org

Stock Options
- **MyOptionValue.com:** www.myoptionvalue.com
- **National Center for Employee Ownership:** www.nceo.org
- **Foundation for Enterprise Development:** http://fed.org

Incentives and Rewards
- **National Association of Employee Recognition:** www.recognition.org
- **Corporate Rewards:** www.corporaterewards.com
- **Bravanta:** www.bravanta.com

Getting in Touch

Make sure you provide plenty of ways candidates can make contact via phone or e-mail. To make it easy, include a *Contact Us* or *Learn More* link on each page that activates a pop-up information form and phone number. Don't send these messages into a general mailbox or to the Webmaster. They should go right to your recruiters, or to an HR professional who understands the importance of building relationships.

By the way, even if you're really busy, it's a great sign when a candidate calls in to ask for help. By taking that proactive step, they are signaling unusually strong interest in your company. If they're a dud, you'll know soon enough, but having the initiative to make personal contact gives them a higher probability of "fit" than a casual job seeker.

An innovative recruiting strategy that extends this idea is Cisco's Buddy Program. When a candidate expresses interest, Cisco pairs them with an e-mail Buddy from the department they would report into. The Buddy's job is to form a relationship and educate the candidate about Cisco's company and culture, while screening the candidate at the same time. If there's a match, it becomes an instant and low-cost win for both sides.

Discouraging Unwanted Candidates

R epel Boarders! While it's great to hear from a qualified, interested candidate, it can be a nightmare to juggle calls from 100 casual job seekers with time on their hands, while you wrestle with another 1,000 resumes from unqualified candidates. When the market is flooded with displaced workers, your immediate problem may be turning candidates away, not attracting more. Here are some thoughts to keep in mind:

1. Chances are your candidate overload is a relatively temporary problem. With 40 percent more baby boomers leaving the market than there are new workers to replace them, candidate shortages are liable to be the rule over the next two decades. Though painful while you're treading water, it's better to plan and invest for the eight years of candidate drought, than for the two years of candidate flood.

2. Even when you're not hiring at all, remember there are valuable people in the mix you'll want to recruit as soon as the faucet opens up again. It's always worth the effort to sort the best candidates to the top, flag them, and begin to build a relationship.

3. The more specifically you describe your culture and it's expectations—and the more exacting your requirements—the more surely you will attract the best of the right people, and repel more of the wrong ones. In times of candidate overflow, you can shape your can-

didate pool by honing your message, tightening your standards, and making it clear you are looking only for the best, most highly qualified candidates. Not just people who are looking for a job—but people who want to share your mission!

A Fast Look Forward

T here are three big ideas driving innovation on the next generation of recruiting Web sites. They are:

1. **Personalization:** Web-savvy recruiting companies and corporations are moving towards individualizing their interaction with the job seeker, in much the same way e-commerce sites have personalized shopping and information gathering on the Web. By collecting information and building comprehensive user profiles, the eventual goal is to be able to present dynamic and highly relevant content as well as to push ever-more-targeted information to prospective candidates via e-mail. Some resulting features might include:

   - A personalized home page that launches when your career site recognizes a cookied visitor.
   - Links to targeted content, matched to the types of jobs searched, or to pages previously viewed by the visitor.
   - Links to new job openings, similar to those searched in the past—but not yet viewed.
   - An instant messaging link to a mentor with similar skills, or from the appropriate department—and to recruiters, HR professionals, and line managers who can answer questions in real time.
   - Skills tests, games, and other assessment features matched to the types of jobs searched.

2. **Relationship Building:** Profiling and personalization are the first steps towards building long-term relationships with high-value, targeted candidates. In Chapter 8, Grow Candidate Communities, we'll look at relationships, and community-building strategies in detail.

3. **A Supply Chain Model:** Since the dawn of the Web, companies have designed their recruiting sites to educate visitors and be a secondary source of applicants—catching the overflow from newspaper campaigns, commercial job postings, career fairs, and search firms.

But today, many are repositioning their own Web sites to the center of the recruiting process itself.

In the new model, the corporate Web site becomes an ever-more primary source of candidates, displacing expensive newspapers, job boards, and search fees along the way. At the same time, it organizes the results of the remaining third-party advertising and search activities—online and off—into a common candidate funnel.

The new recruiting site is the entry point in a supply chain that coordinates sourcing activities, funnels applicants through a screening and assessment process, matches them efficiently to jobs, and passes them to the right desktop in the enterprise.

As we focus next on job boards, digital resumes, traffic, and community building in the chapters ahead, look for these ideas, and notice how they are already beginning to shape the best practices of the most forward-thinking companies.

5

Post Jobs
on Your Site

At this point, your Web-based career center should be dynamic, professional, and simple to navigate. It should offer a compelling view of your marketplace, company, and opportunities, and it should present a clear, vivid picture of your culture and expectations. There should be plenty of deep, drill-down topics for information seekers and a prominent jobs link on every page, for those who want to cut to the chase.

Your job board is the heart of your online career center. It can be as simple as an HTML list of jobs, or as complex and powerful as any commercial job board. In this chapter we'll examine the various build versus buy options, review the best basic and advanced features, and take a fast look at some next-generation tools.

The Build vs. Buy Decision

Do you need a job board? Yes. Even if you have zero real job openings, you should be trolling for great candidates. Advertise your most important positions constantly, and hope that your competitor's top salesperson or best engineer will apply. These perpetual openings aren't meant to track to your current needs, they're designed to snare the odd visitor with a terrific skill set you can use anytime—and fill your resume bank for when you do need candidates.

The better question is, how much of a job board do you need, and when? If you are a stable company with modest hiring needs, you may decide against a searchable job board altogether. A simple list of job openings on a Web page, with e-mail links to your HR administrator might be sufficient for quite some time. This is a simple structure that can be maintained by an office assistant, or updated inexpensively every month or so by your Web outsource partner.

The tipping point occurs when you shift into rapid growth mode, or when you find yourself juggling dozens of new openings every month. In either case, it's time to invest in a database-driven job board application—but there are a series of choices to make along the way.

There are three fairly common job board options. First, you can develop it yourself or have it built for you. Second, you can purchase an off-the-shelf application and integrate it as part of the back-end plumbing of your career site. Third, you can purchase a job board as an integrated module in a larger applicant tracking system.

Choosing the right course is important, as your job board is one of the most critical tools in your career center. You'll want an application that fits your current environment and can scale along with your growth. You'll also want it to be flexible enough to incorporate new features as the need emerges. So, let's take a closer look at each option.

Building Your Own Job Board

Building your own job board is a slippery slope at best. It can be a simple database project—or a never-ending IT nightmare. In the early days, most large companies used their in-house IT resources to design and build their job boards. Smaller companies went to their local IT consultant, or built their own with desktop tools. This process was the genesis and test bed for many of the features that have become commonplace today.

It is a fairly simple project to build the search, retrieve, and display functionalities that form the core of a job board. But building an application past these basic features and staying abreast of new requirements like enterprise-wide management tools, complex editing, job agents, push mail, and other interactive capabilities quickly becomes a full-time development job.

These advanced features—and others of equal complexity—are so common now that building them in-house no longer affords any strategic advantage. In fact, as soon as one vendor announces a compelling new feature, it soon becomes standard among all competitors at little or no additional cost to the end user. As a result, job board software has become a commodity—and the price has fallen to well below the cost of in-house development.

Unless they are intent on developing a proprietary end-to-end system, it's hard to imagine why an employer or recruiter would build a job board from scratch today. Given the proliferation of inexpensive third-party solutions, it's unlikely to make economic sense. So let's take a look at the commercial options.

Commercial Job Board Software

Today, robust job board software is widely available at a low cost. Stand-alone job boards manage your job openings and resume bank, but do not track applicants through the hiring process. They can be integrated into your career center, or deployed as a front-end module to a larger applicant management system.

Job board software can be purchased as shrink-wrapped software, or accessed through a Web-based ASP (application service provider) platform. Shrink-wrapped software is an application you buy or license to deploy within your own IT structure. It can be a mainframe, client-server, desktop or Web-based application—the point is, *you* are responsible for integrating, maintaining, and upgrading it. The ASP model provides access via the Web to software that is developed, maintained, upgraded, and hosted by the vendor.

Shrink-wrapped software is the right choice for organizations that prefer to control and tightly integrate the application with other programs in an in-house system. As with any local software, it's key drawbacks are the time and costs of installation, integration, maintenance, and updating—all of which require capital, management, and IT focus.

The ASP model on the other hand, is a turnkey application; it is entirely Web-based and is accessible from any desktop with a Web browser. The application itself is developed, maintained, updated, and extended with new features by the vendor, entirely in the background. Because the ASP powers a number of boards with a common software and hardware platform, the expenses of maintenance and new development are shared, which results in far lower costs for each user.

Information technology systems are moving rapidly to the Web. Whether you decide to build your own applications or lease services from an ASP, a distributed Web-based architecture makes more sense than localized computing, particularly for large enterprises.

As Web-based systems mature, it's a good bet that the low-cost, turnkey ASP model will continue to gain traction as well. But there are significant barriers to widespread adoption: most notably that mission-critical data may be hosted on a third-party server that can be hacked and that the system is managed by a company that could go out of business at any time.

These are not trivial issues, but there are already a variety of safeguards and contractual measures aimed at ensuring reliable, secure services. Still, the risk-to-reward ratio may still be out of line for some organizations today. The key is to pay close attention as you select your vendor: Apply an appropriate level of due diligence and make sure you examine your safeguards thoroughly.

Whether shrink-wrapped software or Web-based ASP, job board applications share a set of core features, and are continually leapfrogging each other to provide new ones. As a customer, you will be realizing the rewards of this competition, through an expanding feature set, at an ever-lower cost.

Best in Class: Turnkey Job Boards

- **RecruitmentBox:** www.recruitmentbox.com
- **SearchEase:** www.jobboardsoftware.com
- **Jobbex:** www.jobbex.com

A Job Board Module in Your ATS

As with stand-alone job boards, applicant tracking systems (ATS) may be shrink-wrapped or Web-based ASP software. But unlike stand-alone job boards, which offer a fairly consistent feature set; applicant-tracking solutions come in all shapes and sizes. There are over 200 different products aimed at small recruitment offices and employers, midsize companies, and the global enterprise.

Many of the midsize and larger systems now offer job board and resume bank functionalities as standard or optional modules. These modules are typically as robust and feature-rich as a stand-alone job board. The important difference is that they are already integrated into a larger applicant management environment.

Your job board and resume bank are vital links in your recruiting workflow, and there are powerful advantages to a hiring system that is accessible to recruiters, managers, and HR administrators—and that promotes interactivity across the staffing function. Whether you build your own ATS, integrate third-party software, or access an ASP, your applicant systems belong on the Web, too.

Applicant tracking systems are complex and should be carefully evaluated as you plan your recruiting Web site. There are several distinct methodologies that are important to understand and choose from, in order to implement a system that works best with your organizational structure, culture, and recruiting style.

A Checklist of Best Practices

Whether you build you own or choose a stand-alone job board or an ATS with a job board module, there are a variety of core features you'll want to include, and some important options to consider. What follows is a checklist of best practices to help you build your site, or evaluate commercial alternatives.

1. Make It Easy to Manage

- **Keep posting tools simple:** A clean, simple interface for creating, editing, and deleting jobs is important. This is the portion of the application your recruiters are liable to be working with most—and streamlined, time-efficient tools are critical.
- **Employ a job ad wizard:** The more compelling and comprehensive your job ads, the more likely your applicants will become interested and engaged. Tools that help recruiters craft interesting copy, as well as data dictionaries for tech terms and libraries of previously drawn job requirements are ways you can ensure that creative ad content moves quickly from concept to execution.

- **Use job cloning:** A facility that archives closed or deactivated jobs is useful, as is the ability to quickly copy any current or old ad, to create a new one.

2. Spread the Word

- **Display your hot jobs:** Your most critical openings should be featured on your corporate and careers home page. An extension of this practice is to display specifically targeted jobs in areas where you can expect matching traffic. For example, feature some sales and marketing jobs in your product section, where competitors may be surfing for intelligence. Put engineering jobs up in your technical help sections, and post executive positions alongside your executive bios and on your annual report page. The idea, of course, is to present opportunities that match the visitors' interest—and the more you can automate this process, the better.
- **Let your employees help:** If your policies permit it, automatically route new positions to your employee referral system. Jump-start the quest for referral bonuses by e-mailing new openings into the appropriate departments and posting them on your intranet.
- **Put 'em on the Web:** When possible, arrange to export new openings and edits to your job board partners via an automated batch process—or arrange to have them scraped (see the following section for a detailed look at job scraping and cross posting to the Web).

3. Make It Easy to Search

- **Be fast and accurate:** Most job boards offer a full-text search, with an index of key categories for faster retrieval. Job seekers should be able to quickly search by any combination of: title, skills, location, and posting date range as well as by keyword.
- **Be easy to scan:** Highlighted keywords in the search results are a great feature—as is the ability to sort results by any indexed field. The easier your search interface and the more engaging the job titles and content, the more fun it will be for applicants to stay on site and drill down for more.
- **Flag hot jobs:** Also, highlight your most urgent jobs as they appear in the search results. By flagging these opportunities, they move to the foreground and become more visible, and more likely to be clicked and explored.

- **Group similar jobs:** Nesting each job posting into a basket of similar jobs is a fast way to narrow a search and get right to the jobs the applicant is most interested in. Whether you implement a relevance engine (as many Web search engines do), or link similar jobs in a table structure in your database, this is a powerful feature that job seekers appreciate.
- **Help them search:** Salt quick-search boxes all over your site. You don't have to provide a complex search interface—just a simple box for job keywords. The results will take the applicant inside to your job board, where they can refine or run new searches at will.

4. Make It Easy to Apply

- **Keep it fresh:** Update your site as often as possible—at least weekly, and daily if you can. Keep postings current and date-stamp them as you post and edit them, and make sure you promptly remove closed or deactivated jobs.
- **Provide a shopping cart:** The simplest, most efficient way for job seekers to browse and apply is by using a shopping cart. This model allows them to select jobs, save them in their cart, apply to one or any number of them at once, and discard or save the rest.
- **Provide an "apply-now" link:** On the other hand, they may want to go right from the job description to the application. So provide a direct link from each job description, too.
- **Decide to sell or repel:** Your application interface can be simple, to encourage as many job seekers as possible to deposit their resumes—or complex enough to discourage all but the most determined and interested applicants. This is a continuum, of course, and you can select some midway compromise just as easily. The point is, your decision to make it simple or difficult will drive the kind of applicant interface you implement. See Chapter 6, Build a Digital Resume Bank, for a more detailed look at this set of issues.

5. Make Contact and Build Relationships

- **Be responsive:** Make sure you have an auto-responder that thanks each applicant as he or she deposits a resume or leaves behind a profile.
- **Profile your visitors:** The job board is a perfect place to embed skills tests, assessments, polls, and other interactive features that

help you capture information and profile your visitors (See Chapter 8, Grow Candidate Communities, for a detailed look at how to use profiling techniques to build pipelines of qualified, interested candidates).

- **Capture their interest:** Provide links to your skills-specific newsletters in job postings that match. For example, offer a sub-scription to your technical updates in your IT postings. The idea is to engage and connect to prospects who may someday turn into candidates.

- **Push them more jobs:** One of the most powerful features you can implement is a job agent that pushes new opportunities to prospects via e-mail, as they appear. Not only are job agents great profiling tools, they effectively keep prospective applicants inter-ested and in orbit around your company.

  Job agents are a way to automatically stay in touch with candi-dates, without investing more capital or energy in recruiting them. It is a passive way for candidates to continually review new open-ings that match their interests, and a powerful way to reach out to them with new messages.

  Though this is now a common feature of commercial job boards, only a small fraction of employers have implemented it to date. If you are evaluating job boards software, this is a "must have" feature—and if you're running in-house software, it is worth the effort to add.

  Also, remember that any e-mail you send to a prospect is an opportunity to push information above and beyond the job description itself and to link the prospect back to your site. Make good use of these messages by embedding current information. Use links liberally in the body of the message and in your signa-ture line. The object is not only to push them jobs, but also to build an ever-stronger relationship.

- **Help them work with you:** Your visitors may hesitate to sign up for correspondence from your organization that could land on their desktop at work. So, encourage them to use a private e-mail address for their job agent and other correspondence. If they don't have a private account, provide links to Yahoo!, Hotmail, or other free Web-based services, so they can sign up on the spot.

- **Meet their friends:** When a visitor forwards a job from your site to a friend, they are tapping you into their own professional network. Often, they will turn up a prescreened, hidden candidate at no additional cost to you.

    Make it easy to forward any job opening by embedding links—on the results page, posting page, and in the shopping cart—to your own e-mail form. By prompting them to complete the form, you'll collect the visitor's contact information, a contact block for their friend—and be able to tie each person to a specific job interest category.

6. Monitor and Improve Results

- **Measure carefully:** What jobs are getting the most traffic? What time of day is most active? Where are most visitors coming from? How many new job seekers are arriving every week? How many return visitors? How many searches are you serving?

    All of these questions and many, many more are important in evaluating your strategies, refining your content, and targeting opportunities at the right time, in the right place, to the right population of visitors. Make sure you have a robust reporting capability, and take care to monitor the variables that are most critical to your recruiting plan.

- **Be a mystery shopper:** Check it out yourself, and have your friends help. It's important to get the customer viewpoint—and the best way to do that is to become a customer for an hour or two. Start by surfing through and searching your top three or four competitors' sites, and some of the more progressive *Fortune* 100 sites. Then approach your own Web site—first as a casual visitor, then as a job seeker.

    Benchmark your design, navigation, content and features to the other sites you've visited, and answer these key questions about your jobs interface:

    1. Is it easy to get to the jobs from anywhere on your site?
    2. Is the job search engine fast and simple to use?
    3. Can you quickly sort the results and narrow your search?
    4. Are the jobs fresh?
    5. Are the descriptions compelling?
    6. Do they contain all the information you need?

7. Does your cultural message come through, even on the job board?
8. Is it easy to link to more information in your career center?
9. Is it easy (or hard enough) to apply?
10. Are you doing a better job than your competitors?

A Look at Cross-Posting and Job Scraping

M any commercial job boards offer cross-posting options. This means that when you post a job to their board, they automatically pass it along and post it to more boards. This feature is designed to help you reach a broader audience automatically, with no additional effort or expense.

Many corporations today are cross-posting job openings from their own job board to commercial job boards on the Web—whether they know it or not. Often, their jobs are being copied from their career site with "job scraping" technologies that can access any Web page and extract content.

When companies are aware and agreeable to this model, scraping can be a very powerful timesaving tool. For example, if your company has a relationship with a series of job boards that are able to extract the specific postings you designate, you save the time and labor costs of posting and editing multiple jobs over multiple sites. This is a terrific service, and can be a key differentiator for commercial job boards who offer it.

Other commercial job boards have developed a business based on scraping corporate jobs from their public pages, with or without their consent—and aggregating hundreds of thousands of postings as a result. This practice can be helpful in generating candidates—but it has generated its share of controversy, as well.

The logic underlying this model goes something like this: First of all, these jobs are published in the public domain without copyright, therefore, it's a legally permissible practice to scrape them. Second, isn't your objective to broadcast your job openings to the widest audience at the lowest possible cost? After all, this is a free service that may net a valuable candidate, at no cost to you.

These are good arguments, and may be generally true. However, there are some troubling issues. First, there's often a negative reflex to the notion that someone is republishing your content without your prior knowledge and permission. Second, for many employers, there can be a significant time lag between Web site updates. This means there's a good chance that old, closed jobs are being scraped and presented to a wider audience than would normally see them. The result may be a flood of resumes that can't be matched to available opportunities, but must still be reviewed, sorted, and managed.

A Low-Cost Expressway to Your Own Job Board

An early, permission-based version of this aggregation model is experiencing a rebirth. The Online Career Center (OCC), one of the first job boards to appear on the Web, was actually a joint venture launched by a coalition of *Fortune* 500 companies, aiming to share Internet recruiting costs. TMP Worldwide acquired the OCC in 1999.

Today, some of the original OCC founders have formed a new nonprofit organization called E-Recruiting Association, Inc. and have launched directemployers.com, a job board that offers member companies unlimited job posting for a relatively low annual fee. If directemployers.com is successful in generating traffic, this business model could present a meaningful challenge to Monster.com and other sites operating on a pay-per-job posting basis.

Directemployers.com uses job-scraping technology to automate the process of publishing and editing jobs. Job seekers are driven to the directemployers.com site, where they search for openings, as they would at any other job board—but when they click through for more information, they are immediately transported to the members' corporate Web site.

This can be a valuable partnership model, particularly for large corporations who have an enormous number of positions to advertise. Today, many companies are prevented from advertising more than a fraction of their open jobs, due to the rising cost of individual postings. With the directemployers.com model, the cost is capped—and companies are no longer competing with their own vendors for traffic. Instead, their Web partner is driving interested candidates directly to them. The result is a streamlined funnel, less friction, and lower costs overall.

6

Build a Digital Resume Bank

In e-commerce, the sale lives or dies on the credit card page. In Web-based recruiting, the point of sale is the resume submission form. To reach this moment of truth, our prospects have moved steadily from the home page, to the career center, to the job board, and now to the resume interface.

Along the way, they've been engaged, educated, and targeted towards jobs that match their skills and interests. It's time now for them to draw back the bow and send a digitized resume speeding down the wires to your resume bank.

In this chapter, we'll take a look at the digital resume itself, contrast it with an emerging generation of alternate profiling tools, and examine current best practices in resume submission, storage, and retrieval.

200 Million e-Resumes Can't Be Wrong

Before the birth of e-mail and the Web, managing resumes ranged from a tedious chore to a paper nightmare. For decades, the print-ed resume was the lingua franca of the staffing industry and the bane of employers everywhere. But like many other pesky paper documents, its format, distribution, and storage have been transformed by ubiquitous computing and communications. In less than a decade, well over 200 million digital resumes have been created and submitted to corporate and commercial resume banks, posted to job boards, and published on the Web. This migration of the resume from print to the digital realm, and from file cabinet to database represents one of the most significant advances in staffing automation and workflow.

Rise of the Resume Database

D igital resumes are already an essential link in today's recruitment workflow. Many companies now simply require that resumes be submitted by e-mail, and many more strongly encourage it. It's a good bet that as resume banks and applicant tracking systems continue to become desktop commodities, more and more employers will refuse to accept resumes any other way.

For the employer, a database-driven resume bank can transform a big expense into a smart investment overnight. It turns those dusty old piles of paper that are stacked around the office (then moved into a file cabinet, then to an archive box in a storage locker) into digital assets that can be searched and easily retrieved anytime.

Most companies now realize, as recruiters have for decades, that there is enormous value in simple access to past candidates. This is because employers, like third-party recruiters, tend to be hunting for similar candidates, over and over. Yet, before digital resumes and database systems, there was no efficient way to go back and search through records for past applicants who might fit a new position.

As a result, most companies were doomed to repeat each search from scratch, regardless of the fact that many candidates may have applied for a similar position six months before. Repetitive searches would start again with the same newspaper ad or job posting—and if advertising didn't yield a candidate in time, the assignment would be turned over to a third-party recruitment firm.

With any luck, recruiters would immediately find a matching candidate in their Rolodex. If not, they would get on the phone and hunt them down—making sure, of course, to save the new contacts in their Rolodex for the next search. In the 1980s recruiters began to convert their Rolodex cards into database records—and by the early 1990s employers starting wondering why they were paying third-party recruiters 30 percent of an applicant's first year salary to search a database when they could be growing their own.

By the late 1990s, the unequivocal success of Monster.com and other leading job boards had erased concerns about sending resumes over the Internet and posting them into publicly accessible databases—and the single largest barrier to re-engineering the staffing process began to crumble.

The Digital Resume Format

Much of the time and cost savings gained by having applicants submit their resumes electronically is lost if your systems can't read them and you have to preprocess them by hand. An effective e-resume is more than a simple transfer of text from an applicant's old resumes into an e-mail message—and it's well worth educating your prospective applicants about the best ways to create and submit them.

First, remember that you want a machine to read the resume and be able to interpret and retrieve it successfully. That means the message has to arrive in, or be converted to a plain text format. Also, search engines tend to stumble over graphics, fonts, bullets, indents, and strange characters—so very simple and straightforward documents are best. Here are some formatting tips you can make your applicants aware of, to streamline your own workflow:

- Use only Helvetica, Arial, or Times Roman fonts
- Use 10-, 12-, or 14-point type
- Make sure the entire document is left-justified
- Set margins for approximately 65 characters
- Use spaces or dashes to emphasize text
- No bullets
- No graphics
- No dingbats or special characters

Getting Resumes Through the Firewall

There are four principal ways that e-resumes can arrive in your inbox. They can come in as an e-mail, as a document attached to an e-mail, as a link to a Web page, or through a form on your Web site. Providing a form is the most secure method for your visitors, but what about resumes coming from job boards, or over the transom? How do you make sure the data is safe—and that it will flow seamlessly into your applicant management system? Lets take a look at some lessons learned over the past several years of e-recruiting:

First, companies are realizing that document attachments can be dangerous. Opening executable files and attachments that arrive in e-mail are the most common ways of spreading a virus, worm, or other Internet-borne infection. The result of opening the wrong attachment can be deadly for your own files, as well as endanger data throughout your IT system.

In defense, many companies are limiting inbound documents—or even banning them altogether. This is a problem for the legions of candidates who may be routing their resumes as attachments to a brief introductory e-mail. Today, the best way to deliver the goods for all parties is to clip the resume itself (and cover letter) into an e-mail blank, wash out the bullets, fonts, graphics, and other beautifying features, and send it along.

Applicants often struggle over every graphic detail of their resumes in an effort to differentiate themselves and impress a human interviewer. This is still a worthwhile investment prior to a face-to-face meeting or interview, but a beautiful resume can present serious obstacles in an automated workflow. In the new database-driven recruiting environment, the graphic presentation simply doesn't matter—but it is very important that the content is machine-readable, in simple text format.

There are tens of millions of resumes self-published on the Internet, and an increasingly common practice is for applicants to send a link to their HTML Web page instead of sending the resume itself. This is a safe and simple way to view a document, but there's no good way to go out on the Internet, retrieve it, convert it from HTML to text, then route it into your database automatically. It takes human intervention to harvest, reformat, and submit it manually—which interrupts a smooth, automated workflow.

Bottom line, encourage your candidates to keep it simple and to put the cover letter and resume text into the e-mail itself. If they want to attach a formal resume as a Word document, fine—as long as they understand it may not get past your firewall or IT policies. If they want to embed a link to their Web resume, that's great too—but there's no guarantee they'll get into, let alone rise to the top of your database search.

Accidents Waiting to Happen

A widely reported study conducted at the tail end of the 1990s sent volunteers to post their resumes to dozens of *Fortune* 500 career sites. An overwhelming majority reported significant difficulty, and over 40 percent of their attempts failed altogether. This news sent ripples through the ranks of companies who were investing huge sums to build sophisticated recruiting sites—yet a survey of prominent sites today shows not much has changed.

Many sites are still discouraging applicants accidentally, due to overly complicated design—as opposed to filtering candidates on purpose. If you want to cull unqualified applicants at the point of resume submission, there are a number of good strategies you can apply. But an interface that is confusing or difficult to navigate discourages the great candidates, along with the ones you'd like to screen. So clarity and ease of use are particularly important at the point of resume submission.

Another accidental interface problem is being positioned with the wrong features, at the wrong end of the market. You can set the dial on resume submission anywhere from very simple and straightforward —to very complex and time-consuming. The simpler the interface, the more resumes you will receive. Among those resumes may be a great number of unqualified candidates—or a number of great candidates you will not see as your interface becomes more complicated. Let's take a minute to define this issue, and then take a fast look at each option.

The staffing pendulum swings from extreme shortage to extreme surplus, and it is dangerous to craft long-term recruiting strategies, or implement expensive software solutions aimed at only one extreme or the other. If you took a snapshot of the staffing shortage between 1995 and 1999, it was clear that employers needed to open the funnel and encourage as many candidates as possible to apply. If you took the same snapshot between 1991 and 1994—or between 2001 and 2004, for that matter—you'd see a completely different picture.

Of course, there's a natural tendency to focus on problems at the far reaches of the swing, when they are most acute. But a narrow solution aimed at an extreme problem tends to intensify the inverse problem, as the pendulum swings back. Companies who invested in extreme filtering programs in the early 1990s were caught flat-footed when their candidate flood turned into a trickle a year or two later. Conversely, those who spent huge sums to open up candidate flow from the major job boards in the late nineties, today find themselves struggling under a tsunami of resumes from unqualified candidates.

The point is—aim for maximum flexibility, and be wary of solutions designed to solve problems that only exist at either market extreme. Optimally, the mouth of your resume funnel will be easily sized to market conditions across the range. For the largest companies, that means a system that requires candidates to submit a complex profile at one end of the market—and allows a fast, simple resume submission at the other. Smaller companies are less apt to need thousands of prospects in the funnel nor are they likely to be flooded with unwanted resumes—and so should be able to select a simpler solution that works across the board.

Resume Submission Strategies

There are five principal ways to facilitate e-resume submission. Each is appropriate to a particular purpose, and type of Web site, and each serves to open or narrow the funnel of job seekers that apply. Let's look at them from simplest to most complex.

General E-mail Submission

The simplest way for applicants coming from a job board or offline advertisement is to send their resumes to a published e-mail address. In order to streamline the process and keep visitors on their site, job boards usually provide an e-mail pop-up form to clip their resume into or allow them to forward their resume from their database. This method bypasses the need to travel to your corporate site at all.

E-mail from Your Own Site

But there are lots of really good reasons you *want* candidates to visit your site—not the least of which is so they'll get a sense of your company and decide whether they have an affinity for the culture you've described. Once there, the simplest way for them to submit their e-resume is to send it as an e-mail to an address or to a pop-up e-mail linked prominently at the bottom of each job description.

By embedding the address or link in the description page, you can direct resumes to the various members of your team who are working on those openings. Remember to provide pop-up help encouraging applicants to send resumes clipped into the e-mail message, not only as an attachment or link.

Simple Resume Form

A simple form consists of contact information, job interest, and a clip-in resume blank. With the right header information, not only can you route the e-mail to the right recruiter, but automatically submit it to many text-based applicant tracking systems as well. This is still a user-friendly method—and a pretty low hurdle for the job seeker.

Resume Builder

This is a structured form that converts the resume to relational data, field by field. Typically, in addition to contact information and objectives, each title, skill, prior employer, college, degree, certification, and achievement is collected into its own searchable field.

Job boards, recruiters, and employers love resume builders because they force the applicant to arrange data in specific fields that can be easily indexed. The more fields collected, the faster and more accurate the retrieval. But with this method, the tension begins to mount between data collection and ease-of-use.

It's quite an effort to rebuild a lengthy resume field by field—and it could easily take up to half an hour to complete the task. This may be an acceptable time investment in return for the wide exposure a major job board offers, but most candidates will find it a tedious process to repeat over and over on corporate sites. In a market filled with surplus candidates, this can be an effective filter. If the candidate is interested enough in your organization—the theory goes—he or she will invest the energy to complete the form. If not, then it proves the applicant is not serious enough to warrant your own investment in them.

Of course, the reverse theory applies in a candidate shortage market. Applicants are much more sophisticated, knowledgeable, and opinionated today than ever before. If you require them to jump through hoops in order to apply when candidates are scarce and jobs are a dime a dozen, you will be regarded as a callous employer or out-of-touch recruiter.

Best Practice: Key Fields for Your Resume Builder

- Contact Information
- Name
- Address
- Phones
- E-mail
- Experience
- Start and End Dates
- Titles
- Companies
- Locations
- Descriptions of Work
- Years Education
- Colleges
- Degrees
- Certifications
- Honors and Awards
- Job Interests

Profiling System

A true profiling system is the most complex option to manage, but in return, provides the most sophisticated targeting tools and matching capabilities. The concept of profiling, as we know it today, emerged in the late 1990s, at a time when industry pundits were loudly proclaiming the death of the resume (which they seem to do, once a decade or so).

Profilers, they said, would replace the resume—a troublesome, text-intensive, often misleading document—with clean, simple assessment variables that could be administered, evaluated, and scored electronically. Theoretically, hiring managers could determine the core questions that gate any application, and in a matter of minutes apply them online. The profiler would do the work of screening job seekers as they arrived, and route a set of scored applicants to the manager, who at that point could request a resume, if he or she wished.

This is a sound value proposition. Why twist ourselves in knots trying to decipher a resume, when we can simply ask the candidate a series of direct questions? We can learn more, faster, through a well-crafted set of a dozen interrogatories, than by poring over a resume trying to discern the reality behind the prose, followed by tedious attempts to make contact and a time-consuming phone screen. Why not collapse all that effort into one simple Q and A session at the very front end of the process?

Replacing resumes with profilers makes a lot of sense. But like many sensible propositions, it relies on the tacit agreement of many constituencies to gain traction. But there doesn't seem to be wide enough adoption, or a sufficiently compelling payoff yet, to radically transform the way job seekers look for a job.

Today, there are dozens, maybe hundreds of large companies who force candidates to answer profiling questions as a condition of their application. As with resume builders, this is an effective way to determine who is serious about those companies and who is casually surfing for a better opportunity. The tougher the quiz, the fewer casual candidates will apply—and, it would seem to follow, the better the quality of candidates that do. But are they better? Or are they just more desperate? At least we can assume that they're more interested in the opportunity than others who decided against investing their time with the profiler.

To paraphrase the great W. C. Fields, the death of the resume has been greatly exaggerated. There has been no groundswell to date that implies profiling will change the broad shape of resume collection any-time in the near future—no matter how much sense it makes, or how much it streamlines an employer's supply chain.

As a result, even those applicant tracking systems that boldly claimed they would eliminate resumes altogether a year or two ago are now repositioning their profiling systems to coexist as a value-added addendum to the resume, not a replacement. But it's also worth mentioning that many of the competing ATS vendors—including some of those who most publicly proclaimed the profiling paradigm to be wrong-headed and of little value—have added profiling capabilities to their own systems.

Bottom line, profiling can be a powerful tool, and the larger your company, the more important it is that you follow its development and consider its advantages. The natural filter it provides may be just the answer in a surplus market—though it may prove too restrictive and time-consuming in a shortage market. Today, profiling seems to be a powerful and valuable tool to have in your arsenal—as long as you can bypass it when you need to open the mouth of the funnel quickly.

Applicant profiling systems are only one way to profile site visitors. In fact, because they only collect information at the point of application, they are limited to only the most interested segment of a larger population of prospective candidates.

Not every customer buys and not every one of your visitors will want to leave a resume, or be interested enough to go through a profiling process aimed only at active applicants. But you'll still want to capture data that describes their skills, aptitudes, and preferences, and assess them if you can. That's why non-resume-related profiling tools like polls, surveys, and skills games are important to understand as well. We'll take a look at these profiling features and more in Chapter 8, Grow Candidate Communities.

Anonymous Submissions

Do you really want anonymous submissions? Again, this seems to be an idea from the extreme candidate shortage end of the market, when employers are trying everything they can think of to attract people—including promising to send them jobs that fit their qualifications, without knowing who they are in return.

This may seem reasonable in a market where everyone is employed, therefore everyone is a passive candidate—except that for it to work, these "passive" candidates need to be out surfing and going to the trouble of applying for a better job. Hmmm—doesn't that make them an active job seeker? If so, we would like to know who you are, please. Bottom line, it doesn't seem to make a lot of sense unless you just plain can't find candidates any other way.

Fax Submission

Some applicant management systems now accept fax resume delivery. Is this an e-resume? Well, if it goes right into your ATS electronically, it certainly qualifies. If it comes over a fax machine and must be printed and manually keyed or scanned, it's really no better than mailed hard copy.

If you have a system that seamlessly accepts fax transmissions, that's great. If not, it's probably a better time investment to encourage more of your applicants to use e-mail, than to try to get faxes into your ATS. Bottom line, e-mail is replacing the fax machine. Better to focus on this new tool than try to retrofit your organization with the old.

Managing Your Active Resumes

Whichever submission strategy you choose, the resumes that enter your system need to be routed, evaluated, and stored. There are three logical routes they can take. First, in many organizations there are recruiters assigned to the jobs posted on job boards and the corporate site. It makes sense to route resume submissions to the individuals actively working the openings—and from there to a central resume bank when they've finished the search. Second, with the appropriate applicant management system, resumes can be routed directly to the central resume bank, with an e-mail alert to the recruiter. Third, resumes can be routed to both the recruiter and resume bank at the same time.

Recruiters working on a search assignment need their active resumes close at hand—and many store them temporarily in a file linked to your contact management program. You can use a low-cost relationship manager like ACT or Goldmine, a low-end commercial recruiting program, or simply your Outlook e-mail folders.

Best in Class: Low-Cost Relationship Managers

- **ACT:** www.act.com
- **GoldMine:** www.frontrange.com
- **SalesForce.com:** www.salesforce.com

Another handy method is to store active resumes in Word document folders on your hard drive. Name each folder for the appropriate search—then index the entire directory with a text search tool. This enables you to drill down to the folder you need, or to text-search across the pool of documents to find the right resumes.

Best in Class: Index and Search Resumes in Document Folders

- **dtSearch:** www.dtsearch.com
- **AltaVista Desktop Search:** www.altavista.com

As resumes arrive, they can be automatically routed to a designated inbox, reviewed, and then moved manually to each search folder. Or, you can set up a mail folder for each search, and automatically route resumes into them as they arrive. If you are using your mail folders as your desktop resume database, this single step is all you'll need to keep your resumes organized and easily accessible. *Note: Make sure your IT department buys into this plan—and that you're storing these files on your own hard drive, not the company's e-mail server.*

Best Practice: Turn Your Outlook Mail Folders into a Resume Bank

Step 1. Create a Folder to Store Your Resumes:
- Select the View option on the main menu of your Outlook toolbar
- Once you see the Folder List, right click on Outlook Today
- From the pop-up menu, select New Folder
- In the Name field type "Resumes" or other name you designate
- In the Folder Contains field select Mail Items
- Click the OK button
- Move resumes from your e-mail box into the new folder

Step 2. Keyword Search for Candidates in Folder:
- Highlight your new folder by a single left click
- Select the Find button on the Outlook menu bar
- The Find Items in Folder window will open
- Check to "Search all text in the message" box
- Type in the skill keywords you want to find on the resumes
- Only the resumes matching these keywords will be displayed

Step 3. Other Useful Keyword Categories:
- Company names
- College names
- Degrees
- Professional designations
- Locations: cities, states, area codes

Building Your Data Warehouse

It's important that all your resumes, whether they represent an active applicant, or one who has been passed over, are collected into a central resume bank. This can be on your local area network, hosted on a Web server on the Internet, or on your intranet—as long as your recruiters and managers have instant access to the data.

Once a resume is entered into a widely accessible, searchable database, it becomes a digital asset. The argument that old, stale resumes have little value is just plain wrong. There is a wealth of residual value in resumes, regardless of whether they are current or not. Here's why:

A Pool of Passive Candidates

Headhunters know that most people, employed or not, are happy to hear about a new opportunity—and so consider passive prospects as eagerly as active job seekers. In fact, these passive candidates are more highly valued than job seekers, due to the fact that organizations tend to hold on to their top performers at all costs.

Pre-Qualified Prospects

To recruiters, good candidates who are clearly drawn to your company or the position being offered are more highly regarded than candidates with matching skills alone. That means prospects who have taken the time to submit their resumes are pre-qualified, at least to the extent that they've shown interest in your company at one time or another.

As a result, this pool is arguably more valuable than the pool of job seekers you'll reach with a new ad or new job posting. If you can easily reach a population of prospects who were once interested in a particular job, with the prospect of a similar position, it makes sense to do it regardless of their current employment status.

A Data Warehouse

Your resume bank is also a powerful data warehouse. Find a great candidate in your resume bank, and you can find his or her friends on the Web. Find contacts inside your source companies, or people with the same professional certifications or alumni affiliations. Trying to source salespeople from a particular company? Call candidates in that company who may have sent you a resume in the past and ask them about salespeople they work with now. Use your imagination and you'll find many, many more ways to use your resume data to leverage your search.

Cheap Digits, High Return

The burdened cost to store a resume can be a fraction of a penny. Yet, you have lifetime access to a candidate you might otherwise pay a recruiter $20,000 to dig up for you. It doesn't take many placements at that level to pay for your entire resume inventory—and provide a handsome return on investment to boot.

Resume Bank Options

Just like job boards, there are many ways to skin the resume bank cat. If you are a small company or recruiting shop, you may simply want to expand your desktop file system to be more widely accessible. On the other hand, if you are a *Fortune* 1000 company, you'll want a sophisticated Web-based system, capable of storing hundreds of thousands of resumes and retrieving any one of them in seconds, from any recruiting desktop. Here are the broad options in more detail:

Opening up the Desktop

If you are already using desktop tools like Outlook mail folders or Word files to store your own resumes, you can offer wider access by simply moving your resume documents to a shared drive on your local area network—then indexing the directory with your text search tool.

A Simple, Stand-Alone Database

The midpoint between sharing text files and an integrated solution is a simple resume bank developed in Access or a similar desktop database program. This option provides more indexing capability and more refined search capabilities than text files stored in a shared directory, but is difficult to extend with sophisticated features.

If you are at the point where you need to store and retrieve large numbers of resumes—or are supporting a geographically diverse organization—it's time to investigate commercial solutions, most particularly those with Web access.

An Enterprise Resume Bank

Resume banks are standard features in corporate job board programs and applicant management systems today. So, your choices here closely parallel those detailed in Chapter 5, Post Jobs on Your Site. As with job boards, there are solutions designed for recruiters, small companies, and global corporations alike.

Because the resume bank is integrated, it should be evaluated in the context of the overall system, not solely on its own feature set. As a rule, the more robust the overall system, the more sophisticated the resume bank.

Checklist of Best Practices

Here's a checklist of key features, options, and considerations to pay attention to, whether you build your own or buy an integrated system:

1. Simple, Straightforward Design

- **One click away:** Just as your job boards should be no more than one click away from your corporate and career center home pages, your resume submission page should be only one click away from any job description, as well as from the job cart.
- **Clean and simple:** Whether you instruct applicants to e-mail their resume, use your resume builder, submit a profile—or any combination—make your design, navigation, and instructions as simple and straightforward as possible. Remember, you may want to filter unqualified candidates, but you don't want to discourage the good ones along with the bad.

2. Initiate Strong Relationships

- **Say please and thank you:** Make sure your interface is courteous and respectful—and that you take time to acknowledge your submissions with a thank-you note. An auto-responder is fine, but remember to use this message as a further opportunity to sell the prospect on your organization and culture.

Help your applicants understand your internal process, and set their expectations realistically about when or whether they should expect a follow-up. Help them learn more while they're waiting by providing links to information about your company, products, and opportunities.

This is also a great opportunity to personalize the relationship by showing the applicant that his or her resume hasn't disappeared down a black hole. Sign the letter with a name and personalized return e-mail address. The name can be a pseudonym, and the address a general mailbox, but make sure return mail is monitored and answered periodically by a live person.

- **Profile and push:** One of the most powerful recruitment strategies enabled by the Web is to profile, then engage your prospects with value-added information, newsletters or other community features aimed at their skills and preferences. Your resume interface is prime territory for assessment tools, exams, surveys, and other features that collect information at the point of application.

3. Streamline Your Workflow

- **Anywhere access:** It's much more important to provide enterprise-wide access to your resume bank search than to your job board or to most other modules of your applicant management system. Of course every researcher and recruiter should be able to search it—but it's important for managers and executives to have access, too. And the simplest way to provide single point access across all of your teams, units, divisions, and groups, anywhere in the world, is via the Web.

- **Resume agents:** Recruiters should be able to set agents that periodically sweep the resume database, looking for resumes that match their open searches.

- **Resume alerts:** Whenever a resume is submitted that matches a current agent, a copy should be automatically routed to the recruiter assigned through e-mail, or an alert should notify them of the match, along with a link to the resume in the general database.

- **View, share, route, print:** Recruiters should be able to view resumes online, share them in work folders, route them to teammates via e-mail, and print them easily.

4. Find Them Fast

- **Robust search capabilities:** Fast and accurate search and retrieval features are central to your resume bank application. The best search method varies, according to the number of fields you index. If you collect information into a resume builder, you should be able to search on any field. If you sweep e-resumes into your system, make sure your database is full-text searchable by keyword—and use common Boolean expressions wherever you can.

  If you're in between, as most resume banks are, you should provide search options for each indexed field, as well as full-text keyword matching. The most commonly indexed fields are job title, location (city, state, and zip) and posting date.

- **Sorting through quickly:** As with job results, highlighted keywords in the resume title and body are great visual aids. It's also helpful if results can be easily sorted—and relevance-ranked according to the frequency of keywords, the proximity of keywords, or a similar neutral method.

All We Need Are Customers

Well, so far we've built a recruiting Web site with compelling content, an attractive storefront filled with jobs—and a fast, powerful resume bank ready to collect digital resumes. Now, as they say in retail, all we need are customers.

7

Drive Traffic
to Your Jobs

As with Web shopping site, the value of your online career center will be proportional to the number of people who visit. The more interested passive and active job seekers you attract, the faster you will scale your brand, grow your network, and build pools of qualified applicants.

But how do you attract these folks? Your career center is buried inside one of 2 million business Web sites, scattered in a sea of 30 million registered domains—and competing with over 2 billion other pages for traffic. Good grief!

This is the business problem that consumed tens of billions of venture capital dollars in the 1990s as Internet start-ups threw money at Web portals like Yahoo! and banner ad agencies like DoubleClick, in a frenzy of competition for eyeballs and mind share. Traffic is still the principal value driver for career sites like Monster.com whose marketing strategies are to become household names in a mass consumer market.

Today, the land rush has slowed, and solutions have changed, but the underlying problem remains. How do you differentiate yourself, and drive traffic to your career center? More importantly, how do you reach out to the precise population of candidates you need, and get them to visit? The answers are complex, but the challenges are easier to address than ever before. The tools are more straightforward, advertising rates have free-fallen to pennies on the dollar, and there are a variety of proven strategies at hand. In short, it's a great time to interrupt the flow of the right candidates to the big boards and drive traffic to your own corporate Web site.

In this chapter we'll quickly examine the foundational strategies of search engine registration and ranking, look at the most cost-efficient ways to use new pay-for-placement options, and discuss the best ways to find your target candidates where they gather to work and play—get in front of them, so to speak—and drive them to your site.

Consumer Search Engines, Directories, and Portals

Today, America Online (AOL), Yahoo!, and the Microsoft Network (MSN) are the gorillas in the consumer portal space. But each of the second-tier portals has a huge base of unique visitors, too. Because of the aggregate traffic across the dozen or so largest portals, it's important that your career center appear in the search engine index and directory of each.

> ### *Best in Class:* Top Consumer Portals
> - **America Online:** www.aol.com
> - **Microsoft Network:** www.msn.com
> - **Yahoo!:** www.yahoo.com
> - **About.com:** www.about.com
> - **Lycos:** www.lycos.com

Aside from consumer portals, there are pure-play search engines and directories to consider. The most important are those that have influential sites of their own and provide index-for-hire search and directory services to the major portals. Of these, the most prominent are Google, Overture, and the Open Directory Project (ODP).

At this point in time, Google is the most important search engine on the Web, both as a service provider to the portals, and by growing traffic rapidly to its own site. Overture provides the back-end pay-for-placement engine that drives site ranking on most search and directory sites, and the Open Directory Project is the most ubiquitous directory service.

Major consumer portals (and their search service providers), search engines, and directories are the primary tools for navigating the Internet. Your career center pages must be in their indexes, attractively described, and ranked near the top of relevant search results, in order to drive traffic.

Maximum traffic generation from these sites is a function of three principal variables: site submission, site optimization, and paid placement. Let's briefly look at each in turn.

Submitting Your Career Center

If you are a fairly large company, chances are your corporate site is already listed with the major directories and engines. Spiders (programs that are sent out onto the Web to gather information for search engines) tend to automatically pick up substantial business sites. While they are indexing your company's home page, they may also crawl through and index your career center pages as well. But to be safe, it's a good idea to register your career center independently, so that you know the pages are captured, and can ensure that they are categorized correctly and characterized in a compelling way.

There are hundreds of search engines and directories sites that generate enough traffic to care about, but only a handful that can make a huge difference to you. It's a good idea to hand-register your site with the most powerful ones; beyond that, there are a number of reputable, low-cost services that will blast your submission to hundreds more.

The search engines that matter most include Google, Inktomi, Alta Vista, AlltheWeb, Overture, and Ask Jeeves/Teoma. Most operate their own sites, as well as provide third-party search services. Though they seem to change horses fairly frequently, the top consumer portals all use one or another of these engines to power their search. Registering with all of them is a good way to cover the landscape quickly and comprehensively.

The registration process is straightforward wherever you go, but it can take weeks, even months for your site to get sorted, reviewed, and into an index. However, most engines will fast-track your listing for a modest inclusion fee, or if you participate in their pay-for-placement program.

As for directories, Yahoo! is still the most important site to register with. Second is the Open Directory Project—a free, volunteer-run initiative sponsored by Netscape. The ODP is the most widely distributed directory on the Web, fueling over 250 sites—including portals like Terra Lycos, and search engines like Google, Alta Vista, and Hotbot. The third directory to consider is LookSmart, which provides directory services to The Microsoft Network among others.

Register your site by hand with the top dozen or so consumer por-

---

Best in Class: Important Places to Register Your Site

- **Google:** www.google.com
- **AltaVista:** www.altavista.com
- **AlltheWeb:** www.alltheweb.com
- **Inktomi:** www.inktomi.com
- **Teoma:** www.teoma.com
- **Open Directory Project:** www.dmoz.org
- **Looksmart:** www.looksmart.com

---

tals, search engines, and directories—and take advantage of their fast-track services if you can. Most charge between $25 and $50 to speed up your application. Yahoo! Express is by far the most expensive at around $300, but that can be a great investment for the kind of traffic Yahoo! can deliver. Pay-for-placement listings can range from pennies to several hundred dollars, depending on the number of options and search terms you select.

Bottom line, in one day and with a budget of $1,000, you can put your career center in front of a vast Internet audience. If you are budget-challenged, but have more time to wait, there are dozens of reliable site submission services that range from $100 to $300 or so. With these services, you'll fill out one master form and hit go! They do the rest, distributing your URL and abstract to hundreds of sites at once. Many also offer premium services that include site optimization and periodic resubmission of your listing.

Describing Your Career Center

Before you register with any search engine or directory, think carefully about how to describe your career center in compelling terms, using no more than 20 to 25 words. Directory editors don't like market-

---

Best in Class: Site Submission Resources
- **Submit it!:** www.submitit.com
- **AutoSubmit:** www.autosubmit.com
- **Web Site Promotion Directory:**
  www.websitepromotiondirectory.com
- **Self-Promotion.com:** www.selfpromotion.com

---

ing hype, so use a matter-of-fact, descriptive tone. Try to include keywords that your candidates will be searching on. One word is certainly *jobs*—and try to gracefully work several of the key skills you are perpetually hunting for into your abstract along with it. Here are some important tips:

- Write in complete sentences and descriptive phrases.
- Write in sentence case—never in all capital letters or title case.
- Grammar and punctuation count. Be careful and precise.
- Don't use your HTML tag as your abstract.
- Don't use promotional language or hyperbole.
- Don't repeat the title of your page in your text.

Optimization for Free Placement

Free placement is a function of how well your page conforms to a given search engine's criteria for relevance and importance. Page optimization is the process of organizing information on your Web page so it will be found easily, indexed efficiently, and awarded the highest possible ranking in relevant search results.

Web directories are built by hand, so no amount of page optimization will improve your chances of inclusion or ranking—except that professional, useful pages are more likely to be edited in. But search engines are software programs, and they can be gently manipulated into indexing your site so it will appear more often, and with a higher ranking.

Though you may register your important pages by hand, search engines rely on crawling spiders to flesh out their index and stay current. As noted above, spiders are software agents that slip through links from Web page to Web page, examining HTML tags, URLs, page titles, links, and text for information to help categorize and rank them. Each search engine has it's own algorithmic formulas to weight these variables, and those formulas change constantly.

At any given point, any search engine could be looking at only one, or at any combination of the variables. As a result, it has become both great sport and high art to outguess the spiders and improve search engine placement. Though this is a rapidly moving target, there are some fundamentals that apply—and some new strategies to consider:

- **Making the spiders welcome:** You can't have your pages indexed if the spider can't get to them. As a security measure, some Webmasters today annotate company Web pages with a robot exclusion notice. This doesn't physically block spiders that are purposely directed at those pages, but it's meant as a polite discouragement, and most search sites honor them.

  If your career center is flagged as a robot exclusion area, you simply won't be found by the spiders, or represented in most search engine indices. Make sure your Webmaster understands the importance of having your career pages indexed, and makes them accessible to crawlers.
- **Frames:** Many spiders cannot follow framed links. Avoid frames altogether if possible. (Frames divide your browser into sections, which display content from two or more Web pages. Frames are a common device, but they confuse spiders, which cannot follow the links.)
- **Static pages:** Many Web sites generate pages on the fly from a database. Again, spiders cannot follow these links. A good compromise is to create static HTML pages and have them updated periodically from the database, rather than to create each page on demand.
- **Meta tags:** Keywords in the HTML programming code were once a primary method of indexing and ranking pages. Although this is no longer true, they can be important. Make sure you include the right keywords as you build your pages.
- **URLs and page titles:** Search engines generally assume the URL and page title (the bar at the top of your browser window) are good indications of page content. If possible, describe your critical job openings on their own page, with a URL and title that contains your important keywords. Your URL might be *www.yourcompany.*

com/jobs/softwareengineer and your title might be "Software Engineering Jobs."

- **Frequency:** The most basic search algorithms count the frequency of keywords. Your job seekers will be looking for generalized topics like jobs and employment—and for keywords and phrases that describe their skills or titles, like *java* or *marketing manager*. The more often you use the right keywords in different and creative ways, the more relevant the page becomes in the index.

- **Location:** Keywords appearing near the top of your page are considered better indicators of content than keywords at the bottom of the page.

- **Inbound links:** This is fast becoming the most important ranking criteria for search engines. The notion is that the more links to your site, the more valuable it is to others. Analyzing who has linked to your site also refines the idea of what your site does and for whom it is most useful.

  One good way to build inbound links is to run a search on your own keywords and see what comes up. These are the sites that search engines consider most important—and they can be the best links to your site. Call up the Webmaster and offer to swap links. In the case of your career center, your linking partners may turn out to be job boards, with similar openings—and they may be more than happy to exchange a link, as a favor to a prospect that may be purchasing job postings someday.

- **Clicks:** Another ranking method based on relevance is to measure the click-throughs to your pages vs. other pages in the same result set. If your site is selected and clicked on more often than others, you'll be moved up.

- **Bad ideas:** To paraphrase Honest Abe, you can fool some of the search engines some of the time—but you can't fool them all, all of the time. Techniques like spamming keywords or using mirror sites and doorways (different methods of fooling search engines with replicated versions of the same Web site) will make you persona non grata fast, and will result in having your pages ejected from the index. Watch for these terms and be careful of other sketchy strategies you may read or hear about.

This all sounds pretty complicated, and it is. If you have an in-house

IT department, this is a good reason to work closely with the Web gurus. If not, you should seriously consider investing in a good site submission service that offers consulting and ongoing support.

Paying for Placement

E very major search engine today has paid placement options that help your site rise to the top of search results for your target keywords or phrases. Though controversial and relatively new, these options are here to stay.

The essential player in this space is Overture—a search engine whose offerings are based on a pay-per-click model. Customers select, and then place a bid on the keywords and terms they want to match. Bids can range from a penny to dollars a click—and the paid results are ranked from highest to lowest bid. Unpaid results follow.

For example, if your company is recruiting semiconductor engineers, you might "bid" for the term *semiconductor jobs* or *jobs for hardware engineers*. If you are the top bid, your career site will come up whenever a candidate enters that term for a search. As you can see, this is a powerful way to step in front of targeted candidates, and drive them to your career center first..

Overture provides paid placement services to the majority of major search engines and is the key vendor in this space—but most search engines offer paid placement options of their own, as well. Paid placement is a powerful and relatively low-cost strategy for driving traffic today. It may be penny-wise and pound-foolish to ignore it.

Banners, Buttons, and Sponsored Links

T he time-honored Internet advertising model is to figure out where your prospects are gathering to search, shop, read the news, get information, or download music—and slap a banner ad or sponsored link on the site. Executives go to WSJ.com (the Wall Street Journal), teens to MTV.com and job seekers to Monster.com—allowing advertisers to focus on these populations, instead of blasting ads into a generalized pool of consumers.

Of course it's not as simple as all that, and Internet sites and advertising agencies are still struggling to prove that consumers can be profiled accurately, neatly segmented, and compelled to click through the ads. This uncertainty has cratered the banner ad market for now, creating a window of competitive advantage for recruiters who know how to exploit it:

- First, the prospects you're after don't have to be cut from the herd of a large, generalized audience at Yahoo! or AOL. Many are self-selected into homogeneous Web communities and destination sites, focused on their industry and their professional or skills niche.
- Second, there has been a wholesale discounting of ad prices. They're really cheap—and increasingly billed on a performance-only basis.
- Third, your competitors are still paying to post jobs in the same crowded job boards full of active job seekers. Very few yet realize the advantages of growing their own brands and driving passive candidates to the jobs in their own career centers. This method is more focused and can be less expensive—and it virtually guarantees a higher caliber of passive candidate.

Monster.com spent tens of millions of dollars annually to build its consumer traffic base, at a time when Internet ad prices were at their peak. But you don't need mass consumer traffic for your own job board—and Internet ads are now a low-priced commodity. This is the time to be building awareness, relationships, and driving the best candidates to your career center.

> ### *Best Practice:* How Ads Are Priced
> - CPM—Cost per 1,000 Impressions
> - CPC—Cost per Click
> - CPL—Cost per Lead
> - CPS—Cost per Sale

Banners, Pricing, and Networks

Banners and buttons are simple and low-cost to design—and text links are a few words or a brief, well-chosen phrase. The days of obsessing over which shocking images and blinking words get the most click-throughs are pretty much over for now. Here's a fast primer for today's ad landscape:

Design

The best ads are attractive, but very straightforward, consisting of a single compelling message, or a simple rotation of no more than three panels in a banner. You can use any of a dozen simple graphics programs to create your own ads, or any of thousands of services specializing in banners and buttons.

Pricing

Internet advertising is universally priced by performance, usually expressed in impressions. The most common are cost per thousand views of the ad (CPM) or cost per click (CPC). CPC is the preferred method of the two, as you are paying only for visitors who actually click through to your site.

Networks

Ad networks are designed to automatically serve your ads to a targeted audience. Targeted services promise to display your ads only on sites that match your demographics. So, if you're aiming at college students, your ads will be served to pages on major youth-oriented sites and if you're aiming at high-income earners, your ads may be served to stock trading or financial news sites.

General ad networks and link exchange services swap banners relatively at random with other network participants. So, an ad for a job board may appear on a pet food site or on an individual's home page at AOL.

The Power of Sponsorships

Sponsorship ads are text blocks inserted into mail list digests, e-newsletters and other push content. E-mail is the hands-down killer app on the Internet, and there are literally hundreds of thousands of publications, news services, and vendors who send periodic messages to a base of interested readers.

Just like with banners, the process is to figure out which newsletters go to your target population and buy an ad in those. Because e-mail tends to be even more targeted and is actively pushed to the consumer, sponsorship prices can be steep. The key for recruiters is to go off the beaten track to sites that are highly targeted to your professional audience, but low cost—sometimes even free.

Guerrilla Traffic Strategies

A mazon and e-Bay attract tens of millions of visitors every month with expensive ad campaigns targeted at the biggest, most expensive sites on the Web. But you don't need a lot of visitors—you need the right visitors, from the right industries, with the right skills.

You can't reach these highly targeted prospects cost-efficiently by advertising on general consumer sites—you need to head off the road and into the Web, looking for pockets of just the right folks. As a recruiter, you are interested in people who work in specific industries, have graduated from the right colleges, possess the skills you need, and hang out with other people just like them. Here's your map to where they are:

1. **Community Sites:** Similar people gather together in Internet communities to work, play, share, and collaborate. There are all kinds of communities, from 12-step self-help groups to dog lovers, antique collectors to Metallica fans. The ones we're interested in are communities where people meet to address industry, skills-based, or professional interests. These include:
   - Organizations
   - Alumni groups
   - Web forums
   - Mail lists
   - User groups

2. **Destinations:** Similar people go to the same sites for industry and skills-related news, information, and tools. These include:
   - Trade publications
   - Industry vortals (Vortal is shorthand for vertical portal. Vortals are sites filled with information and links targeted to a specific industry, skill, location or other vertical topic.)
   - Skills vortals
   - Local vortals

In later chapters we'll examine techniques for mining each of these kinds of sites quickly and simply, for candidates with specific attributes. For now, let's look at how you can inexpensively advertise your company's brand and opportunities—in places and ways that guarantee the most targeted exposure, with the least competition, at the lowest cost.

Advertising into Communities

Online communities don't exist to advertise jobs, they are gathering places for people with similar interests. In a community strategy, your objective is to drive the members to your career center. By the way, if they have a job board—go ahead and post a few. But be alert to the ways you can drive their members back to your career center where all your jobs are listed.

Banners, buttons, and text links are common ways to advertise on community Web sites. Most community sites charge significantly less than the going Internet ad rates, simply because their primary focus is not to generate revenue, but to serve their members. And one great way to help is to make them aware of your company and jobs.

Many communities have minimal Web sites, so banners may not be the most effective approach. Mail lists, forums, and other communities are almost entirely organized around e-mail. And virtually every type of community uses an e-mail discussion platform or e-newsletters to keep members in touch. Sponsorship ads in community e-mail are powerful options today. Also, think about ways to sponsor activities for the community: their events, meetings, etc.—these are great ways to get an ad in front of the group, drive candidates to your Web site, and build relationships in one fell swoop.

Finding the Right Communities

Locating communities may be easier said than done, which is one reason they offer you a great competitive advantage. Communities often represent untapped pools of people with the precise skills you're looking for. Becoming a supporter and advisor to the group can result in a full harvest of candidates for years to come.

Of course, communities are self-profiling—at least to the extent that they publish the interests of the group. The Society of Human Resource Managers (SHRM) is full of human resource professionals. The Chicago Java Developers Forum is full of Java programmers from the Chicago area, and the Wharton Business School Alumni site is filled with MBAs.

There are tens of thousands of prominent and less obvious communities hosted on the Web. Most have been aggregated into one database or another or are listed in a directory maintained by an interested individual, company, or vertical portal.

To start, think about the keywords that define your target candidate:

- What industry do they work in?
- What are their titles?
- What skills do they have?
- What tools do they work with?
- What companies have they worked for?
- Where did they go to school?
- Where do they live?

Find communities that match those keywords and you'll find your candidates. There are databases and lists of communities for every type of candidate on the Internet—and more that can be found with search engines. As we look at each model, we'll provide some key resources and search strings to help.

Organizations

Industry, professional, and skills-based organizations are the most traditional and formally organized business communities. Virtually every business association has moved onto the Web, and most offer a variety of resources online, including meeting schedules, training programs, and membership directories. Many also host community forums and publish newsletters—and the larger groups are installing their own job boards at a rapid clip.

Organizations should be happy to help companies who might hire their members. Make contact and explore the possibilities with local chapters (usually listed on the site) and the national headquarters. There can be a number of low-cost ways to reach their membership, including advertising on their site, in their forums and newsletters, and sponsoring or speaking at meetings and events.

Professional organizations are easy to find—there are numerous free, searchable sites that list thousands of the prominent professional organizations.

If you need to look further, you can use a search engine to locate even more. Here are some search strings you can copy into Google to

---

Best in Class: Organizational Lookups
- **American Society of Association Executives:** A searchable database of over 6,500 organizations. Go to: www.asaenet.org
- **Associations Central:** A gateway to association-related information on the Net. Go to: www.associationcentral.com
- **Google Directory:** Drill down to Society > Organizations > Directory.

---

find organizations in your target market, industry, or skill set:

Organizational Search Strings

- association AND members AND *<your keywords>*
- site:org AND *<your keywords>*

College Alumni Sites

Active college alumni range from recent graduates to the top officers in the world's largest corporations. Alumni groups exist to serve their members, and many are highly organized, well funded, and administered by employees of the college, university, or grad school.

Some are self-profiling to the extent that their members tend towards specific professions, skills, or business sectors. For example, the country's top business schools tend to provide a large number of the MBAs hired by consulting firms and Wall Street, and those who eventually migrate into the senior executive ranks of the *Fortune* 500. Law schools obviously graduate lawyers, medical schools graduate doctors, and engineering schools produce engineers.

Four-year liberal arts colleges are less easily profiled, except to note that a high percentage of their graduates may be from surrounding markets, or have developed an affinity for the community in which their alma mater resides. In other words, because they have friends and relationships in place, Berkeley and Stanford grads may be more attracted to relocating back to the San Francisco Bay Area, NYU grads to Manhattan or the environs, or MIT grads back to Boston.

College alumni groups can be powerful networks to tap into. There is an affinity among graduates of the same college, and a sense of responsibility to help others, particularly with career opportunities. Yet very few employers are approaching these organizations directly today, aside from brushing up against them in the course of their normal college recruiting activities. Remember, the object in advertising into college alumni sites is not to reach this year's grads—it's to reach seasoned professionals who remain in touch with their college or grad school networks.

Like professional organizations, there are free, searchable directories of college alumni Web sites. If you are targeting specific colleges and cannot locate their alumni groups otherwise, contact the school's annual fund drive or development department. The folks who are responsible for raising money always know where the alumni are. And, if you have specific opportunities to share, they may be happy to send an e-mail message for you to a particular segment of the group. Like recruiters, good fundraisers are always looking for ways to touch base with their network and pass along a message of value. The fact that you have job opportunities for their members should motivate them to help you.

Alumni sites aren't usually huge traffic generators, but some well-funded organizations do provide sophisticated services for their group. Check out the site to see if ads make sense—but the best opportunities may be sponsoring push newsletters or bulletins.

Best in Class: College Alumni Lookups

- **Alumni.net:** Vertical portal for schools, worldwide. Go to: www.alumni.net
- **Gradschools.com:** A database of grad schools searchable by degree or program. Go to: www.gradschools.com

---

Many alumni groups are private efforts, organized and hosted by an eager swim team captain or class secretary. That means they won't be listed in the official directory sites, but can still be found with search engines. Here's a search string you can clip into Google to find more college alumni sites:

College Alumni Search String

- site:edu AND intitle:alumni OR inurl:alumni AND <*your keywords*>

Corporate Alumni Sites

C ompanies fresh from the talent wars of the late 1990s realize that they are outplacing employees today whom they will be scrambling to replace in a few short years. As a result, they are much more sensitive to how they displace these workers, and are thinking about ways to keep them close and in contact with the company. Building alumni communities is emerging as a key strategy to keep departed workers friendly and within reach.

Corporate alumni sites are relatively new arrows in the recruiting quiver. They originated as private networks of former employees who wanted to stay in touch with each other after moving on to new jobs or retiring. The earliest sites were hosted and often guarded closely by individuals who considered recruiting to be a crass intrusion. Today, most realize that networking new job opportunities is an important and valuable focus for the group.

The first commercial corporate forums were launched by Vault.com—and were characterized as virtual water coolers where current and prospective employees of a company could meet to chew the fat. The forums were designed to give grad students and early career professionals a glimpse inside the cultures of a variety of prominent firms. However, much to the dismay of many employers, early conversations often devolved into angry diatribes posted by disgruntled employees.

The second generation of corporate alumni sites aimed to give employers a networking tool of their own. These third-party sites typically charge employers to host forums for their workers—and provide networking tools that include membership directories, company news, and access to other community features.

In paying for hosted forums, most employers aren't looking to control the conversation—they are preserving relationships and maintaining a link to former employees whom they may want to hire back, or who may have friends that can be tapped. In short, the primary purpose of these sites is to enable community-based recruitment platforms. For detailed information about how to build an alumni network for your own company—and for a list of major players, see Chapter 3, Turn Your Alumni into Recruiters.

There are many more informal corporate alumni networks on the Web than company- sponsored groups. Here's a Google search string that will help you find them:

Corporate Alumni Search String

- "corporate alumni" OR "ex employees" AND <your keywords>

Web Forums and Discussion Groups

Many trade publication sites, industry news sites, and individuals host business Web forums—where people gather to share information. Many of these sites are highly targeted and self-profiling, as they are organized around specific industries, professions, or skills. Find the right conversations and you'll find the right people. Here are some thoughts once you get there:

It Pays to Listen

If you can join and follow the conversation for a while, do so. Some groups are more about posting jokes and gripes than serious business issues. Make sure the group is large enough and professional enough to be worth the effort. If you can't join, it doesn't mean you can't advertise. Contact the moderator and discuss the character of the group and the media opportunities.

It's Not a Job Board

Good forums are designed to stay on topic, and unless job posting is explicitly permitted in the rules of the group, don't do it. Instead, send a message to the moderator and ask how you should approach the group—perhaps they know of some members you can send your jobs to offline, or mention them in one of their own posts.

Build a Relationship

Make it clear you are not interested in turning the forum into a job board, but would like to create a long-term relationship as a partner to the group. Is there something your company might bring to the party? Is your firm knowledgeable in some key area? Can you help with tools? Can you encourage some of your own experts to join the group and make friends? Remember, your long-term goal is to find a few great communities you can nourish and grow into an automated recruiting pipeline.

Plant the Seeds of Commerce

Many Web forums are already hip to the fact that they can make money by helping you advertise into their groups. In fact, there are huge forum platforms like Yahoo! Clubs or Topica, whose entire business model is traffic aggregation and advertising.

But there are still many forums hosted or moderated by firms and individuals who are focused on their topics and members—but not revenue. It may be up to you to educate and help them understand the value of alerting their members to your jobs. After all, jobs aimed at the people in a particular group are an important and valuable resource.

Perhaps your advertising support can help defray the costs of new equipment or software—or allow them to offer more services to their members. Be creative and offer something the site manager may not have thought of. With a fairly large community of the right people, an investment to become a sponsor and friend can pay great dividends.

Mail Lists

Mail lists are forum conversations distributed via e-mail, either as individual messages or in a periodic digest. Some mail lists invite participation from recruiters, but again, if not explicitly stated in the rules, make sure you contact the moderator first and get the lay of the land.

Mail lists are great, because they are pushed to the participants—and so are more closely followed, and garner better participation than most Web-only forums. The best opportunities to pursue are placing sponsorship ads or threads in the forum, containing links to your career center. Alternatively, you might put a banner on the registration or in the help section.

There are mail lists focused on every business topic you can imagine—from broad strategic issues to arcane technical considerations. As long as it's worth chatting about, you'll find it somewhere on the Web, with an e-mail newsletter attached.

Many mail lists are maintained by individuals and small organizations, and may not be listed in the major directories. Others may not publish their conversations on the Web at all, and take place entirely via e-mail.

However, often you'll find that members will archive threads on a

> ***Best in Class:*** **Hosted Forums and Mail Lists**
> - **Yahoo! Groups:** http://groups.yahoo.com
> - **Topica:** www.topica.com
> - **Cool List:** www.coollist.com
> - **Delphi Forums:** www.delphiforums.com

Web site for their own use or post them on a Web site to share with others. If you can find those threads, you can usually follow them back to the source. Here's a Google search string that can help:

Forum Archives Search String

- intitle:archive AND "mailing list" OR "mail list" AND *<your keywords>*

User Groups

The Internet began as a series of interconnected technical user groups—sharing ideas between colleges, government sites and a network of defense think tanks. Today, there are tens of thousands of user groups with active Web sites serving every part of the globe.

Technical user groups can be important recruiting assets—partly because they're still an uncharted wilderness area for most employers and recruiters—but also because of the perpetual shortage of skilled information technology workers in our knowledge-based economy and workforce. Looking forward over the next decade, competition for the best IT and engineering candidates will remain red hot. That means you'll be more liable to find the best candidates sharing ideas with their colleagues in user groups than surfing job boards looking for jobs.

There are user groups formed around broad industry issues, and others minutely focused on a single platform, language, or tool. Most offer forums or mail lists, and many large groups operate sophisticated Web sites, some with their own job boards and resume banks. User groups are highly localized, and there are targeted resources for most metro areas, states, and regions—as well as thousands of international groups.

User groups offer a wide range of advertising options. Though many are now actively pursuing a revenue plan, many others are still operating Web sites, moderating forums, and publishing newsletters on a shoestring—and can use all the help they can get. As with other communities, it's important that you are sensitive to their mission and approach them as a relationship-builder, not a salesperson. But help them understand how beneficial your support can be for them—and your jobs can be for their members.

Best in Class: User Group Directories
- **American Personal Computer User Groups Directory:** http://cdb.apcug.org/loclist.asp
- **Google Directory Listings:** Drill down to Computers > Organizations > User Groups

---

Today, every company in every industry has some technical need—whether it's engineers to design and build products or simply skilled technicians to install computers, servers, a network, or software. Understanding your company's technical needs and building strong bridges to the right user groups in your area can be the best way to ensure a steady supply of these increasingly difficult-to-recruit candidates.

User Group Search String

n intitle:"user group" OR intitle:"discussion group" AND < *your keywords*>

Communities Are Viral Networks

Remember, advertising into communities of any type represents a broader opportunity than posting a job on a job board. Communities are collaborative mediums—and are fertile grounds for the type of viral message that can turn you instantly into the preferred recruiter or employer for the entire group.

The best viral marketing programs are built on the same low-friction transmission and network dynamics you are tapping into by advertising into communities. Social scientists tell us that the average person has an immediate network of 15 to 20 people, and has regular contact with an extended network of scores, even hundreds more. A significant percentage of acquaintances in adult networks are related by skill set, profession, or a current or past shared workplace. Hence, there are very good odds your ad will be forwarded to a number of prospects outside the core of the community audience, either by chance along with other content, or by design as a referral.

Advertising at Destination Sites

The Web destinations we care about are the sites that your target candidate visits regularly for news, information, or tools related to their occupation or specialties. These tend to be a trade news source, online newsletter, Webzine—or a vertical portal with links to targeted skills, industry, or product sites.

Destination sites are more liable than communities to have a formal ad model already in place. Many are commercial media ventures, after all—though there are also many amateur enthusiasts who have grown a loyal following by publishing directories of links to specific industry or skills resources.

Whether they offer news, articles, or links, these sites attract a targeted audience. Most provide low-cost banner or text ad options on article or links pages; some have forums, and many have newsletters as well. Like associations and user groups, the more sophisticated sites are beginning to add job boards of their own.

Best in Class: General News Directories
- **Local and National Online Newspaper Directory:** A huge meta-list of local newspaper sites. Go to: http://newslink.org/met-news.html
- **Business Journal Directory:** Business news for over 40 metro areas. Go to: www.bizjournals.com
- **Google News:** News portal, linked to thousands of publications. Go to: www.google.com/news/

Trade News and Publication Sites

The trade publishing industry covers every conceivable skills and industry niche—and virtually all have a Web presence today.

Many smaller publications may not be listed, but provide Web content to other sites in their industry or skills niche. Also, larger publications are

> **Best in Class: Trade Directories**
> - **Trade Publications Search Engine:** Just what the name says. Go to: www.newsdirectory.com
> - **Google Directory Listing:** Drill down to Business > Resources > News and Publications > By Industry

often syndicated or hosted on a variety of personal and business Web sites. If you find an article aimed at your target candidate, chances are it will be on a site full of other resources aimed at them—or you can follow it back to a source that does. Here's a Google search string to find articles:

Article Search String

- intitle:"press release" OR intitle:article AND *<your keywords>*

Skills or Industry Vortals

The term "vortal" is shorthand for vertical portal, and denotes a site that provides comprehensive information and links to a specific topic. There are sports vortals for tennis, basketball, and soccer; science vortals for astronomy, biology, and physics—and business vortals representing a variety of targeted industries, professions, and skills. Though vortals are a common feature of trade publication sites, many individuals offer valuable sites as well. Here are some Google search strings to help you find them:

Vortal Search Strings

- intitle:links AND intitle:*<your keywords>*
- intitle:resources AND intitle:*<your keywords>* AND *<your location>*

If you are targeting generalized pools of candidates in specific locations, there are vortals aimed at literally every metro area, and many out there in the white space on the map. Go to: www.citysearch.com to find a directory of sites for major metro areas—and check the newspapers. The *San Francisco Chronicle's* site at www.sfgate.com and the New York Times www.nytimes.com are great examples of local vortals.

Also, you will find industry, skills, and professional vortals aimed at specific cities, states, and regions—simply add AND *<your location keywords>* to your search string to narrow the results to your location.

Internet Advertising Networks

Ad networks like DoubleClick and 24/7 Media have formed networks of Internet sites—and serve ads to them in the course of targeted advertising campaigns. The notion is that advertisers can fine-tune their campaigns to the specific characteristics of people found on the various sites in the networks. It's a great idea, and an extraordinarily powerful channel for some types of advertisers.

But these agencies are struggling today—not only with low banner prices, which severely affects their revenue—but also with delivering on the promise that they can serve ads to a precise set of eyeballs. For these reasons, and because their networks tend to be built around the largest, most highly trafficked sites possible, they are not a compelling resource for a guerrilla ad campaign. You'll do better finding your own communities and destinations, and contacting them directly. But keep an eye on this model, as it may evolve into an efficient tool set for recruiting as well.

Best in Class: Banner Networks
- **DoubleClick:** www.doubleclick.com
- **24/7 Real Media:** www.247realmedia.com
- **Link Exchange:** www.bcentral.com

Budgeting Your Media

The key to an effective, low-cost campaign is to go off the beaten path to find communities and vortals with highly targeted traffic, but very inexpensive advertising rates. This is a guerrilla strategy and takes more time and effort than simply advertising at well-known media sites, but the payoff in savings and competitive advantage can make this a great investment.

There are pools of people everywhere on the Web, but very few recruiters or employers know how to find them and reach them effectively. This is precisely why sites like Yahoo! and Monster.com, who have invested huge amounts of capital to become well known and easy to find, can command premium fees. In a business world where time is often the scarce resource, this expensive branding strategy is very effective.

At the same time, though, these sites trade high traffic numbers for specificity. As a result, audience characteristics are very diffuse, so you end up paying a premium price to reach a large group of people who may not be right for you. As the Web matures, narrow-casting into highly specific pools will become easier—today, you have to hunt around a bit for a good, low-cost spot to fish.

Recruiters and employers who are looking for great people will find more of them in their own communities and vortals than in job boards—simply because the most valuable candidates aren't looking for a job. Though this type of advertising may be non-intuitive to staffing professionals accustomed to advertising in newspapers and job boards, it is a powerful tool, and belongs in the growth column of your media budget.

8

Grow Candidate Communities

Y ou've built a great recruiting Web site that attracts and educates job seekers and passive candidates alike. They arrive, browse your content, and search for jobs—and a handful leave a resume behind. The rest disappear into the ether of the World Wide Web.

How many might have been a perfect candidate? How many will ever be back? This chapter explores ways to learn about the people that visit your site, attract them into targeted communities based on their skills and interests, and build long-term relationships with them.

Why would recruiters be interested in this? Because Web communities are self-selecting pools of qualified, interested candidates who can be assessed continuously and recruited quickly. They become a pipeline of just-in-time candidates.

A Next Generation Strategy

T he concepts in this chapter are another look forward for recruiters, recruitment managers and executives. The notion of using value-added information to grow communities filled with just-in-time candidates represents as radical a paradigm shift today as job boards were a decade ago.

A small population of early adopters has been successfully tending communities of candidates for years. But the practice of creating a supply of people who share information with you, who come to trust your brand and so become de facto qualified and interested candidates is simply not in the mainstream yet.

But it's coming fast. As recruitment strategists digest the new models enabled by the Web, it's simply a matter of time before global corporations and small recruitment shops alike build clusters of targeted candidates ready to be activated as the right job openings appear.

This paradigm requires a closer collaboration of technology, marketing, and recruiting than is typical today. It is a solution that requires a greater number of parts to be moving forward in concert, and may require a significant shift in traditional recruitment activities and management structure to be fully realized.

A Community of Candidates

We define a Web community for recruiting purposes as a pool of people with similar skills, who are drawn together by common interests. For example, if you publish a newsletter for emergency room nurses, chances are your subscribers will be nurses with ER experience. By providing information of value (your newsletter), you can draw interested parties into your orbit. To the extent those people are the same candidates you hunt for continuously, you've built a successful recruiting community.

Today, most employers and recruiters still open each search by advertising or hunting through their database for resumes on hand. Most search assignments start from scratch—and go through a repetitive and time-consuming cycle of identification, contact, relationship building, screening, and assessment, until a pool of candidates emerge.

Wouldn't it be great if that pool of candidates were already identified, screened, and ready to go? When Amazon.com gets a new business best-seller on its shelves, it knows immediately who to pitch it to. Their database tells them which prospects have previously browsed or purchased business books on their site, and what specific topics within the business category they have shown interest in. As a result, they can send a targeted message to exactly the right prospects among millions of registered users, immediately.

This idea can be extended to recruiting by simply tracking, profiling, and pooling prospective candidates into communities defined by their skill or function. Just like Amazon, you can collect information about your prospects, encourage them to come back by providing targeted information of interest to them, and learn more about them over time—effectively creating a relationship, encouraging interest in your company, and screening them as you go.

A major portion of every recruiting assignment is finding the initial candidates, assessing their skills, and determining interest. A well-run community performs these three functions in real time, enabling recruiters to reach into an interested pool of qualified candidates within minutes of receiving a new search.

Just-in-Time Recruiting

Building large pools of people may seem counterintuitive, since for decades industry has aimed to reduce inventories of every other type, lowering risk by sizing just-in-time production to demand, at the latest possible moment.

This makes perfect sense in the material world, given the potentially lethal cost of creating or committing to surplus inventory. But the investment required to build information-based communities can be nominal, the carrying costs are extraordinarily low, and a ready inventory of skilled people is a valuable competitive asset. Web communities can be one of the most powerful recruiting strategies in your plan.

For third-party recruiters, Web communities are farms filled with qualified candidates ready to pluck and sell to interested clients. For corporations, Web communities are a way to grow their own candidates and bypass expensive headhunting fees. Either way, harvesting candidates is faster than searching for them. If you've planted the right seeds and tended your fields well, your communities will save you time and money and will provide a handsome return.

One Too Many Relationships

As we've discussed, communities draw similar people around a camp-fire of common interest. Yahoo!, for example, is a media company whose entire business model is based on community building. It creates relationships by offering free information, news, forums, and services. It aggregates visitors, profiles their activities, and creates ever-more targeted ads and personally relevant offerings for them. In the process, it also becomes a familiar and trusted ally at the center of a community of users.

But recruiters have been trained to create relationships one at a time, through a traditional contact management process. They sort their most valuable candidates to the top and make an investment in nurturing long-term personal relationships with them. They may set an alert in their calendar to call quarterly or regularly send a card, an article of interest, or some other offering. Of course, this is precisely the mechanism of relationship development that Yahoo! follows—continual contact, mutual interest, trust, and eventually the offer of an opportunity—except that Yahoo! uses the Web, it's forums and e-mail, to communicate with millions of people, in many groups, continuously.

Some recruiters have learned to automate their periodic contact by using bulk e-mail to send a number of messages at once. This one-to-many contact is, in fact, the seed of a candidate community. It is a relatively small step from sending the occasional note to a variety of individual candidates, to sending them all a brief monthly newsletter. If you then encourage them to pass the newsletter to interested friends—in fact, make clear that anyone with the appropriate skills is welcome to join—you will have created a community of interest.

To the extent your newsletter narrows its content to topics of special interest for particular skills, your subscribers will soon be narrowed to those with the skills and interests to match. Voila! A pool of self-selected, qualified candidates with similar skills of a definable type.

Attracting a specific audience to specifically targeted information can be accomplished by publishing a newsletter, providing content on a Web site, or hosting a forum where similar people can collaborate. Yahoo! uses all three very effectively—and so can you.

Community Building

The Web itself, simple publishing tools, list management software, and e-mail are the most effective tools for building communities today. Today's recruiting tools, including contact management and applicant tracking systems are designed to store, retrieve, and route digits and documents, not create and grow relationships. But the Web is by nature a relationship platform, where people tend to gather, collaborate, and communicate.

The object of building a candidate community is not only to put people in orbit around your enterprise. Over time, your goal is to build stronger relationships—educating and strengthening trust—while you learn more about them by monitoring discussions, pushing them surveys, assessments, and other profiling tools.

Soon, like Yahoo! or Amazon, you'll be able to collaborate and advertise into your pools. As you do, your enterprise becomes a valued host and the employer or recruiter of choice for community members, which helps you reach in and recruit very quickly and effectively.

Creating the community relationship is a two-step process. Step one is gathering information and profiling your prospects to define some basics about their skills and interests. Step two is inviting those prospects back to participate in a community of some kind. As with Yahoo!, it may be a community of newsletter subscribers, information seekers, a forum, or all three. We'll look at each model in turn later in this chapter. For now, let's understand how to collect information and profile candidates.

The More They Click, the More They Stick

Remember our premise that recruitment is a sales process, and so your recruiting Web site should be modeled on e-commerce lessons? Well, successful e-commerce starts with understanding the customer, moves on to a continual relationship, and then on to the sale.

Understanding the customer is a process that takes place over time. Some of the ways Amazon and Yahoo! collect information are very straightforward, some are not entirely obvious, and some are downright sneaky. But they're all aimed at collecting as much data as possible into a detailed profile of the prospect's behavior and interests.

You'll want to understand everything you can about your prospects, too, so that you can offer them the right information, put them in the right pool, and eventually sort the best ones to the top. The profiling process starts when they arrive on your Web site—and your first objective is to keep them there as long as possible, so that you can record their moves and ask them questions.

There are two proven ways to keep visitors clicking. The first is to organize your content into the bite-sized, "scan and drill down" format we've discussed earlier. If you make each page a distinct topic area, you not only encourage visitors to click around and stay longer, you can later map their travels to specific interests. You'd be amazed at how much you can deduce about a visitor by following these clicks.

The second way to keep them engaged is with interactive features. The Web is more like a video game than a book, and people are conditioned to be constantly moving. They want to surf, scan, click—maybe check some boxes, vote on a survey, answer a question, chat a bit—then surf, scan, and click some more.

Profiling and Permission

So while they're clicking, what exactly are we looking for—and how do we get it?

Well, we're looking for any data that will help us contact, understand, and assess our visitors. We want to know who they are, where they live, where they're employed, what role they play, their skills and aptitudes, educational background, the tools they use, and whether they will fit into our culture. We need to understand them in detail, so we can match them to a community and measure their value. Here's how we do it—1, 2, 3:

1. **Follow the clicks:** See where they came from, where they go, and what they stop to look at. Your Webmaster probably does some of this already. If not, there are a host of simple, inexpensive Web tools that can help.

2. **Ask questions:** Use interactive features to gather precise information about the visitor's background and preferences. Surveys, polls, contests, and games are some of the features commonly used to gather contact information, interests, and aptitudes.

3. **Stay in touch:** Get them into orbit and keep them there. Make sure they're coming back for more information: Sign them up for your forums and get permission to send newsletters, product updates, special offers, or jobs.

The more you know up front, the more compelling you can make the offer to stay in touch. And of course, the longer you stay in touch, the more you'll learn, and the faster you can recruit.

Best in Class: Monitor Your Web Traffic
- **WebTrends:** www.webtrends.com
- **Accesswatch:** www.accesswatch.com

Who, What, When, Where, Why—and How?

Tracking a visitor's movements across your site and simply asking questions can yield an amazing trove of information. Think like a good newspaper reporter and organize your queries to answer the journalistic five W's. The bonus question is: How can I stay in touch and learn more?

Let's take a closer look at these questions, and the various methods you can use to gather answers:

Who Are You?

This is the most basic and important question of all. Complete contact information is the first objective of a good marketer. For recruiting purposes, recording your visitor's name, location, e-mail address, and phone number is a critical step in the profile.

You can naturally gather contact data as your visitors sign up for news, request more information, respond to a survey, or set up job agents. And of course, their survey answers, the jobs they select, and the news they sign up for should provide answers to other parts of their profile.

Where possible, coordinate your profiling activities with data gathered by your marketing group on other portions of the site. All visitors, even those coming for sales and product information, are potential candidates. As we've said before, the simple fact that they are on your Web site qualifies them as likely participants in your industry. Customers, partners, consultants, and competitors are all interested and knowledgeable about what you do. In fact, the best passive candidates come from these categories.

Marketing promotions often use giveaways and special offers as prospecting tools to collect contact information. A downloadable white paper, free trial, or chance to win a prize are all effective ways to exchange something of value for more extensive profile information. Put the offer on your career site, and have your prospects complete a profile form to download or qualify for it. In order to gather structured, searchable information for your contact database, remember to use drop-down options as opposed to blank fields in your forms. Also, for recruiting purposes, it's important to ask for personal e-mail addresses and home phone numbers.

What Are You?

This is an abbreviated way to ask: What is your title? What is your function? What are your skills? What jobs would fit you best?

If you pay attention, you can infer a great deal by simply following a visitor's path through your Web site. For example, if someone spends a lot of time on your sales pages, they are liable to be a prospective client (or competitor). If they go directly to customer support, log in with a password, and focus on technical help for Java implementation, they are certainly a customer, and very likely a software engineer with java programming skills.

The key to this type of intelligence is a system that tags each visitor's unique IP address as the visitor arrives, monitors the page views, and records the specific pages traveled to.

In this system, Web pages are catalogued into a database by topic, and the visitor's IP and page view history are matched to a prospect record, as soon as contact data is acquired. A cookie is then passed to the visitor's browser, so that as new information is collected—every time they are on your site—the new data is stored in the profile.

Following a visitor around your site has limitations, of course. The best way to gather precise data is to use interactive tools that query and assess. These can be surveys, polls, games, contests, exams, or sign-ups. Of course, if you use a candidate profiling system, you've already collected this information from applicants. Similarly, if you have a job agent, you can tell very precisely who your visitors are, what skills they have, and the types of positions they might fit, by the jobs they select to be pushed to them. But how do you learn more about the passive visitors that make up the vast majority of your traffic?

Best Practice: Serving Those Delicious Cookies

Cookies are text snippets that you can serve to your visitors as they travel about your site. Your cookie will assign a unique code to their browser, so it will recognize them each time they return. With a simple database, you can begin to collect information into a profile, linked to that cookied i.d.

The information you gather can be as simple as the time of their visit—or as complex as the pages they've viewed, a list of the topics they seem most interested in, the kinds of jobs they search, and more.

As a recruiter, you can use cookies to greet repeat visitors to your career center with pop-up ads of the kinds of jobs they viewed on their last visit. Or, you can collect information about them as they use the various interactive information traps you've set around the site.

Over time, the cookie can alert you to the fact that Susan Smith, a software engineer from Seattle, Washington, who scored highly on your Java assessment, is visiting from your competitor's company for the third time—searching for project manager jobs.

To capture detailed data on skills, aptitudes, experience, employers, and interests, you must ask for it—and you will be most successful if your query is a natural step in an interactive exercise of some sort. In other words, if you challenge someone to a game that tests their technical knowledge, it is natural to ask whether they want to play the Windows, Unix, or Linux version. If you ask someone to take an industry survey or a poll, it is natural to inquire about his or her job title and function. If you provide an activity that helps someone determine their aptitudes, it is logical that you would ask about their education, background, and current occupation.

These interactive exercises should be sprinkled throughout your entire Web site. Put a skills assessment inside your Product Help section, and not only will you identify your visitor as a customer, you may learn exactly what skills they have. If they are skills you're looking for, automatically push them an invitation to join your forum or subscribe to a skills-specific newsletter. Use your imagination and set these traps wherever you think your quarry is liable to travel on your site.

> ### *Best Practice:* Gather Information with These Interactive Features
>
> - Special offers
> - Product news
> - Industry news
> - Polls
> - Surveys
> - Quizzes
> - Games
> - Assessments
> - Profilers
> - Job agents
> - Tell a friend
> - Help and live help
> - Information request

When Can I Meet Your Friends?

People congregate in communities based on common interests, online and off. So, a software engineer or sales executive visiting your Web site is a member of a larger professional community of software engineers or sales executives. They may be best friends or casual acquaintances, may work in the same company, may be alumni of the same college, participate in the same organizations, attend the same conferences—whatever the case, your prospects certainly know more people just like them.

The only thing better than having an e-mail and phone number for your perfect candidate, is having an e-mail and phone number for all their friends, too. So, no matter what special offer, valuable download, newsletter, article, job, or interesting fact you present to your visitors, *always* help them share it. Put a link to *Send This Page (or Job, Article, Tip, etc.) to a Friend* wherever you can. Your link should pop up a form that allows the sender to designate multiple friends, by name and e-mail address, and type a brief accompanying message. Of course, the nature of the information forwarded provides the first clues about the interests, function, or skills of each recipient.

Where Are You?

An old saw says, "All employment is local." Of course that's not true anymore. We live in a highly mobile society, and most executives, managers, and corporate workers realize they may have to relocate for better opportunities. The migration of job advertising to the Web has been both a driver and a result of this mobility. It's possible for job seekers today to find new openings instantly, anywhere in the U.S. and in many locations overseas—not just on commercial job boards, but on corporate sites as well.

In fact, most career sites are a centralized view of *all* the jobs open across the enterprise in *all* locations.

So it's important to determine where the visitors are now—and where they might be willing to relocate should they become candidates. Current city and state should be standard queries in any form you use to collect contact information. And make sure that your job agent and profiler forms determine whether relocation is an option—and if so, where?

Why Are You Here?

This question really means: Are you an active job seeker? If they submit a resume, complete a skills profile or set up a job agent—the answer is yes. In that case, the agent alone can serve the community function. The visitors have already identified themselves, shared their skills and background—and you know where they are and how to get hold of them.

If they are a casual visitor, you'll have to work harder to encourage them to click around, answer questions, and grant permission to let you push them news, surveys, and polls that will help you profile them over time.

How Do We Stay in Touch?

This is the $65,000 question. To find the answer, walk awhile in your target candidates' moccasins. What information is valuable to them? Is it industry or product-related? Is it ideas they can use to grow their skills or advance their career? Is it tips and techniques to make their jobs easier? Do you or your company have a special perspective, or access to otherwise-unavailable data? The key is to promise true value—in exchange for the relationship itself.

Once you've determined what constitutes value to your prospect, it's time to select the type(s) of community you'll build.

Three Ways to Build Communities

There are three principal community models, each with its own challenges and advantages. Let's take a fast look at each:

Vertical Portal

A portal is a generalized gateway to information on the Web. A vertical portal is an organized set of links and content aimed at a specific audience. The object of the portal model is to attract targeted visitors to a Web site, and keep them coming back.

Portals offer free information in exchange for eyeballs. They may offer a directory of specialized links, a library of original content, collaborative tools, a calendar of events—basically whatever it takes to draw the right traffic to the site.

Portal building can be an extensive project or a simple page of important links. The key is to provide something of unique value to the community. A successful portal is great for recruiters, because it draws potential candidates back to your site continuously, where you can keep learning about them, perhaps even find their friends—all the while providing value that strengthens their trust and regard for your company.

Web publishing tools are simple to use and inexpensive (even free), and site hosting is a low-cost commodity today. But portals can be high-maintenance affairs. Offering an old, stale site with dated materials and broken links is a poor way to attract the best people. That means that new content, new links, and attention to detail are extremely important. But the time to find and publish new content is an entirely reasonable investment for recruiters who search for the same types of people over and over—and for whom each placement may be worth 20 to 30 percent of the first year's salary, not to mention for corporations who are tired of paying those headhunting fees.

News Service

The news model is an umbrella for any correspondence that is regularly pushed to a prospect's desktop via e-mail. Most commonly, this takes the form of a weekly or monthly newsletter that provides targeted information to the community.

Depending on your audience, the topic might be important product announcements, industry updates, "how to" tutorials—whatever you can count on your prospect to be interested in. The newsletter itself can be brief; in fact, it can consist of links to articles on the Web, in lieu of original content. As with the portal model, the key to newsletter success is providing information of unique value.

News sign-ups can be fairly detailed, so there's an opportunity to collect much more than contact information. If the newsletter is skills-focused, it's reasonable to embed questions about your subscribers' current skills (in order that you might better serve them). Once subscribed, your readers should be presented periodically with polls and surveys related to their profession. Promising to share the results among those who respond can be a good way to jump-start participation.

Before you push e-mail to a prospect, make sure he or she agrees to receive it. The process is called "opting-in," and it is what differentiates your newsletter from unsolicited commercial e-mail, or spam. By completing the subscription form, your prospect has opted to receive specific information.

Make sure that the various types of mail you may send are options that can be selected, or de-selected. In other words, if your prospect signs up for skills information, he or she should be able to select or refuse to receive sales promotions at the same time.

Newsletters are common and simple to produce, either in text or HTML format. The e-mail tools required to mail from your database are easy to find and easy to use—or you can outsource mailing to any of a number of inexpensive services.

- If you are sending messages inviting people to subscribe to a newsletter or visit your career center, make sure you give them an opportunity to refuse further mail from you.
- If people do opt-out, be scrupulous about removing them immediately and permanently from your mail list.
- No matter how you may be provoked, simply don't respond to flames—just remove the offender and move on.
- You are not selling anything—so don't sound like a salesperson. You are offering value added information that will assist your community members with professional issues. Your tone should be helpful, but businesslike.
- E-mail is never private—the Internet is a public medium and as your message travels through it, others can read your mail. Don't

---

Best in Class: E-mail Services

- **List Builder:** Low-cost, solid Microsoft application puts you in control of your mailing. Go to: www.bcentral.com
- **Messagemedia:** The deluxe service, recently acquired by Doubleclick. Go to www.messagemedia.com
- **L-Soft:** Another strong contender for managing mail lists and campaigns. Go to: www.lsoft.com

---

> ### *Best Practice:* E-mail Netiquette
> As you grow your communities, you will be reaching out to inter-
> ested prospects via e-mail. This professional, targeted correspon-
> dence is not spam, but you're liable to run into a Web terrorist or
> two who just can't see the difference. Don't give these extremists
> the satisfaction of pointing fingers and calling you names—make
> sure you are a courteous, thoughtful, and knowledgeable netizen.

---

send confidential correspondence over the Web.

- Document attachments will always be impossible for some members of your community to open. Worse, they might not make it
  through your members' firewalls. And worst of all, they can carry
  viruses and other nasty critters. Just don't send them.
- Be friendly but professional. You are building business communities—you can assume your audience is there to grow their career
  and skills, not tell each other off-color jokes.
- Respect your community's time and inbox by only sending necessary, periodic e-mail.

Discussion Groups

A Discussion Group can be a Web forum, mail list, or both. The object is
to provide a platform for community members to share ideas and information with their peers.

A Web forum is a discussion group hosted on a Web site. Visitors travel to the site to participate and post questions and answers. Most forums
provide a daily or weekly e-mail digest of the posts. That way, subscribers
can monitor the conversation, see new questions, and click to the site to
respond. A mail list is simply the digest, without a Web site. To post, subscribers send an e-mail to a moderator, who then includes the thread in
the next digest.

Forums and mail lists are powerful recruiting tools. As you monitor
or join the discussion, you'll quickly identify the old pros as the ones providing the answers to the questions posted by the less experienced folks.
You'll see the quality of the question, the nature of the response, and get
a sense for individual personalities—in effect, pre-screening the group for
candidates as you go.

Participating in a value-added way, by moderating the group, or simply adding your thoughts, will make you one of the gang—and the

---

Best in Class: Forums

Web Forum and Digest Platforms

- **Web Crossing:** Powers Adobe, Apple, New York Times, and AIRS Forums. Go to: www.webcrossing.com
- **Vbulletin:** A robust, low-cost solution. Go to: www.vbulletin.com

Free Ad-Sponsored Forums and Lists

- **YAHOO! Groups:** Over 5,000 groups in the employment subcategory alone. Go to: www.groupsyahoo.com
- **Topica:** A great free resource. Start a mail list or forum in minutes. Go to www.topica.com

---

recruiter or employer of choice members turn to when they are looking for a new opportunity. As a bonus, forums provide an inside look at the issues your candidates deal with every day. And of course, the better you understand your candidates, the more effectively you can recruit them.

Turnkey Web forum and digest software is available at a reasonable cost, and there are a number of freeware options available. Another route is to use Yahoo!, or other service providers that offer a free forum platform, in return for being able to advertise into your group. Either way, forums are becoming a low-cost staple for corporations who host user groups, and customer service organizations are implementing them to provide interactive help desk tools. Now, recruiters too are discovering how effective they can be in attracting, profiling, and building relationships with targeted candidates.

Part Three

Advertise Your Job Openings

9

Organize Your Web Job Posting Campaign

J ob boards are the largest line items in e-recruiting budgets today. But thousands of competitors, shifting alliances, and new technologies make the job board market anything but stable. This year's best media buy may become next year's overpriced, underproducing channel. It's important to understand the players and plan carefully.

Job postings have exploded over the past decade, principally at the expense of newspaper classifieds—once the unchallenged medium for recruitment advertising. Newspapers are losing more ad revenue every year to job boards—in fact, even as the number of recruitment ads fell sharply with the economy in 2001 and 2002, job boards continued to grow.

As the Internet matures, it's hard to imagine that the newspapers can stuff this genie back in the bottle. So far, their attempts to counterattack have been clumsy at best—like a deer in the headlights, most are stuck between competing headlong and refusing to cannibalize their own best revenue streams in the process. While they dither, more and more job ads are simply moving online to a new audience.

But if newspapers are the biggest losers so far, who will the winners be? Once it seemed that the big career hubs were unstoppable juggernauts. But will the Monster.com, Yahoo! HotJobs, and CareerBuilder troika become the career equivalent of the big three credit repositories? Or will they die the death of a thousand paper cuts at the hands of niche and local job boards?

More likely, they will be interrupted by their own clients, as corporate recruiters become more skilled at driving traffic to their own sites. Already, virtually every large company posts jobs on their own site—yet only half of the *Fortune* 500 post on any of the big career sites. There are many times more jobs on corporate sites than on career sites today—and employers are learning that it can be less costly to bring applicants to all of them than advertise a fraction of them on job boards.

In this chapter, we'll think about planning and media options, we'll look at an array of important partners and tools—and we'll learn to craft great job ads, aimed at the highest-performing candidates.

In the chapters following, we'll look at the dynamics and challenges you'll face at the biggest job boards, examine the universe of niche boards, and look at the emerging models in each.

Allocating Your Time and Resources

A Web media plan allocates time and resources over the arc of your recruiting objectives. Here's a view of its components parts:

- **Objectives:** Your recruiting goals are the sum of the type and number of candidates you need, where and when you need them. Your plan then, is a projection of the capital and labor resources required to complete your objectives within the necessary time frames.
- **Time:** Your overall sourcing plan should look a year ahead and be revised quarterly. Within that frame, you will have deadlines for specific interim objectives. These should be clearly defined with a timeline, resources list, and task list for each.
- **Resources:** You have two principal resources to deploy: capital and labor. Capital is the sum of budget dollars and goodwill that can be exchanged for assets. Labor is the sum of management focus and team bandwidth that can be allocated to execute the plan.

- **Results:** Tracking your cost-to-hire and measuring return on investment (ROI) across your media placement are the only ways you'll understand what works and what doesn't. The Web is a new medium, in a state of rapid change—what worked last year may not work now.

Whether you use a spreadsheet, or end-to-end applicant tracking system—make sure your process is transparent from ad placement through to the hire. Use the data to do more of what works, and less of what doesn't.

Who you need to hire, when, and where will drive the number, frequency, and geographic reach of your ads and job postings. If you have more money than time, you should aim towards more traditional methods and use easy-to-find, branded job boards. If you have more time than money, use it to explore niche sites, communities, and low-cost traffic strategies. Your planning goal is to allocate time and capital most efficiently across your range of options.

Considering Your Web Options

The lion's share of media placement on the Web is routinely funneled to the largest job boards—often at the expense of more targeted and more efficient resources. Yet, for all the budget dollars spent on the major boards, employers are reporting relatively dismal results.

In a 2001 study conducted by Career X-Roads—18 public corporations reported that in a sample of 122,000 positions filled, less than 8 percent of hires came from job boards—and only a fraction of those from the largest sites. By contrast, 12 percent of hires came through the corporate career center.

Job seekers are also reporting that a low percentage of their jobs are coming directly from these boards. A recent survey by Drake Beam Morin indicated that over 60 percent of its career transition clients are finding new positions via networking—while only 6 percent are being hired from job board applications.

Now, remember, these are data collected at the recession end of the pendulum, in a market where higher referrals and more active visits to company hiring sites can be expected. In a labor shortage market, fewer employees have friends who are out of work, and fewer people will be visiting company Web sites to actively look for jobs.

But it is startling nonetheless—perhaps even a wake-up call if you've been automatically signing over the greater portion of your e-recruiting budget to a handful of job boards based on their traffic and brand name.

A more diversified Web media plan should consider:

- The power of employee and partner referral, and a campaign to advertise and manage it on the Web.
- Banners, buttons, links, and sponsorships in targeted communities and destinations, to drive passive candidate traffic to your own Web site.
- Pushing ads to your own candidate communities through newsletters and agents.
- Choosing one or two major job boards, if your company is large enough and adequately branded to benefit. (See Chapter 10, Broadcast to Job Seekers at the Monster Job Boards, to better understand your chances of success, if you are a smaller company or recruiter.)
- Choosing a handful of the best niche boards, based on the industries, professions, or skills you are targeting.
- Choosing the best local job boards based on the importance of various cities or metro areas in your plan.
- Broadcasting and cross-posting to free sites and news groups.

We've discussed Web-based employee referral, driving traffic to your own career center, and community building in earlier chapters. As Web recruiting strategies mature, these options will certainly become more prominent in media planning. At the same time, it's important to weigh the opportunities that the major boards, niche boards, local, and free boards offer.

Thinking Through Your Plan

Your Web media plan is an important part of your recruiting plan, which should be integral to your strategic and business forecasting process. It should be built annually, reviewed at least quarterly, and adjusted where necessary.

Your plan starts with a series of headcount projections:

- How many people will your company need to achieve its business goals in the upcoming year?
- How many in each region or facility?
- How many to replace turnover, normal attrition, promotions, and transfers?
- How many will be added through planned or likely mergers and acquisitions?

Then goes to timing, by region:

- When will the gaps appear?
- When will you have to proactively start recruiting to ensure continuity?

Then to strategies:

- What functions and skills will you need, in which locations?
- Where are those candidates on the Web? How do you get in front of them?
- Who are you competing with? How will you position yourself against them?
- What is your core value proposition? What will your ads say?

Then to tools:

- How many jobs will you post? How many sites will you post to?
- Will you use a recruitment ad agency?
- Will you use posting tools?
- How many ads do you need? Banners? Text? Sponsorships?

Then to resources:

- How will you allocate your capital and labor over the plan?
- What combination of activities will deliver the highest return on investment?
- What kind of contingency resources should you hold in reserve?

Pricing Your Plan

How long is a piece of string? Well, it depends on where it starts and where it ends. Like string, there's no standard size or cost when it comes to a media campaign. You'll need a sufficient amount of money and time to execute crisply and attain your objectives—with a little in reserve in case things don't work out as planned.

In the short term, job posting prices have fallen along with ad rates from their highs in 2000 and 2001. As of this writing, the market shake-out is continuing and many sites remain under pressure. Over the longer term, you can expect this cycle to reverse, and prices will eventually begin to trend upwards again. But barring the return of a torrid staffing market before mid-decade, rates won't be exploding to the upside—they are more likely to rise in modest increments as the market progressively firms.

For media planning today, here are some broad guidelines:

- Individual job postings at the major sites have fallen from $250 to $350 per month to a similar price for two to three months. In other words, the entry price is the same, but your listing will be posted longer. You can cut these numbers in half again, if you'll commit to volume packs of jobs.
- Niche boards today typically range from $100 to $200 per two- to three-month period. Here again, there is significant flexibility and further discounting available for volume posting.
- Ad rates have fallen to a fraction of their bubble-era schedules. Though it's more difficult to generalize in this market, it seems that non-targeted consumer sites have fallen farthest—some from as high as $200 to just over $2 CPM.

  Targeted rate cards have suffered less, though many are now below $10 CPM. It's safe to project that you can reach into even the best candidate communities for under $15 CPM.

If you are posting hundreds or thousands of jobs over the course of a campaign, you'll need to factor in posting and administration, expressed in labor and tools costs. Figure it takes fifteen minutes of burdened admin-level cost to enter and check a single job—and extrapolate that over your campaign.

If you decide to invest in meta-posting software or services, your labor costs can be exchanged for fees ranging from several dollars per job, per board for low volumes, down to pennies per posting for a large, flat-rate contract. If you use a full-service recruitment ad agency, your posting costs may disappear entirely into the agreement. Let's take a brief look at these two models.

Recruitment Ad Agencies

For decades, the largest corporations have used recruitment ad agencies to help them develop their employment brands, plan media campaigns, create ads, and negotiate placement in newspapers and trade publications. The niche is tiny relative to the overall advertising market, but recruitment ad agencies are important advisors and allies to companies that purchase and schedule vast amounts of media.

Major recruitment ad agencies such as Bernard Hodes helped lead the industry to the Web, and they continue to help their clients move online. Web-only agencies and consultants also help employers plan and place job postings. These boutique agencies compete with the majors in the *Fortune* 1000 tier—and have taken the model down market to mid-size employers. Small companies and third-party recruiters rarely use agencies to plan or place media.

Recruitment ad agencies can be powerful partners and valuable allies. Here's why their services are so compelling to large companies:

- **Knowledge:** Because media is their core business, agencies know the landscape and players and can navigate their clients past low-producing or overly expensive options.
- **Planning:** National and international media campaigns can be extraordinarily complex. Agencies have the experience and resources to streamline the plan-building process.
- **Pricing:** Agencies derive significant revenues from the media provider, not directly from the client. That means that they can provide planning, placement, and management services at a lower cost to the end user.
- **Relationships:** Agencies have close relationships with primary media outlets, and can help you cut through the tape and get to decision makers quickly.
- **Pass-through:** Because agencies are negotiating huge media placement on behalf of multiple clients, they can drive prices down, then package and pass those discounts to their clients.
- **Posting:** Agencies are beginning to bundle job posting services into their media contract. This can be a great answer to a tedious and time-consuming administrative chore.
- **Contracts:** Agencies negotiate individual media deals with each

vendor, and send you one integrated invoice. This is particularly valuable with online job postings that extend over dozens of sites, all with different pricing and terms.

There are some caveats. First, agencies are bound to the networks they've created, which are typically composed of the largest career hubs and most prominent niche sites. This is an important portion of most large media plans but should not consume your entire budget. If you hand off your entire plan to an agency, you may be painting yourself into a corner that is more profitable for the agency than optimal for you.

Second, it's a mistake to rely on most agencies for cutting-edge strategies. Their business is traditional media placement—and they won't be taking your budget deep into the Web to ferret out untapped communities of passive candidates. As valuable as they are in the mainstream media world, most simply don't have the time, inclination, or expertise to help you craft guerrilla media campaigns.

Best in Class: Recruitment Ad Agencies

- **Bernard Hodes Group:** Now a subsidiary of Omnicom, Hodes is a pioneer, market leader, and one of the biggest and best resources out there. Go to: www.hodes.com
- **TMP Worldwide:** Yellow-pages advertising company, now famous for owning Monster.com. Go to: www.tmpworldwide.com
- **Davis Advertising:** Very progressive, great agency with lots of Web-savvy. Go to: www.davisadv.com

---

Job Ad Distribution Tools and Services

There's a clear line between full-service, all-media recruitment ad agencies and their Internet-only brethren. And another line between the Web-based agencies and the pure-play job posting software and services for job ad distribution—but this line is getting blurry. Most job posting software firms are now wrapping their tools with some level of consulting or media services, or both.

For companies that don't use full-service Web agencies, these companies offer varying combinations of lower-cost tools and services that can post your jobs to a variety of sites automatically. Ad distribution software provides a single interface for entering or editing jobs and a meta-posting engine that sends them to a variety of boards at once. The most sophisticated tools then send an agent to make sure the job was posted promptly and in the right category.

But no ad distribution engine or service can post your jobs everywhere. Like the big agencies, they are designed to post jobs at the largest, most prominent sites—though many offer a low-cost broadcast option that will cross-post to hundreds, even thousands of free boards, portals, classified ad sites, and newsgroups. Most vendors tout the breadth of these networks as a competitive differentiator, but in fact their real value is dubious.

Job ad distribution is well on its way to becoming a commodity software add-on, or invisibly bundled service. Smaller companies won't pay much to post several jobs to several job boards. Larger companies are negotiating ad distribution into their agency service agreements—or posting through agency-provided software built into their applicant tracking systems. And there doesn't seem to be broad enough demand in the middle to build a market on the software alone.

But automated ad distribution is a great timesaver if the tool you choose matches the boards you want to post to. It makes sense if you are posting dozens of jobs to more than a handful of job boards every month—or if you want to blast a job all over the Web.

If you are planning a large media campaign, be sure to ask your agency about these services. If you are evaluating applicant tracking systems, make sure there is a built-in option that fits your organization—or an easy way to export job data to the one you choose. If you are in need of occasional help, familiarize yourself with the stand-alone service providers in this space.

Creating Great Job Ads

Advertising behaves differently on the Web—and the key to creating great job ads is optimizing them to fit the medium. First, there are significant advantages that job postings offer in contrast to newspaper advertising:

1. **Lower cost:** Newspaper advertising rates scale upward with publishing and distribution costs. But once platform costs are recovered,

---

Best in Class: Job Ad Distributors

- **IIRC:** Somewhere between a job distributor and a full-service recruitment ad agency, IIRC provides a solutions-based approach and customized posting platform. Go to: www.iirc.com
- **Hodes iQ Post:** Part of Hodes iQ applicant tracking suite, this is a powerful engine that can be unbundled to post to all the major boards, and to 75 pre-built media packs. Go to: www.hodesiq.com
- **AIRSPost:** Sophisticated engine that posts your jobs, then sends a spider to make sure they're in the right place on the board. Go to: www.airsdirectory.com/products/technologies/post
- **WhotoChoose:** Swipe your credit card and post. Fast, simple-to-use network of major and niche boards. Go to: www.whoto-choose.com

---

hosting jobs on a Web server is almost free—resulting in lower costs to the advertiser.

2. **Lots of space:** Ads in newspapers are highly space-constrained. Job postings can provide deep rich information—and lots of it.

3. **Ubiquitous:** Newspapers are published once or twice a day—but job postings can be updated and viewed in real time at any moment, from any desktop on the globe.

4. **Media rich:** Newspapers are an analog text medium. Job folios can be enabled with voice, video, and interactive content.

5. **Connected:** Newspapers arrive on your doorstep. Job postings are a two-way digital highway running to and from any node on the global network.

But along with these benefits come new challenges:

1. Your ads are hidden inside databases, and can't be browsed until they're retrieved in some way.

2. Searches are matched to keywords in the title and body of the ad, so when you use the right words, your ad is easily found. Use the wrong words, and it won't be found at all.

3. Though you can buy banners on most job boards, there are no display ads in search results. So all jobs are created equal—until you differentiate your ad with a strong title.

4. Brief ads are the norm in newspapers—but on the Web, they can be hundreds or thousands of words long. You're expected to provide fully drawn, comprehensive descriptions of each opportunity.
5. Job postings stay up forever (or at least as long as your posting contract) unless you take them down. This creates some level of management and maintenance overhead.

Swimming in a Sea of Job Postings

With more than 2 million openings advertised on the top sites alone, job boards can be vast oceans of similar-sounding ads. A search on any common job title at Monster.com can deliver more than 5,000 matches—that's 100 pages of similar-appearing results.

There are two challenges for you here. First, making sure your ad appears on the first several result pages of the right search—and second, making the title stand out enough to compel a prospect to click. Good luck!

Studies show that users tend to click on brand names first. That means if you're a small company on a big job board, competing with Microsoft, Disney, or Coca-Cola, you're already in trouble. There's not much you can do about that, but there are some tactics you can use to become more visible.

Here's a checklist of best practices to make sure your job ads get clicked:

1. **Make the match:** Job board search engines are, after all, search engines. Use the techniques you've learned in organizing your own job board. Frequency and placement of matching keywords and phrases are the principal variables that drive a match in most text databases.

   Describe the position in the most common terms—and in as many varied ways as possible in the title and body of the ad. Search the job boards you'll be posting to— as well as the ones you aren't planning to post to—to see what comes up and why.
2. **Make sure:** Post your jobs, go back and search—then tweak and repost them until they hit the first page of search results. If your ads are on page three, they're too far down to be effective.
3. **Update often:** Many job boards automatically rank (or enable the

user to sort results) by most recent posting date. It can be frustrating when 1,000 new ads are posted on top of yours in the first day or two. If possible, negotiate a contract that allows you to repost, and do so as often as you can.

4. **Know your audience:** Every position has a jargon that resonates. Your titles and ad should be phrased in the language of the positions you're staffing. Use warm language and keywords that reflect the syntax and nuances that apply to the role.

5. **Create interest:** A title is worth a thousand words—but you have maybe ten words to work with. Make it as compelling as you can, without sounding like you're selling moon rocks in a late-night infomercial. Use all the space, and as many keywords as possible to help the match—but stay away from all caps, asterisks, stars, or other exclamatory characters.

People are drawn to adjectives that describe their positive traits. Words like savvy, expert, enlightened, accomplished, discerning, talented, inventive, excellent, skilled, ingenious, gifted, learned, lettered, experienced, eager, and aspiring can create immediate interest.

Also, remember that job seeker eyeballs go automatically to brands and the locations they're interested in. If your brand is a story in itself, use it as part of the title—and add city, region, or state names and abbreviations.

Building a Job Template

If you are posting new jobs every month, someone on your team will be writing a lot of ad copy. If you don't already have a system that provides one, it's a good idea to develop a Web template that can be used as a form by your writers. Here is a sample structure:

- **Job identification:** The requisition number, originating group or location, the author, hiring manager, principal recruiting contacts, dates, and deadlines are all important to tracking the job through your system.
- **Job title:** Use the same number of characters your job boards allow. Write titles that are upbeat, differentiated, interesting—and highly clickable.

- **Job opportunity:** This is the most critical body of content in the ad. It should draw a vivid and attractive picture of the opportunities and growth the prospect will achieve by joining your organization.
- **Environmental description:** Your culture, mission, and shared values are important considerations and key selling points. Is your company casual, team-centered, highly competitive? Do you offer unique working conditions or benefits? What are your expectations and success drivers? The more clearly you describe your organization, the more you're liable to attract the right candidates and repel the wrong ones.
- **Skills/Education:** In traditional recruitment media this is the centerpiece of your ad. But on the Web, it is secondary to the preceding opportunity and cultural information. State your requirements but remember this is a sales brochure—your opportunity statements are more critical than a detailed list of skills and degrees.
- **Other requirements:** Clearly articulate soft skills, communications skills, organizational skills, willingness to travel, flexibility, and other requirements or valuable traits.
- **Closing and contact:** Embed a personal contact name or nom de plume, with an e-mail link. Even if you use a common mailbox, assigning a name to each job personalizes the process for the applicant. Include your URL or a link to your company Web site if possible—and your standard EOE statement.

Remember, the postings you create for job boards and your corporate career center have different architectures. Your job board posting must present the opportunity, company, culture, and requirements concisely in the ad. Postings on your Web site can consist entirely of opportunities and requirements—then link to comprehensive information in your career center. If you are posting to both, it's a good idea to develop two versions at the outset. Create the job board ad first, and then pare it down for your Web site.

Selling Your Opportunities

Aim your ads at highly motivated, top performers who are inspired by the prospect of personal growth, challenge, and professional advancement. The best ads focus on these opportunities first and foremost—here's how:

- **Achievement:** Describe what your prospects can accomplish within your company and culture. Your expectation that they will contribute in a significant and valuable way is a key to attracting high-performing individuals.
- **Growth:** The best people are attracted to a compelling future. Paint a clear picture of how your prospects can grow and develop over the first several years—and give them something to reach for and beyond.
- **Success:** Avoid detailed lists of skills, degrees, and designations, unless you are trying to closely filter your applications (see below). Focus instead on the kinds of prior success that can be pulled forward and applied in the new position.
- **Excitement:** If you don't sound passionate about your opportunities, how will you attract others who are? The best people are cathedral-builders, not bricklayers—engage them with your mission, your culture, and the promise of your opportunities!

Filtering Unwanted Candidates

One of the consequences of 50 million job seekers surfing job boards every month, can be a tsunami of unwelcome resumes from unqualified candidates. Unwanted resumes divert administrative and systems resources, and interfere with a good applicant pipeline. Here are several tactics you can use to lower the volume—diplomatically:

- The stronger and more forcefully you state requirements in the title and body of your ad, the more you'll discourage unqualified applicants. Make your "must have" skills and experience requirements prominent and firm.
- Focusing on what a prospect will *do* once hired, discourages those who do not care to do what you describe.

- Requiring candidates to send a cover letter explaining why they are interested may discourage the casual resume submission. Another approach is to send an auto-responder requesting this letter—and focus on the candidates who respond.
- Omit fax and mail contact information. Try to discourage paper at all costs; even unwanted resumes are more easily managed in digital format.

Ready, Set—Go!

Your media plan is ready to be fleshed out and budgeted, and you have a career center Web site to drive job seekers to, a resume bank to store their qualifications, and a set of communities underway to keep them close by.

It's time to head out on the Web and understand the universe of 40,000 job boards—starting with the monster boards at the top of the heap!

10

Broadcast to Job Seekers at the Monster Job Boards

The three largest job boards are astride the market like a colossus. According to Media Metrix, at the midpoint of 2002, Monster.com, Yahoo! HotJobs, and CareerBuilder accounted for an astounding 84 percent share of unique visitors to the top ten job boards. Nearly 15 million people visited Monster.com alone in July—over three times the traffic of its nearest competitor—in fact, more than all other nine boards combined.

So, there are two kinds of job boards today: the top three, and everyone else. The numbers seem to say the war is over, and competing job boards should pound their search engines into plowshares and just go home. Well, who knows? The big job boards are among the few category killers on the Web so far. Monster.com has become to jobs what Amazon.com is to books, and e-Bay is to auctions—which seems to bear out the boom-era prediction that one early mover in each space will take home most of the marbles.

But as the big three consolidate the summit, the job board market seems to be fragmenting at the base. There aren't ten job boards to compete with—there are tens of thousands. It seems every portal, alumni group; trade organization, chamber of commerce, and specialty recruiting firm is jumping in, instead of pulling out. As the market gets hammered by falling ad rates and fewer job openings, the options seem to be proliferating—at the same time a more sophisticated base of Internet job seekers are bypassing the boards altogether and going straight to the company sites instead.

But niche job boards, professional groups, and employers have a long way to go before they unseat the big three. It's hard to argue against the effectiveness of Monster.com's 15 million monthly job seekers, on top of another 15 million in their resume bank. This kind of scale virtually guarantees performance, and Monster.com has some strong supporters and fans in its corner. At the same time, reports are surfacing of poor results, widespread customer defection, and disappointed job seekers.

So, where's the reality? Are the big three an automatic no-brainer for your recruiting plan, or an accident waiting to happen? In this chapter we'll look at the business model and dynamics of posting to the big career hubs, examine the challenges and provide some strategies to optimize your success.

The Big Board Marketplace

Even with a sagging economy in 2001 and 2002, there were at least 5 million unique jobs posted on commercial sites on the Web, and millions more posted only on corporate and free sites. A survey by iLogos Research in early 2002 found 75,000 job openings on *Fortune* 500 sites alone. Assuming a churn of 120 days, that suggests a quarter of a million job postings just in the upper one percentile of companies on the Internet.

The same survey found that 70 percent of *Fortune* 500 companies use one or more of the big three job boards, but fewer than 10 percent use all three. Monster.com was the share leader with 54 percent of the aggregate postings over the three boards, comprising approximately 25,000 jobs—and that's only 2.5 percent of the 1 million jobs Monster claimed at the time.

In short, the big boards are extremely well positioned. The market is vast, they are well diversified over a broad distribution of clients, and there's plenty of room to grow.

> **Best in Class: The Big Three**
> - **#1 Monster.com:** www.monster.com
> - **#2 Yahoo! HotJobs:** www.hotjobs.com
> - **#3 CareerBuilder:** www.careerbuilder.com

The Rest of The Universe

No one really knows how many free and pay job boards are on the Web today. Several years ago, a pundit wrote that there were 40,000 job boards on the Web, as if it were a scientifically derived count—and that urban legend has been published as fact, ever since. Actually, it's as good a guess as any, give or take 10,000 or so—the fact is, no one knows and it's virtually impossible to extrapolate.

In 2000, AIRS launched the Job Board Genome Project to find out—by mapping and categorizing every third-party site that offers job openings on the Web. To date, the project has mapped just over 11,000 boards, with no end in sight. Interestingly, over 20 percent of the 4,500 boards mapped by early 2001, were gone by mid-2002—yet the universe continues to grow, with new entrants added constantly.

The commercial job board marketplace is a complex and often confusing mix of models, media strategies, and ever-more-narrow niche prospects. Let's define the landscape a bit, by starting at 35,000 feet and working our way down.

Job Seekers Versus Passive Candidates

Job boards are for job seekers: The truly passive candidate is not looking for a job, and so will not be traveling out to Monster.com to search job postings. Commercial job boards have been twisting themselves into pretzels for years, claiming to attract passive candidates. But the fact is, they only attract job seekers. Those job seekers may be currently employed—but they are job seekers just the same. When you post jobs in job boards, you are advertising to active job seekers.

Resume banks are for passive candidates: One of the best things active job seekers can do while they're at a job board is to submit their resumes to the resume bank. Once in the bank, each resume is the gift that keeps on giving. As long as it's in the bank—even after the job seeker is no longer seeking a job (hence, is now a passive candidate)—employers can find his or her resume, call the former job seeker, and try to recruit him or her.

Information Exchange Versus Media Models

In the early days of the Web there was some confusion about whether job boards were a way to lower costs for employers by providing a frictionless information exchange—or a media business that could lower costs to advertisers, by providing more space and more reach for less money.

The long-term information play would be to aggregate resumes into a third-party career repository that updates education and jobs, much like the way today's credit industry updates payment information. There's a huge front-end cost to this—but once built, a credentials bureau would produce high margins at a fraction of what customers pay today to post jobs.

But in round one, boards found they could make lots more money with a media play than they could serving information—and so job boards today behave more like the newspapers moved online than a credit repository.

However, looking forward to a day when job postings might cost a penny—it's possible the model could reverse. The big three job boards have accumulated tens of millions of resumes so far, and thousands more are flooding in every day. If ad prices were driven through the floor, that data would become an unassailable barrier to competition, should they choose to change the game.

Broadcast Versus Narrowcast Strategies

Media is traditionally priced on the actual or projected readership of the ad vehicle. Whether you use the term traffic, impressions, readership, or subscribers—it all means pretty much the same thing: How many people are apt to see your product or service over the run of the ad? If you are aiming for sheer numbers, select a medium that will broadcast your message as widely as possible, at the lowest cost.

But ads can also be aimed at a particular demographic—in fact, the more precisely targeted, the higher the ad value. If you are advertising BMWs, targeting factors like location, income level, or profession are key. For a job opening, the best targeting factor may be a particular industry, skill, degree, or certification. If you are searching for a few individuals with specific attributes, select a medium that will narrowcast your message directly to them.

Commercial job boards can be neatly organized by these two media models—broadcast and narrowcast—and then by target market, as follows:

1. Career hubs "broadcast" jobs to a general population of job seekers, targeted by location. They may be focused internationally, or by country, state, region, metro area, or city. The defining characteristic is that the job seeking audience is everyone, regardless of skills or experience.
2. Niche boards "narrowcast" to a specialty audience defined by industry, profession, business function, skills, or candidate characteristic (college, executive, or diversity)—or a combination of any of these attributes, within a specific location.

The big boards are firmly in the broadcast camp. Let's take a closer look at how they work.

Broadcasting to Job Seekers

When you buy ads based on newspaper circulation or television network share, you are paying for a generalized population of eyeballs. In other words, your job ad in *The Boston Globe* is distributed to everyone who subscribes in the Boston area—regardless of who they are, what they do for a living, or whether they want a job or not.

This is an attractive model because it reaches lots of people—but you never know how many job seekers are in your sample, let alone how many might be qualified for the position you're advertising. Arguably, career hubs are one step more valuable than newspapers, because you know the eyeballs you pay for belong to job seekers—yet job postings cost much less than newspaper ads today.

Conversely, ads on niche boards that target very specific audiences are a step more valuable yet, because the eyeballs you pay for there are pre-qualified as to industry, skills, or other criteria—and niche boards are often even less expensive than the career hubs.

And advertising into professional organizations, trade groups should be even more valuable than niche boards, because their members are not only pre-qualified, but tend to be experienced passive candidates, not job seekers.

If career hubs can charge more for generalized visitors than niche or community sites can for their highly targeted audiences, it seems that job ad values on the Web are driven more by brand recognition and mass readership than by specificity. This is upside down logic for the media market—and for recruiters. After all, recruiters know that the best candidates are the most targeted, most hidden, and most happily employed. And media buyers expect to pay less for a mass audience than they do for a targeted one.

But the reason the universe lines up this way today—and will for awhile—is that brands and familiar models are the brightest stars by which Internet travelers can navigate. The only way to find anything fast in a soup of 2 billion Web pages is to remember a few key names. And the more the new Web business resembles a familiar terrestrial model, the easier it is for investors and customers alike to grasp. By this logic, career hubs like Monster.com are among the killer apps of the early Internet. They are the newspaper classified sections, moved online.

Trouble in Paradise

The big boards are the gorillas today, and they're not in imminent danger of being marginalized by the niche market, communities, or employers. But there is a distinct undercurrent of unease among customers—and signs that the market is casting about for alternatives.

Employers and recruiters alike are concerned about a growing set of issues, including the potential for monopolistic and competitive behaviors at the big boards. As these sites grow, so grows pressure to find new solutions. The key complaints are:

1. **Pricing:** It's become expensive to post lots of jobs on the big boards, even after negotiating volume-rate posting contracts. As a result, many large companies are rationing job postings to fewer than 25 percent of their open jobs—and that delta is liable to be even wider for cash-constrained smaller companies who pay retail.

2. **Control:** Aware that many large employers had become dependent on posting large packages of jobs, some big boards increased contract prices dramatically in 2000—reportedly by as much as 400 percent in the case of some *Fortune* 500 customers.

   That level of pricing power was both astonishing and infuriating to customers. Though prices have fallen slightly since, as a result of the recession economy in 2001 and 2002—some gun-shy customers are reducing their exposure to the big boards, to limit the risk of a similar jolt when the market swings back.

3. **Competing interests:** Through aggressive acquisition of executive search and recruitment companies, Monster.com has built a vertically integrated staffing firm alongside its job board, which competes directly with third-party recruiters—many of whom are its customers today.

   Monster.com's parent TMP Worldwide recently announced plans to spin these holdings off as a separate public company. However, unless they're fully divested, these siblings may continue to be regarded as a threat.

   Though ownership of a vertically integrated suite of staffing services is a logical growth strategy, it may create resentment and fear within the client community. Many recruiters, including the largest global staffing firms, correctly perceive the big boards as very dangerous potential competitors once coupled with a service arm.

4. **Diminishing returns:** By the time a board has half a million jobs and 10 million resumes on hand, recruiters, employers, and job seekers are all fighting an uphill battle to be noticed.

   Job searches on the big boards routinely return dozens of pages of results filled with similar-sounding job titles. Employers are beginning to question whether showing up as job number 765 on results page number 14 is really worth $300.

5. **A flood of unqualified candidates:** Niche boards tend to attract experienced candidates from a target industry or skills group. But the big boards are a clearinghouse for all types of job seekers, and so attract a high number of college students and other entry-level and inexperienced workers.

   To complicate matters further, it is simple for a job seeker to send dozens, even hundreds of resumes at a time from the big boards. As a result, employers are finding themselves flooded with unwanted resumes from unqualified candidates. A recent example is a modest-sized, but high-profile employer on the Boston Route 128 corridor that posted 30 jobs—and received 9,600 resumes in the next three weeks.

Even unwanted resumes demand attention. In order to even determine their value, resumes must be manually reviewed, electronically scanned, or keyed into an applicant tracking system. Either way, it's an expensive drain on HR and IT resources.

6. **A dearth of quality hires:** Bottom line, it's all about making high-quality hires. Yet there seems to be quite a bit of anecdotal concern about the bang-to-buck ratio—in both the number and quality of hires from the big boards to date.

For example, Lockheed Martin recently reported that it spent $1.8 million on job boards in 2001. In return, it sorted through 300,000 resumes to complete 900 hires. A 2001 survey of a dozen public companies in 2001 also reported that, though they were active users, fewer than 2 percent of their hires came from Monster.com. These are troubling stories—all the more so because none of the major boards are tracking or publishing information about postings-to-hire or cost-to-hire ratios.

Look, every business has problems, and these troubles pale in comparison to the travails of many mature companies—not to mention the bloodbath of Internet start-ups. The big job boards are young, but very successful companies so far. They have access to public capital, a proven business model, and a huge marketplace. But looking forward, they're not liable to be the only game in town for long.

Monster Job Board Strategies

Posting jobs to the big boards has become a pretty straightforward process, and the competitive edges that early adopters once enjoyed have been smoothed down to a nub. As a result, there are not many magic tricks left—but there are some best practices to keep in mind:

Brands Rule

Job seekers click on major brands five times more often than non-branded jobs. This is great if you are a well-known *Fortune* 500 company like Intel or AOL Time-Warner, but not so great if you are Acme Paint Supply, in Fontana, California.

If you are a brand company with lots of openings, you almost have to have some chips on these tables. Chances are your competitors are there, and it's a good idea to make sure your story is being told alongside theirs.

If you're a smaller company, think about your investment. Do a search for similar titles and see what comes up. If the competition is too fierce, you may be better off with a local job board, or even sticking to the newspaper for now.

Step One—Diversify

A single big job board may not be the best basket for all your eggs. Jupiter Media Metrix recently reported that 76 percent of job seekers are loyal to one board. At the time of the survey, HotJobs had the most loyal user base; Monster.com came in second, and CareerBuilder third. Only 15 percent of the job seeking population used two boards—and less than 10 percent used all three. Bottom line, if all your jobs are on one big board, you will miss a sizable population of job seekers on the other two.

It's also important to diversify into the niche boards and communities. In fact, more jobs than ever are flowing to this emerging market. Again, you are liable to miss a vast audience of seasoned, passive candidates by ignoring the niches. Target your complex, hard-to-fill positions to these boards.

Step Two—Measure

Unlike consumer or business-to-business advertising, recruitment ads are rarely based on targeted media strategies. Recruitment ad agencies and job boards aren't out doing customer surveys in malls or sending questionnaires to job seekers—nor do they provide especially strategic advice when it comes to posting jobs. So, you're basically on your own.

Whether you use a sophisticated applicant tracking system or a simple spreadsheet, it is very important to connect the hire all the way back to the source. This may be as simple as tying each resume to the job board as it arrives—or as complex as requiring each new employee to detail the route they took to your company. But without keeping track and measuring results, it's impossible to understand what works and what doesn't.

Step Three—Consolidate

Once you know what works, put your wood behind that arrow fast. It may turn out that 90 percent of your good hires are coming from the distinct population that only uses HotJobs—or from specific niche sites—or from searching the resume bank, instead of posting jobs. The point is, if your data tells you one source is markedly hotter than others, double down. This doesn't mean consolidating every resource you have on one board—it means pulling your investment from underperforming channels as soon as you have identified better ones.

Location, Location, Location

The three most important value drivers in real estate and job ads are location, location, and location. Get your ad to the top of the first page of search results, and your click-throughs will improve dramatically. (See Chapter 9, Organize Your Web Campaign, for tips on how to get there.) Invest in a *hot jobs* text link or a banner on a major job board home page—and stand aside.

Do the math—if you have a really tough mission-critical job to fill, what's more expensive: a premium placement on one of the big three, or a 30 percent search fee? If you're planning an enterprise ad campaign, it's a good idea to budget in a few big ads, along with your postings.

Wave Your Arms

If you're drowning in pages of similar job postings, wave your arms and get noticed. The best way to attract attention is with a catchy, interesting title. This is the most commonly prescribed antidote to being lost on the boards. It's kind of a thin lifeline, but you've got to grab onto something—so take a few extra minutes to make sure your titles are as compelling as possible. And remember, it's always important to repost often, so you'll stay near the top of the results—and pay attention to those all-important keywords.

Stop the Flood

But you may be wrestling with too many resumes today—and if you are, better placement doesn't matter. Why post more jobs if you're already flooded with resumes? If you have more resumes than you can sort through already, stop posting—in fact, you may want to remove your job openings altogether and focus on getting to the bottom of your stack. If you are only finding one or two good resumes for every 200 resumes you review, chuck the stack and start over.

It's sometimes simpler, less costly, and faster to just go search the resume banks. Today, the big boards offer literally tens of millions of resumes—and all of them do a fine job of providing search tools to sort through them quickly. Create an e-mail template for each job opening, surf the banks, and send the right e-mail off as you find good candidates that match. There are lots and lots of motivated job seekers out there who will be very happy to hear from you.

Stay Ahead of the Curve

The big boards are doing a good job of anticipating needs and are moving fast to provide more features. Make sure you are well informed about new ways to present your opportunities and find the best candidates.

This is a fast-moving market, it's getting expensive to play in, and you need all the edge you can get. It's a good idea to build a relationship with your customer rep, and make sure you are briefed quarterly on what's changed—you may find new features that can offer you an early advantage.

Portals Versus Pipelines

Speaking of new features, there are some significant trends that seem to be influencing development on the big boards today. The first is a new war looming between job board business models.

Because the big boards operate in a media model based on traffic and length of stay, they are moving steadily to offer more career information, job search tools, and affiliated services. This provides line extension and new revenue streams—and serves to keep visitors browsing on-site longer. In short, it is a portal model.

But portal strategies are being challenged by a new paradigm. Job aggregators have turned the ad model upside down by offering a new value proposition. Instead of selling the notion that visitors spending more time on a portal is good for advertisers, it promises to present bare-bones job opportunities and send prospects immediately to the corporate site. This is a low-friction pipeline model.

FlipDog.com was the first aggregator to enter the space—by spidering corporate Web sites (not necessarily with their knowledge or consent) and offering a central place to view them. The idea was controversial, and the site was immediately rewarded with a shower of press and traffic. But FlipDog had a hard time figuring out how to turn clicks into revenue, and soon fell on hard times—eventually crashing down to become a low-cost, but high-value acquisition for TMP Worldwide, Monster.com's corporate parent.

High value? You bet. Had FlipDog behaved less like a technology provider and more like a nimble, market-driven competitor, the Monster model may have come under intense pressure. After all, FlipDog was aiming to provide many times more jobs than the big boards—including hundreds of thousands of jobs that are otherwise hidden. This is a powerful message and could have been tough to sell against. Luckily for Monster, FlipDog didn't have the sales and marketing chops to monetize it—and so, Monster was able to take it out, presumably with a big sigh of relief.

But the model has reared its ugly head again—this time in the form of a new site called DirectEmployers.com (see Chapter 5, Post Jobs on Your Site, for more information on how the job aggregation model works). It is run by a consortium of large employers, all of which are huge customers for the big three. This is a new kind of threat that should make all the big boards sit up and listen carefully—here's why:

1. It is a relatively low-cost, flat-fee model that threatens to divert job posting revenue flowing to the big three in precisely the way they've interrupted the flow of revenues to newspapers—by providing more ad space at a lower cost.

2. Anytime your leading clients form an organization to compete with you, it's a bad thing. If you see a thought bubble above your client's head that reads, "Why don't we just do this ourselves?"—it's time to re-evaluate your business model, your barriers to entry, your pricing, or all three.

3. This model fits neatly into the front end of another emerging trend—employers and recruiters who are building comprehensive career centers, and want to drive traffic to them.

This is a model that is easily replicated in a niche—in fact, it is a logical way to organize job boards for lawyers, or doctors, or software engineers of one type or another. If DirectEmployers.com gains traction, it could make the job board market a horse race again.

All Employment Is Local

The next huge wave of hiring is coming toward us, and should start breaking on the beach in a year or two. By mid-decade, we should all be way under water. But this wave is different from the last one—when the great telecom build-out, year 2000 fear, and a frenzy of Internet start-ups combined to create deep shortages in the IT, managerial, and executive benches. This time around, it's the hourly employees, those folks who put the products together, answer the phones, and drive the delivery vans.

The overall labor shortage is projected to hit 20 percent by the end of the decade. Of course, the NASDAQ was supposed to hit 10,000 by this year—so don't build a staffing plan around that statistic alone. But it is clear that the baby boomers are heading for the rest home—and that there is a big valley before the next bulge.

According to current labor projections, the first and deepest shortages will be in lower to midlevel service and product categories. In fact, the first waves may be lapping at the beach, as the health care, hospitality, and retail industries are already struggling with worker shortages.

This new market will require different recruiting skills and tools. First and foremost, these workers are local—it's hard to imagine that Safeway will be relocating supermarket checkers from Chicago to San Francisco, or that Domino delivery people in Atlanta will be looking for Pizza Hut jobs in Seattle. This is a whole new challenge—and as the fulcrum shifts down market and to the strip mall, so must the major job boards.

Today, there is a Maginot line of local career hubs and newspaper Web sites around every town and city—filled with jobs at the local mall and Jiffy Lube. If the big boards go after these ads and win, the newspapers are in real trouble. In fact, even if the job boards lose—but cut ad prices by half as a result—it's bad news. So the last stand of the local classifieds is coming, and it may turn into a nasty house-to-house street fight before it's through.

Big Boards, Big Brands, Big Traffic, Big Money

No matter what happens in the long term, for the foreseeable future, the big three job boards set the pace—and the prices. They may rule forever, or they may be just like the three television networks in the 1970s—unchallenged, prosperous, and ruling the airwaves, while the first lines of cable TV were being run underground.

11

Narrowcast to Targeted Candidates in Niche Job Boards

The big three job boards, Monster.com, Yahoo! HotJobs, and CareerBuilder, are mass consumer advertising platforms, like the big three TV networks—while the niche boards are a 40,000 channel cable system, filled with highly specialized programming and waiting to pounce.

Though the targeted niche model has been around since the early days of the Web, the number of niche boards has exploded over the past several years, as local newspapers, trade publications, professional groups, and vertical portals have established job boards for their target audiences.

Some niche boards have become an attractive alternative to big boards—by offering a lower priced and clearly non-competitive value proposition, a more targeted advertising opportunity, and access to specialized pools of more experienced candidates. Many others are languishing on the Web, with too few jobs to generate traffic and too few visitors to make them worth posting to.

Today, there are niche boards aimed at virtually every industry, function, and business skill, as well as specialty boards designed for recent college grads, diversity candidates, and other population pools. Because these boards are highly focused, they can be a great recruiting resource.

But they can also be hard to find, time-consuming to assess, and cumbersome to manage.

In this chapter we'll look at the benefits that niche boards offer today, provide some signposts to help navigate this often-confusing market, examine the challenges you'll encounter, and offer solutions to streamline your workflow and save time and money.

First, let's focus on the paradigm of narrowcasting—and understand its fundamental strategy, cost advantages, and results.

Mass Eyeballs vs. Targeted Eyeballs

If advertisers want to sell something with mass appeal—say, aspirin, credit cards, or automobiles—they head for the TV networks. But if they're selling bell-bottom jeans or pimple cream, they go to MTV.

Today, the cable networks have neatly segmented the TV population into special interest categories—aspiring chefs go to the Food Channel, investors go to CNBC, and kids are at Nickelodeon or The Cartoon Channel. Niche boards have migrated similar choices online for job seekers and employers alike.

Niche advertising makes good sense in today's staffing market. After all, individual job postings are highly specific as to skills, location, and other criteria—shouldn't they be targeted as precisely as possible? Is there any reason to advertise jobs for a marketing manager to Windows programmers? Or nursing jobs to salespeople? Of course not, but in a newspaper or career hub, that's precisely what your ads are doing—and to some extent, what you are paying for.

The High Cost of Building an Audience

Newspapers, TV networks, and big job boards rely on expensive consumer branding to grow their audiences, and large distribution engines to reach them—and so customer acquisition and delivery costs scale upwards with sheer audience size. To use a well-known job board example, Monster.com has invested tens of millions of dollars in Super Bowl ads, billboards, banners, newspaper ads, and TV infomercials to grow their brand and audience—and tens of millions more to build data centers, develop sophisticated software, and staff their distribution.

As a result, Monster.com has grown an enormous audience, which is attracting a huge customer base. Of course, this requires Monster.com to invest in attracting more audience share to satisfy new customers, while scaling operating and distribution to meet audience demands. This can be a virtuous and profitable cycle, if the company has sufficient capital to meet its investment needs. On the other hand, the expensive process of growing a mass audience almost guarantees high media prices.

Though ad prices have softened with the economy in the last year, the big boards remain at the very top of the rate card for Internet job posting. Regardless of market conditions, they must generate sufficient revenue to overcome their consumer-branding engine and wide distribution costs. And though you may only be interested in reaching the 2 percent of their audience who are nurses, you are paying a premium to help them attract the other 98 percent of their traffic.

Narrowcasting via niche boards, on the other hand, tends to be more cost efficient. Audience acquisition costs are low, since niche consumers form their own viral networks around community services or information, and distribution costs are generally lower, as the audience is more static, easier to pool, and more accessible.

Because these capital barriers are low and operating costs are modest, niche boards return high margins on lower ad prices. As a result, niche boards tend to be less costly—in fact, ad prices are often 30 to 50 percent less than the big boards.

Targeting vs. Screening

With broadcast strategies you pay to reach the widest population possible—then sort through the results to find the qualified candidates. With narrowcast strategies, you pre-qualify the applicant up front, by advertising into pools of candidates with known characteristics.

A flood of unwanted, unqualified candidates from the major job boards can be an enormous data management headache. Targeted ads tend to produce fewer resumes, but of higher quality, simply because niche audiences have been pre-sorted out of the general population on the basis of skill, industry, or other special characteristics.

Because good niche boards are harder to find and take time to assess, narrowcasting requires more focus and investment up front. But the pay-off can be an efficient pipeline of pre-qualified candidates—instead of a tidal wave of generalized resumes that must be sorted, reviewed, and screened for relevance before being qualified for skills and attributes.

An Experienced, Professional Audience

By examining the model, it's clear that narrowcasting via niche boards can offer a more targeted ad, at a lower cost point than the big boards. But there are additional important benefits to consider—most markedly, the caliber of audience drawn to a niche community versus a big job board.

Niche boards tend to attract a more professional, passive candidate pool than general job boards, because:

1. Many niche boards spring from existing communities of business professionals, and so are born with an audience of seasoned, experienced candidates.
2. Many niche boards are embedded in vertical portals designed primarily to attract passive candidates, not active job seekers. Happily employed professionals visit these sites daily for industry or skills news, information, and tools.
3. Many niche boards can't afford expensive consumer advertising, and so grow their traffic through a network effect—as recommendations pass through the business community of similar candidates.
4. Most niche boards are hidden from the general Web surfer, and so most job seekers (like most employers today) simply default to the colorfully branded, easy-to-find, big boards.
5. The big job boards are designed for massive numbers of general job seekers—and so attract a high percentage of college grads, career starters, and laid-off workers.

Job Seekers vs. Passive Candidates

Ultimately, the objective of your recruiting efforts should be to find the most talented, most highly skilled people for your organization or clients. That means going after the most productive workers, wherever they can be found—and most recruiters agree that they are often buried inside your best competitor's company. Fair or not, it's a recruiting tenet that "the best candidates are too busy working to be looking for a job."

In fact, some recruiters discount job seekers entirely, on the basis that this small percentage of the workforce is most apt to contain the unsuccessful, the disgruntled, or the opportunistic candidate. This may be a harsh notion in a market driven by economic downsizing, but can be very true in a labor shortage market. Bottom line, most recruiters and employers tend to value passive, employed workers more than active job seekers.

You won't find passive candidates on the big job boards, but they are often on a niche site with a "jobs" tab.

A Growing Consensus

Niche job boards are a rapidly emerging market force. Most staffing industry stakeholders agree that niche sites are more cost-effective, offer less competition, and can deliver better, more targeted candidates. This recognition is creating a new inflection point in the e-recruitment market.

In 2001, Forrester reported that 40 percent of recruiters preferred niche boards to general career hubs. Though barriers remain, it's likely that community-based recruiting strategies will be a key to the next market wave—and as a result, niche boards should have a clean shot at interrupting the automatic flow of job postings to the big boards.

Barriers to Niche Board Success

Better candidates, cheaper! If that was the whole story, the niche boards would have run right over the career hubs already—but they haven't. Why not?

While the niche market is maturing rapidly, there are still some monster-sized issues to overcome. The keys to unlocking the potential of niche job boards are:

1. **Improved visibility:** Niche sites are hard to find. There are tens of thousands of places to post jobs on the Web, but finding the right job boards for a particular industry, skill, or location is a difficult and

time-consuming research task. This drives employers and recruiters to the default purchase of the well-branded, highly visible career hubs.

2. **Simpler job distribution:** Niche sites are hard to use. It's simple to place a package of 100 different jobs on CareerBuilder or HotJobs. But it's very difficult to take that same package of jobs, organize them into sub-packages according to skills, and then key each job individually into multiple niche sites. Add the complexity of varying price schedules and customer interfaces, and the task becomes even more daunting.

3. **Greater reliability:** Niche boards offer uneven results. Though there are thousands of niche boards, there tend to be only a few really competent ones in each specialty branch. Many sites offer very few jobs, and little or no candidate traffic. Many are run poorly by a skeleton crew of techies—or by a staff with only a passing regard for customer service.

These shortcomings may not be readily apparent. So added to the frustration of searching out niche boards, is the process of vetting them against reasonable performance and service requirements. Finding the few reliable sites in each niche can become a difficult, time-consuming research project.

Bottom line, despite growing demand for narrowcast solutions, it's still much easier to buy and manage job ads on the well-known, highly capitalized big boards. Though niche boards offer more targeted ads, better pricing, and higher-quality candidates—the time commitment required to locate, screen, and work with them remains a significant barrier for resource-challenged recruiters and employers.

As niche boards struggle with these challenges, the weaker sites continue to auger in, only to be replaced by even more new entries. It's hard to predict whether this market will explode out of the box in the next few years, continue to clump along in the shadow of the big three—or shake itself out to a much smaller number of well-run sites in each niche.

> ### Best Practice: There's a Growing Consensus That Niche Boards Are on to Something
>
> "Many savvy job seekers are eschewing big career sites such as Monster.com, HotJobs.com and Headhunter.net [nee CareerBuilder] despite those sites' vast databases and fancy tools. Instead, they find their time is better spent zeroing in on niche boards with more focused listings."
>
> — Alex Salkever, *Business Week*
>
> "The future is all about niche, specificity, and focus. The sloppy, generic and untargeted messages we have been sending are too expensive and do not get results. Start simply and begin using the niche job boards for sourcing candidates, focus your online advertising toward those groups."
>
> — Ken Gaffey, Electronic Recruiting Exchange
>
> "Niche recruiting sites are burgeoning at the rate of nearly 100 a month. [These] boards attract users the same way community boards do, by offering career advice, networking opportunities, links to vendors, and other services. Those inducements lead users to check in often, creating more exposure for job postings."
>
> — Donna Fenn, *Inc. Magazine*
>
> "Niche job boards are career sites that specialize in job seekers with specific profiles—lawyers, accountants, financial planners, for instance. By contrast, the big national boards handle all types of workers. And they are flooded with resumes. Monster.com, for instance, earlier announced it had collected its 10 millionth resume. That kind of heavy volume is one reason why recruiters and job seekers are turning their attention to specialty boutiques rather than big-box marketplaces."
>
> — Joyce Lain Kennedy, Syndicated Career Columnist

Hub vs. Niche—In the United States and Abroad

Before we jump into the niche market, let's revisit our definition of a career hub. The big three career hubs are the best-known examples of sites that aim to attract "everyone, everywhere." In general, these sites, along with a large second tier of competitors, focus from border to border on the United States and Canada.

There are now similar career hubs serving most regions and major countries of the world. Few sites try to reach a completely international audience in one fell swoop, as experience shows there is value in designing regional or country-specific sites—even if they are merely a separate interface to a common jobs and resume engine, partitioned and served from a common host.

Niche boards are also being launched to serve targeted populations across the globe. In fact, in many countries, the best niche boards are more able competitors for their country's technology and business populations than their U.S. counterparts. As with domestic sites, it's almost impossible to gauge the number of niche boards in other world regions, but it's clear the market is growing internationally.

Navigating the Niche Board Universe

Whew! With tens of thousands of niche sites targeted to every industry, skill, business function, ethnic group, career status, and location imaginable, the marketplace has become a maze. To plot a course quickly to the best sites in a given niche, it's important to understand how niche boards are organized.

As the niche market has developed, eight principal categories have emerged—each with its own sectors. There may be dozens of sectors, and hundreds of niches within each category. Here's a brief look at each:

1. **Local career hubs:** Boards in this category are aimed at all types of candidates, but with a strictly local focus on a city, metro area, state, or region. Many local career hubs are sponsored or owned by local news, radio, or government agencies.
2. **Industries:** Boards in this category are aimed at industries and sectors within those industries. For example, there are boards aimed at the general health care industry—and others aimed at the hospital, biotech, or pharmaceutical sectors. There are boards aimed at the general financial services industry—and others aimed at the banking, insurance, and brokerage sectors.

3. **Vertical skills:** Boards in this category are aimed at specialized skills within a vertical industry or sector. For example, nursing, radiology, and hospital administration are specialized skills niches in both the general health care industry and the hospital sector. Commercial lending, real estate appraisal, and loan underwriting are specialized skills within both the financial services industry and the banking sector.

4. **Horizontal skills:** Boards in this category are aimed at business functions that extend horizontally across industries and sectors. General management, finance, human resources, marketing, and sales are fluid skills found in virtually every business.

5. **Technical skills:** The tech marketplace is so vast, diversified, and important to recruiters that it rates its own niche category. General tech sites offer a variety of jobs. Specialized tech skills such as semiconductor design are vertically focused, while IT skills cut horizontally across all industries and sectors. Tech niches may be defined by a hardware platform, operating system, language, tool, or product—or a combination of several at once.

6. **Career status:** Boards in this category are aimed at candidates with experience at a particular point along the career spectrum, from hourly service workers, to recent college graduates, to senior executives.

7. **Diversity:** Boards in this category are aimed at candidates defined by ethnic origin, gender, sexual preference, age, or abilities.

8. **Free agents:** Boards in this category provide a labor exchange for contract, temporary, part-time, and distance workers.

AIRS surveys report that the best, most successful niche boards tend to focus on a skill, industry, or other attribute *and* a specific metro area or regional focus. So niche boards for Java programmers in the Northeast or sales professionals in Los Angeles are more likely to yield better candidates, faster than their more general counterparts.

Of course, as with the big career hubs, the wider the geographic focus—the more traffic, the higher the profile, and the bigger the board. So it follows that the largest, best-known niche boards are the most general in nature. They tend to be hubs that serve many sectors within a category, and so they're a good foundation for a niche campaign.

Find the Right Boards, Fast

Today, at the top level of most niche categories, the clear market leaders are relatively simple to find. They're a good, fast place to start—though you may end up struggling with some of the issues you'll find at the big three: high prices, more job seekers than more passive candidates, and lots of competition.

The more difficult niche boards are to find, the more likely they are to be duds—or to be the exclusive pool of passive candidates you've been hoping for. If you can commit the time, it's definitely worth the effort to go off the beaten track and be among the first to cast a line into new waters. Whether you're looking for the leaders or the hidden pools, the process is the same:

1. Check the TV Guide.
2. Think like your candidate and look for a job.
3. Scan the sites and sort the best to the top.
4. Make contact, screen, and test the finalists.

Check the TV Guide

In the niche market, aspiring job boards share your pain. Just as there's no easy way for job seekers or recruiters to find them, they're having a hard time becoming visible. What this 40,000-channel cable network really needs is a *TV Guide*.

Before you start searching the Web, check out the closest thing available today. AIRS Job Board Genome Project offers a free job board directory of over 10,000 sites—and the majority, of course, are niche boards. Other key resources are the free, Web-based Riley Guide, and the Career X-Roads and Weddle's Guidebooks (see box on next page).

Another guidelike resource is the plethora of meta-posting tools and job ad distribution services (see Chapter 9, Organize Your Web Job Posting Campaign). These sites do list a lot of niche boards, and they can be a good reference, but they're not designed to find new sites for you, or take you deep into the Web to high-value niche communities.

In fact, though many claim to have mapped to thousands of niche boards—most of these representations are fairly bogus. Most ad distribution services are plugged into the big three as well as a number of well-

---

Best in Class: TV Guides for Niche Boards

- **AIRS Job Board Directory:** Free to recruiters and employers. AIRS researchers have assembled and organized the largest job board directory on the Web. Users can drill down through a Yahoo!-style directory interface, or use a keyword search to find sites. Go to: www.airsdirectory.com
- **Riley Guide:** Librarian Margaret Dikel (nee Riley) is the grande dame of Internet career resources. The outstanding Riley Guide to employment resources of all kinds has been published—and growing—since the early days of the Internet. Go to: www.riley-guide.com
- **Career X-Roads:** Published annually by career gurus Gerry Crispin and Mark Mehler, this is the industry standard text today. Each year, the authors comprehensively review thousands of sites, then select and profile the top 500. Go to: www.careerxroads.com
- **Weddle's Web Guides:** Author Peter Weddle has aggregated detailed information on thousands of Internet job boards and career-related sites. Weddle's approach is fact- and features-based and is very comprehensive. These are outstanding resources. Go to: www.weddles.com

---

traveled niche boards (usually the top several sites in large niche categories). The rest tends to be a lot of smoke and mirrors.

The "thousands of job boards for one low price" offers are actually postings to a handful of networked sites, which then cross-post your jobs automatically to a bunch of free bulletin boards, low-traffic local boards, Usenet groups, and Internet classified sites. There's really not a lot of value in this untargeted blast to fairly random destinations.

Ask Your Friends

A fast way to find good sites can be to tap knowledgeable recommendations from people with experience to share. The most accurate evaluation tools are often real-life results—and most recruiters are happy to share what works and what doesn't.

A fast phone call or e-mail to your colleagues will work—or you can pass your questions to thousands of recruiters at once in an industry forum. Here are the top three forums today:

- **ERE:** Electronic Recruitment Exchange is the largest daily mail list for recruitment and HR professionals, with 30,000 subscribers. These are mostly top-notch corporate professionals, and much of the discussion is focused on corporate recruiting strategies and technologies. The discussions are moderated, so they stay on-topic and useful. Go to: www.erexchange.com.
- **AIRS:** AIRS Forums are part of the AIRS News Network, which serves daily recruitment news to over 50,000 recruitment and HR desktops daily. There are 11,000 Forums subscribers—and like ERE, they participate in moderated, on-topic discussions daily. Go to: www.airsdirectory.com.
- **RecNet:** The Recruiter's Network is an unmoderated mail list with several thousand subscribers. There are some very knowledgeable participants who regularly offer helpful tips—but readers may have to sift through a stack of personal notes, goofy advice, and off-color jokes to get to them. Go to: www.recruitersnetwork.com.

Identifying which sites work best and which to avoid are common topics in the forums. It's a good idea to monitor them all, so you can follow interesting threads—and join at least one, so you can ask questions quickly when you need to.

ERE and AIRS also provide searchable archives with thousands of past conversation threads. Because job boards are such a popular point of discussion, there are lots of tips to help you search, as well as specific recommendations and warnings.

Think Like Your Candidate

Your candidates are out looking for you with some of the same tools you're using to find them. By replicating their methods, you'll get to the same primary boards the active job seeker will find—and with some advanced techniques, you can reach deep into the Web to find hidden, more passive communities.

Like most consumers, job seekers chart their way through the Web using one of the top consumer portals. AOL, MSN, Yahoo!, Google, Lycos and About.com are consistently the favorites—in fact, according to

Media Metrix, by mid-2002 these sites were logging an aggregate of 300 million unique visitors a month.

All of these sites offer a Web directory and a search engine. To find the most prominent niche boards, start with the directory. It's a simple process to use your candidate keywords or drill down to a list of niche sites in your candidate categories.

Because directories are built by hand, they reflect someone's initial opinion that the site is worthwhile—the listing then drives more traffic to the site, helping to create the virtuous cycle that successful job boards rely on to grow. Drill into each directory until you see a clear pattern of boards that appear on most or all lists—chances are you'll be able to triangulate the leaders pretty thoroughly.

Remember, in most categories there are niche hubs and subordinate sectors. For example, you can find Oracle developers at DICE, a technical hub serving a number of tech skills, or at Oraclejobs.com, a site specifically tailored to Oracle developers. Make sure your keywords are sufficiently broad to return the general sites, and targeted enough to reach the specific sites.

If your target niche is too narrow, too specialized—or if you're not finding the right niche leaders in the major directories, it's time to turn to the search engines.

Searching for More Niche Boards

Most consumers use very simple search terms to find jobs. For example, to find niche boards that specialize in sales positions, they might search: *sales AND jobs*. To find teaching jobs, they might try: *teach OR education AND jobs*. These searches actually work pretty well for job seekers—they often turn up jobs on the major boards and on corporate career sites, as well as on niche boards.

But those results are less valuable for recruiters trying to get off the beaten track to find untapped boards. First, recruiters don't want to see results from corporate sites—and second, this simple search tends to turn up the same higher-traffic niche boards you can find in the directory. There are less intuitive, but more effective ways to reach down into the Web.

In a Web with over 2 billion pages, it's very possible that trade publications, niche news sources, or interested individuals have already found and published links to valuable job boards that aren't listed in the major directories or otherwise easy to find.

Here are two good ways to tap into their research:

1. **Find the page:** We're looking for pages filled with information about how to find a particular kind of job—and looking for lists of job boards in the process. Pages titled "Engineering Jobs" are liable to contain jobs for engineers. Here's how that search is run in Google: *intitle:jobs AND <your keywords>*

2. **Find the vortal:** The pages we're looking for are usually part of a vertical portal (vortal) filled with news and information about your target niche. Find the portal, rummage around—and you'll often find links to targeted job resources. Here is a Google strings designed to surface niche portals: *intitle:links AND intitle <your keywords>*

Vortals often have job boards of their own or offer other ways to target job ads to their visitors. As you search for pages with information about other job boards, look for other ways to reach through the vortal, to its audience.

Finding the Communities

The deeper you go into the Web, the more valuable the candidates. Active job seekers can easily find the most prominent niche boards, which has helped them become the niche market leaders. But vortals are off the main highway, and so tend to take you one step closer to those passive candidates.

Vortals also tend to publish links to more places passive candidates gather—including other vortals, professional organizations, publications, and user groups. In Chapter 7, Drive Traffic to Your Jobs, in the section entitled "Finding the Right Communities," you'll find detailed instructions and resources that will quickly take you into the Web and to these targeted community sites.

You may have already mapped them as places to advertise with banners and links—to drive candidates to your career center using Guerrilla Traffic Strategies (again, see Chapter 7 for details). If you have, chances are you've mapped their job boards as well. If not, now is a good time to head out and see what these communities offer. Keep your eyes open—

not only for a job board, but also for ways you can attract candidates to the jobs posted on your own Web site.

Scanning the Sites

With some organization and a little search experience, you'll be able to cut right to the vortals, find lots of communities—and lots of niche boards, pretty quickly. The next time-consuming problem is that so many of them turn out to be duds.

That's why it's important to triage the boards you find as quickly as you can, discarding the obvious losers and sorting the best contenders to the top.

There are some pretty obvious clues to niche sites you'll want to avoid. Here are the most common reasons to move on and keep looking:

1. **Poor design:** An attractive site, attention to detail, and simple competence are not too much to ask—in fact, if they're not apparent at first blush, chances are you'll have an unhappy experience in the long run.

   Even if the site promises access to great candidates (as may be the case with some local user groups, for example), you'll need to go through the site owner to get to them. If basic business sensibilities are absent in the site, chances are they'll be absent in your relationship.

2. **Poor content:** A lack of jobs may mean the site is brand-new—or may signal a lack of interest. Take a minute to figure out which it is. A new site may mean lots of opportunity—an old, unused site means lots of wasted time.

3. **Old content:** If the jobs are old, nobody cares about the site—move on.

You may be surprised at how many niche boards share these problems. Their communities may be too small to generate meaningful traffic, there may be no compelling reason to visit the community Web site (since many provide information to members via e-mail), they may not have the energy to devote to building the board—or they may just be inept.

Whatever the case, the key is recognizing the problem and moving on quickly. Two more things to think about as you go:

- **Keep a log:** Sorting quickly through dozens, maybe even hundreds of boards can become a bleary business. Make sure you log your travels and a brief comment, so you don't have to start over again six months down the road—and if you are working in a team, post the list on the Web or your intranet, where others can get to it efficiently and share their experiences, as well.
- **Try, try again:** Don't confuse the quality of the job board with the quality of the candidates in the community. If you're looking for database engineers in Denver, the Rocky Mountain Oracle User's Group may have a junky-looking job board with little or no traffic—but if they have 300 members, you still want to get in front of them.

Use your site visit to shoot a fast note to the Webmaster or chapter head, to explore other ways you can reach their community.

Vetting the Finalists

Once you've sorted the most compelling contenders to the top, it's time to get on the phone and make contact. Many sites will only offer an e-mail contact option. Okay, this is a bummer, and not a good way to start a business relationship. If the site is already on the borderline, you may want to knock it into the second string right now.

If not, shoot the site manager a note, but make it clear you need to chat, and soon. Suggest a time and request a phone number. If they take too long to respond, that's another flag—if you don't get a note back at all…bam! Those sites should go right to the bench.

Once you do get the site on the phone, you're going to want to know about:

The Audience

- What are the principal types of candidates?
- Are the candidates you're looking for there?
- How many are in the community?
- How experienced are they?
- What is the geographic reach?

The Traffic

- Are traffic statistics tracked, and if so, how?
- How many unique visitors to the site each month?
- How many page views?

The Features

- Is there a resume bank?
- How many resumes are there?
- Are there premium placement opportunities?
- Are there resume or job agents?
- Are jobs cross-posted, and if so, where?
- Will they provide a link to your Web site?

The Competition

- How many companies are using the site?
- How similar are their jobs to yours?
- Are they recruiters or employers?
- Are they your direct competitors?
- If so, make sure you get the competitive picture: Are they successful? What kind of candidates are they sourcing? How can you out-post them?

The Cost

- How much to post jobs?
- What is the standard posting period?
- How much are job packages?
- Are there all-inclusive options? Are they annual ones?
- Bottom line, what is the most economical way to use the site?

The Results

- Nothing succeeds like success—always request current references.
- The proof is in the pudding—always request a free trial.

That's pretty much it—don't expect much in the way of formal traffic statistics, or other traditional media metrics. These boards are small, resource-constrained, and off the beaten track. If you feel comfortable with the answers you're given, and trust the voice on the other end of the phone line, you're past the first hurdle—if not, cut them to the second string and move on.

The second hurdle is a real-world trial. Whether free or not—post a few jobs, and monitor and measure your results. In the process you'll find out how easy it really is to post, manage, and edit your ads—and what it's like to work with the board. If you aren't getting results, phone in and see what they'll do, if anything, to help.

If the board is great to work with and you're seeing the results you're hoping for, bam! Good choice. If either side of the equation is shaky, you'll have to judge whether it's worth investing more to see if it will turn around, or whether you should cut your losses.

Kiss a Lot of Frogs

As the old saying goes, "You've got to be willing to kiss a lot of frogs to find a Prince." There are a lot of crummy niche boards out there, and scattered among them are some really terrific resources. It's a numbers game—the faster you can move contenders into the chute, evaluate, decide and test them, the better all around.

Don't linger over your kiss. If it's not working, move on and try more boards. Someday there will be standard metering tools that advertisers can rely on to evaluate career hubs and niche boards alike—just as network and cable advertisers today rely on the Nielsen ratings. Until then—it's go fast, use your intuition, and good luck!

Part Four

Searching for Passive Candidates

12

Passive Candidates: Find One, Find Them All

There are three overlapping candidate pools in the employment marketplace. First, there are the unemployed job seekers. The size of this group fluctuates with the economic pendulum, but tends to hover around five percent of the working population—about 6.5 million people.

Second are employed job seekers. These are folks who have a job, but may be unhappy, would like to relocate, or feel their careers are at a standstill, and so are actively looking for a new employer. Let's say this group represents 10 percent of the working population at any given time (this is an educated guess; no one really knows)—that's another 13.5 million people.

Third are non-job seeking employees, or passive candidates, in today's parlance. These are employees who are making a productive contribution to their current employer, neither planning nor taking active steps to look for another job—but who would consider moving if a better opportunity presented itself. This pool constitutes the remaining 80 percent of the workforce, or 115 million people.

A decade ago, only a small percentage of non-job seeking employees were considered passive candidates—meaning that only a few would enthusiastically listen to a recruiting pitch. The only way to reach the rest was to use a headhunter's Rolodex and persuasive sales skills. But the world has changed dramatically since then, and new realities have taken shape.

Today, the tacit employment contract is a temporary agreement. Most workers realize that the "job-for-life" model is dead, and that no matter how well they perform, they are at risk of being part of an economic downsizing beyond their control, driven by falling stock prices or the market imperative to grow short-term earnings. As a result, former life-long employees now consider themselves to be free agents, with an average tenure of three to five years in any one job—and the radar is always on for the next opportunity.

The second sweeping change is that most of these 115 million passive candidates are wired to the Net through a business desktop, or a computer at home. That means they're not hidden inside a recruiter's drawer anymore—if you know how to search, you can find them.

In this chapter, we'll take a closer look at passive candidates—why they're important, where they tend to gather, the clues they leave behind, and the search tools you'll use to find them, and their friends. In the following chapters of this section, we'll share specific techniques for finding the millions of resumes and people hidden in every nook and cranny of the Web.

Past the Job Boards

Let's review: Job boards are a convenient way to find active job seekers, but you won't find passive candidates there, because they're not looking for a job. Passive candidates are out past the job boards—hidden in home pages, staff directories, alumni groups, Web forums, virtual communities, attendee lists, membership directories, and many more kinds of documents, scattered over 165 million domains on the Web.

The only way to reach passive candidates is to go out and find them. Here's why it's important to know how to do that:

1. **Passive candidates are better than job seekers:** In a sudden recession, many unemployed job seekers are innocent victims of being in the wrong position, in the wrong company, at the wrong

time. But many more are out of work because they are unseasoned and underskilled or have failed to make the cut somewhere.

On the other hand, regardless of the economic climate, most companies will do everything they can to hold onto their best and brightest. And aren't these your target employees? If you are building your company to compete and win, you need to find the very best contributors in the talent market. It's a good bet those workers are hidden inside your competitors' companies, not surfing job ads at Monster.com.

2. **The most resourceful recruiters win:** There's no trick to searching a job board's resume bank—and plenty of recruiters and employers fight each other to do just that, every day. Job boards are pretty old news in Internet time, and they're the first stop for every newbie on both sides of the hiring table. Why jostle with a herd of competitors for a few job seekers, when you can leave them behind and reach many more passive candidates?

3. **There are more resumes outside resume banks than inside:** As popular as job boards have become, only a fraction of the Internet population ever visits any given one, and even fewer leave their resume behind. There may be as many as 50 million unique resumes inside the thousands of commercial resume banks—but there are many times that number of resumes, home pages, and bios hidden in the billions of pages in the Web and Deep Web.

4. **You'll lower the cost of hard-to-find candidates:** The most highly skilled, successful candidates are headhunted from one position to the next; they'll never download their resumes to a job board and will never surface as visible candidates in the job market. Before the Web, the only way to find those candidates was to hire a search firm to network by phone, wait at least six weeks, and pay the 30 percent bounty. But with the right Internet search skills, anyone can dig up the same hard-to-find candidates in a matter of hours, at a small fraction of the cost.

5. **You'll gain a powerful advantage:** There is no competitive upside in sorting through an overfished pond of job seekers at a job board. But being able to reach inside a target company, root around, and pluck out their best contributors can make a real difference, fast. As an employer, can you think of a surer way to win a talent war? As

a recruiter, can you name a better way to impress your clients and make more money?

Bottom line, employers have always had access to job seekers through the Sunday classifieds and job board advertising. But reaching passive candidates has long been the exclusive province of third-party search specialists with deep niche contacts and great phone skills.

Well, not anymore. The Internet has leveled the playing field by putting massive amounts of profiling and contact information into the free, public domain of the Web. It's difficult to imagine that any contact buried inside a recruiter's Rolodex is not also represented somewhere, in some way, on the Web. That means the information itself is not the competitive lever anymore—it is the ability to find it.

Market leading companies know this and guard their best employees jealously. In fact, as a rule the better they're hidden, the better the catch. The good news is, if you understand the structure of the Web and how communities of people behave, and if you know some simple search commands, you can find virtually anyone today—even in the bowels of your fiercest competitor.

Remember, people are not the most strategic resource—the *right* people are. A basic truth in recruitment is that the better your candidates are, the more competitive *you* are. As a search professional or third-party recruiter, you're exactly as valuable as the quality of candidates you find. As a manager or employer, you need outstanding contributors to win. You're more likely to find those kinds of people deep in the Internet, a long ways from a job board.

Networking Your Way Upstream

There are two approaches to searching for passive candidates. The first is to try to find a resume for the exact candidate with the precise skills you're searching for. The second is to drill in somewhere close, and network your way over the last mile.

Finding the right resume is certainly possible. There are several hundred million home pages, resumes, and other "people pages" on the Web with sufficient information to let you know if you hit pay dirt. You may be able to go right to the perfect candidate—in fact, it makes sense to look for resumes before you drill down farther. In the chapters ahead, we'll be looking at how to filter through billions of Web pages quickly to do just that.

The second, and most reliable way to turn up the really great candidates is through good old-fashioned networking savvy. Good headhunters know that if they can just get in the right ballpark, they'll be able to work their way to the right candidate, one contact at a time. It is exactly the same game on the Web, except that you'll be working with new, more powerful networking tools.

The Web offers an array of better, faster, cheaper ways to zero in on candidates. Here are a few examples:

- Using the phone is a tedious, serial process. Make a call, leave a voice mail, make another call, leave another voice mail—until finally you make contact and have a conversation that you hope will take you one step closer to the candidate.

  Strong Web researchers can find a good contact, link themselves to more good contacts, and on to the right candidate in a fraction of the time—because they don't have to wait, and don't have to build relationships or trust in order to ask for the information they need. They just go find it.

- In the physical world, you may spend three days and $3,000 to attend a national conference and collect business cards. On the Web, you can find the event, find the speakers, link to many of the attendees, and send them all e-mail before the conference even begins.

- Getting past receptionists and administrators can be tough, so recruiters are often trained to ruse (the polite way to say "lie") their way inside a company and on to their target candidate. Of course, this particular tactic makes many recruiters squeamish.

But there is no need to mislead the gatekeepers when so much informaition is available on the Web. Using this public information, savvy recruiters can easily find documents with names, titles, and contact information on them. Once you've made contact with someone inside, you've bypassed the gatekeeper—and you can network your way quickly from your first contact to your target candidate.

While some recruiters are wrestling with gatekeepers, others simply find people with similar skills, linked to the company on the Web. Using this public information, they can easily get inside, and surf from contact to contact until they find the right candidate.

Close counts in horseshoes and recruiting. Find their friends, co-workers, former associates, partners, or college buddies—and you'll find your candidate. In other words, find the right community and your candidate can't be far away.

Communities on the Web

People are social animals, and gather in communities that share a belief, purpose, or need. To the extent communities are organized to pursue social or business ventures, share information, or accomplish an objective, they tend to be composed of people with similar characteristics. Most groups are not entirely homogeneous, of course—but many are sufficiently self-profiling to predict the skills, experiences, or preferences of its members. Here some fast examples:

- An alumni group for the Harvard Business School class of 1980 will be filled with experienced, seasoned Harvard MBAs. Because Harvard degrees are highly valued by *Fortune* 500 companies and big government, there will likely be lots of corporate executives, and some politicians, in the mix.
- The IEEE is the largest professional organization for electrical engineering professionals. When it holds a national conference about wireless networking, you can bet the speakers and attendees are all interested in wireless networks—in fact, most are probably working with them today, and some will be the experts in this field.
- Lucent's Bell Labs is a premier communications research facility, renowned for its innovation and intellectual firepower. Though not everyone there is a research scientist, Bell Labs is a community built around cutting-edge science. So, when you find a page on the Web entitled "Meet the People of Bell Labs," it's a safe bet that it will be filled with distinguished communications experts.

Because the Web is both an information repository and communications medium, it offers communities a way of storing membership and other collaborative documents—and the means to communicate via a free, common platform. These are powerful advantages, and communities of every type have migrated to the Web.

When communities publish information and conduct conversations on public Web pages, recruiters can sort through them, and listen in. If you know how to search and what you're looking for, the sheer volume and quality of the information you can harvest is astonishing.

Here are the top ten Web and Deep Web communities that your candidate may be hiding inside, or linked to:

1. Companies
2. Colleges
3. Alumni groups
4. Organizations
5. News and publications
6. Conferences and events
7. Discussion groups
8. Virtual communities
9. Local or national ISPs
10. User groups

These self-profiling communities are often untapped pools of passive candidates. In the coming chapters, we'll look closely at the types of documents and people you'll find in each—and we'll learn to search through them to harvest the best prospects.

But first, it's important to understand the basic architecture of the Web, the various ways people are represented, and the tools we'll use to search for them.

People Are in the Pages

The Web and Deep Web are vast oceans of documents and pages. Hidden in those pages are the tracks of millions and millions of job seekers and passive candidates.

Here is a brief primer on how data is stored on the Web.

The Internet Is a Database

The Web is not a single monolithic system, but a loosely configured network of individual computers called servers. Though "located" in millions of different servers, Web pages are stored using a standard data format.

This means there is a searchable structure to the Web. If you understand the rules, the Web becomes a powerful free database, filled with people.

People Are in the Pages

There are billions of Web pages on the Internet. Tens of millions are resumes, or profiling pages that perform the same function—i.e., they so thoroughly describe a person's skills and background that they are obvious recruiting tools.

But there are many other kinds of pages on the Web that describe people, many of which are useful to recruiters. Employee directories, project pages, white papers, annual reports, articles and press releases,

---

Domain Name Extensions

Top-level domains are the suffix (called the "extension") attached to a class of domain names. The extension indicates the purpose of the site.

Common U.S. Top-Level Domains

- **.com**—Commercial business site
- **.edu**—Educational site
- **.gov**—Government (non-military) site
- **.mil**—Military sites and agencies
- **.net**—Networks and ISPs
- **.org**—Non-profit organizations

New Top-Level Domains

In 2000, the Internet Corporation for Assigned Names and Numbers (ICANN) approved seven new top-level domains, indicated by the extensions below:

- **.biz**—General business
- **.info**—General information
- **.name**—General individual
- **.museum**—Museum only
- **.coop**—Cooperatives only
- **.aero**—Air transport industry only
- **.pro**—Certified professionals only

Key Domain Resources

- **Internic:** A public clearinghouse for information related to domain name registration. Go to: www.internic.net

- **Accredited Registrars:** A list of companies authorized to assign Internet domain names. Go to: www.internic.net/regist.html
- **ICANN:** The Internet Corporation for Assigned Names and Numbers is the non-profit corporation responsible for IP addressing and the domain naming system. Go to: www.icann.org
- **Verisign:** Formerly Network Solutions, Verisign is a one-stop shop for domain verification, registration, and information. Go to: www.netsol.com
- **International Organization for Standards:** Maintains list of country codes. Go to: www.iso.ch/iso/en/prods-services/iso3166ma/02iso-3166-code-lists/list-en1.htmlwww

alumni rosters, speaker's lists, forum threads, and more—all have people and profile information in them.

Pages Are Stored in Web sites

Web sites are hosted on servers connected to the Internet. Each Web site (there might be multiple Web sites on a given server) has a unique identifier called a domain name—and each page has a unique identifier called a uniform resource locator (URL). This means you can find any individual page on the Web—and trace it back to its domain to find more like it.

Pages Are Organized into Directories

Pages are organized in a directory structure, exactly like the folders and subfolders on your desktop computer. The directory tree is represented in the URL displayed in your browser. Here's an example, using a theoretical Web site, folders, and pages:

http://www.bigcollege.edu/alumnidirectory/engineering/~bobsmith/resume.html

This is Bob Smith's resume. It is attached to Bob's alumni home page (the tilde (~) usually denotes a home page), inside a subfolder called **engineering**, which is inside a folder called **alumni directory**, which is stored on a domain called **bigcollege.edu** (the extension .edu confirms this is a school (see box on previous page), which is stored on a server connected to the World Wide Web.

Bob is obviously an engineering alumnus of Big College. Now, here's the really good news—Bob is not alone. Just like you keep lots of similarly named documents in your folders, so do Web sites. So there's a really good chance that there are more resumes in the subfolder named **engineering**. To find out, simply delete the URL back to the engineering subfolder and hit Enter.

This AIRS technique is called PeelBack, because it peels back the URL to a folder with more candidates in it. If you peeled Bob's URL back a little farther, to the **alumnidirectory** folder, you should find the entire alumni directory, not just the engineering section. This is a powerful tool that can be used anytime you see folder names with employees, staff, people, team, roster, directory, contacts, or other "people" words in the URL.

Let's look at one more hypothetical example:

http://www.softwareleaders.org/q3salesconf/
mondayspeakers/mary_bio.html.

This is Mary's biography page. Mary seems to be a software sales guru, since she was speaker at the third-quarter sales conference of an industry association called "Software Leaders" (the .org extension confirms this is an organization).

If you peel this URL back to the first subfolder, you should find links to the rest of the speakers for Monday. Peel it back one more time and you'll find the conference folder, which may link you to Tuesday and Wednesday's speakers, or to the sponsors—or maybe even to attendees.

How to Read a Web Address
http://www.college.edu/cs/~bsmith/resume.html

- **http:** (hypertext transfer protocol) This is the format used to transfer information
- **www:** (World Wide Web) While not all sites use it, it is the host server that supports text, graphics, and sound files
- **college:** Server's location and the second-level domain name
- **edu:** Top-level domain name
- **cs:** Directory name (in this example, cs stands for "computer science")
- **~bsmith:** Subdirectory name (in this example, it is the home page for bsmith)
- **resume:** The file name
- **html:** File type (in this example, it is for hypertext mark-up language)

Peel it all the way back and you'll be on the Software Leaders Web site—a good place to look for officers, chapter heads, and members.

Pages Are Linked to Related Pages

It's simple to put a link on a Web page, and linking topics to deeper information hosted on other Web sites is a fundamental paradigm of the Web—and for recruiters, it is a powerful device that enables them to find more of the same kinds of candidates.

Let's think about Bob's resume and Mary's biography for a moment. It's likely both will have links to their companies and colleges—and to the professional organizations they belong to. Follow any of these links and you'll find communities of people with similar education, skills, or industry experience.

Find One, Find Them All

L et's take a linking example from the ground up. Ariel Martin is the new marketing director for Amalgamated Tech, a maker of computer peripherals in San Jose, California. She graduated magna cum laude from the University of Michigan and has an MBA from Stanford. She belongs to the local chapter of Women in Technology International (WITI) and is a member of the American Marketing Women's Association. Before Amalgamated, she worked in marketing positions at GE and American Express.

When Ariel puts a home page up on her local ISP, what will she tell us—and what will she link to? Well, if she's like most professionals, her links will take us to her most important milestones, achievements, and relationships. These include:

1. **Companies:** "I'm a marketing director at Amalgamated." It's a good bet this is the way Ariel would introduce herself at a professional gathering—and on her Web page. Ariel will almost certainly link us to her new employer, Amalgamated, and probably to GE and American Express as well.

   With any luck, she'll include a *meet my team* link that takes us inside Amalgamated to her colleagues there—and may have links to her corporate alumni groups at GE and American Express.

2. **Colleges:** It's a good bet she'll link to both Michigan and Stanford—and with any luck, to her former roommates, or fellow debate team members (who are all in marketing or sales at *Fortune* 500 companies now), or to her favorite professor, who knows a lot of other former students who now have marketing positions with leading organizations.

3. **Organizations:** Ariel is on two committees for WITI in San Jose, and so will link us to their local chapter—which just so happens to have an officer's directory with names, titles, and contact information for a dozen other executives from similar technology companies—as well as the minutes of every meeting for the last year, with an attendance list for each.

 She will be presenting at the AMWA conference in New Orleans soon—and so will also link us to the conference site, where we'll find lots more marketing gurus just like her.

4. **Friends:** Ariel's friends include people from GE, American Express, Amalgamated, WITI, and AMWA. She's great at networking, likes to stay in touch—and hopefully will link us to Dan's home page to see his cat, to Suzie's home page for the world's best chocolate chip cookie recipe, and to her boss Meredith's home page to see pictures of her new boat.

5. **Resumes:** Most people who build a personal home page today link their resume to it. That means we'll be able to see Ariel's qualifications in detail—and with any luck, find resumes attached to Dan, Suzie, and Meredith's pages, too.

Peeling back URLs to find folders full of related people, and following the links between related documents, are two ways to turn a contact with specific characteristics into the first link in a chain that leads to more and more people like them—until you find the perfect candidate. We'll examine more ways to do this in the chapters ahead.

Searching for People

In a text database where several hundred million people are represented by hundreds of different kinds of documents scattered over billions of pages, where do you start?

Well, that depends on the candidates you're hunting, on where they're liable to gather, and on the resources you have available. Let's take a 35,000-foot look at searching the Web, and work our way down to finding your candidates.

First, there are two ways to search for people on the Web:

1. **Web-wide search:** Plug in your keywords and a search engine will take you across every document in its index, looking for a match. It doesn't matter if the pages it retrieves are hosted on a corporate server, at a local ISP, inside a college, or on a personal computer in Juneau, Alaska. If the keywords match, you'll get it back. This is the best way to survey the Web for resumes, home pages, and profiles.

2. **Destination search:** If you can predict the community your candidate is liable to be represented in, or linked to, you can go right to that Web site—turn it upside down, shake out all the documents and follow all the links. This is the best way to find non-resume documents like employee directories, staff lists, e-mail contacts, and more.

Second, it helps a lot if you have a search plan. Here are some key steps:

1. **Profile your candidate thoroughly:** The secret to successfully searching any text database is the quality of your keywords. In order to have great keywords, you must have a detailed understanding of your candidates—their skills, their experience, their college, their degrees, their certifications, where they probably work, where they probably used to work, where they go for information—all the way down to the jargon they use every day (we will examine keywords in greater detail farther on).

2. **Start with your resume banks:** The first places to search are the resources you have at hand. Your candidate may have already applied for a position with your firm in the past—or may be inside one of the commercial resume banks your company already pays to access.

   If you're looking for high-quality, hard-to-find passive candidates, it's unlikely they'll be in either place. But you never know, and you definitely have to check; just go through as fast as you can, and on to the next step.

3. **Search for Web resumes:** There's a better chance your passive can-

didates will have a resume or detailed home page published on the Web somewhere. This is an important step—and we'll examine it thoroughly in the next chapter.

4. **Rank your destinations:** If you haven't found the right resume, don't worry—there are plenty of other ways to find your candidate. Chances are they are inside a community site, or linked to one. The question is where?

At this point, you need to make some predictions about where your target candidates work today and where they have worked in the past, where they went to college and what professional associations they maintain. These are the primary destinations in a people search—companies, colleges, and organizations.

Secondary destinations include publications, conferences, forums, virtual communities, ISPs, and user groups. What do they read? What events will they attend? Do they participate in discussion groups? Where is their local ISP? Are they active in a technical user group?

Think about your candidate, make a list of the places where he or she is likely to be hiding, rank your list, then do a search. In the chapters ahead we'll take a detailed look at how to find and evaluate each kind of destination.

5. **Search your destinations:** There are three ways to search any destination.

- First, go right through the front door. Surf out to the home page and wander around looking for people documents lying around in plain sight. These might be executive lists, press releases, sales contacts, articles, or any number of other pages with names and contact information on them.

- Second, go through the side door. Use AIRS X-ray process to bring every page in the Web site to the surface—including hidden sections with no visible links to them. These pages are *not* behind a firewall, they are in the public Web domain—in fact, if they weren't already indexed by a public search engine, we wouldn't be able to find them. These hidden areas are where you're most liable to find documents like employee directories, staff lists, and project teams.

- Third, go through the back door. Use AIRS FlipSearch process to find every page linked to the Web site. Who links themselves to a company? You'll find employees, former employees, vendors, partners, and other related people. You'll find alumni, research fellows, professors, speakers, and others linked to colleges, and officers, chapter heads, and members linked to their organizations.

6. **Find their friends:** Every time you collect a new name, e-mail address, or phone number, you've added an important keyword to

---

AIRS Search Terms

- **PeelBack:** The process of sequentially examining subfolders in the URL directory tree to find more of the same kind of candidate. By deleting the tree back to folders with "people words" like *staff, attendee, member,* or *employee* and then refreshing the page, you may find more resumes, more home pages, or more leads to passive candidates.

- **PowerSearch:** The process of combining standard Boolean terms with advanced field commands to create powerfully targeted, very precise search strings. When you're looking for a few great candidates, you don't want to sort through 100 pages of general results—you want to go right to them. The more precise your string, the more precise your results will be.

- **X-Ray:** The process of using various search engines to examine all of the indexed documents—or to search for particular documents—inside a target Web site. For example, you might X-ray a source company using the keywords *staff directory*, or a college site using the string *alumni AND executive.* Your results will be pages inside the site, with those keywords on them.

- **FlipSearch:** The process of using various search engines to surface documents linked to a page in a target Web site. For example, several engineers may have linked their personal home pages to a project they've worked on, inside a source company's site. By flipping that project page, you'll find those engineers. Or flip an organization's home page and find all the current and past members who have linked to it from their resumes.

- **PeerSearch:** The process of using names, e-mail addresses, land addresses, and phone numbers as search terms to find similar people on lists.

your search. If you are looking for network engineers, you're liable to find them on a phone list with other network engineers. If you've found one salesperson at a target company, using his or her name as a search term might bring back a list of the entire sales group.

As you go along, use AIRS PeerSearch process to find people related to those you've already found. Doctors are on lists with other doctors, software gurus with other software gurus, and finance executives with other finance executives. Find one, find them all.

Your Search Tool Set

There are three principal categories of search tools on the Web. First are directories like Yahoo! and About.com, which examine and catalogue Web sites into pre-named categories, much like the Yellow Pages do for business phone numbers. Second are search engines like Google, AltaVista, and HotBot, that match your keywords to words appearing in text documents on the Web. Third are meta-tools that search multiple search engine indices from a single interface. Let's take a fast look at each:

Directories

Most large directories have collected a significant number of personal home pages and resumes. You can assume these are the second most picked over resumes on the Web (the big three jobs boards are in first place here). Take a fast look if you want, but you'll find lots more, lots faster with a search engine.

Though their candidate pools may be fairly weak, directories are great for finding lists of companies, colleges, organizations, and other destinations that could be hiding your target candidates.

Search Engines

Search engines rule the complicated text-search universe of the Web. No hand-built directory could ever keep up with the ever-changing bubble and boil of pages on the Web. In fact, the Web is growing and changing so fast that even search engines with automated spiders can't keep up. That said, a good search engine is the fastest road to passive candidates.

Unfortunately, the search engine marketplace is still young, fragmented, and confusing. There is no all-inclusive index of the entire Web—and no standardized way to collect, index, or serve data. Here are some fundamental issues to keep in mind:

- Search engines send spider programs out onto the Web, to crawl through links and retrieve information. No search engine can cover the entire Web, and since spider programs are all different, they are each working from their own subset of the pages on the Web.

- As spiders return with data, it is analyzed, stored in a database, and indexed according to each engine's proprietary algorithm. Most search engines today store the full text of a document, but their methods for ranking relevancy are markedly different. That means when you run the same search in two search engines, you are likely to see very different results—not only because they've stored different documents, but because they're working from a different ordering of the data.

- All search engines use keyword matching to return your search results. But to get to those results, you have to know the syntax and range of commands the engine offers—and each is different. As a result, users are stuck with their knowledge of one or two engines that search part of the Web—or doomed to working from a cheat sheet with dozens of variables for the rest.

- Since early 2002, the sweepstakes for the largest Web index has been a horse race between Google and Alltheweb. Both have passed 2 billion pages and seem to be neck and neck at this point. If you have a choice, bigger is better.

- The current trend in relevancy is to consider the number of links to a page as the principal indicator of its value. This is actually a breakthrough of sorts, in that pages with more inbound links probably are more useful and should be sorted to the top.

This trend toward relevancy ranking contributes to another, longer-term tendency for search engines to conserve cycles, or speed up the process by spidering only the "best" pages (i.e. pages that have some commercial value), and skipping over the rest. The result is that fewer personal documents, like home pages or resumes are being broadly indexed. Of course this is bad news for recruiters who need access to those passive candidates. We'll look at this issue in more depth—and show you how to find these missing pages in Chapter 14: Find Resumes in the Deep Web.

We're going to be using search engines a lot in the following chapters. We like Google best today because it is so simple and powerful and has the largest (for this week, anyway) index.

If you feel like you're missing out with just Google, go to Alltheweb next—it's a close second. And if you feel ambitious and want to cover as wide a swath as possible, use all four of our top headhunting search engines.

Here they are, and here's why they're on the list:

- **Google:** A great second-generation Internet success story. Its clean design and sharp focus on search have vaulted it to the top of the popularity charts. It's a great headhunting engine because its index is huge, it's really fast—and it offers features like cached documents (no more 404 errors) and the ability to retrieve PDF and Word documents, Excel spreadsheets, and PowerPoint presentations. Go to: www.google.com.
- **AlltheWeb:** A close second to Google, this engine offers a similar mix of huge index and sophisticated search features. Go to: www.alltheweb.com.
- **AltaVista:** A reliable old warhorse for power search gurus who like to write pages and pages of Boolean expressions. This is arguably the most versatile engine for the really advanced user—but it just doesn't have the reach of the two leaders. Go to :www.altavista.com.
- **Hotbot:** A formidable weapon in its day—like AltaVista, still powerful, but behind the curve. Hotbot was the original FlipSearch engine in 1998—and rumor has it that it will be coming back for a run to the top, soon. Go to: www.hotbot.com.

These search engines represent the best combination of reach, stability, and advanced search capabilities available today. It's a good idea to try them all out—and prioritize them based on your own results.

Meta-search Tools

At first blush, meta-tools seem like the perfect answer to searching across the Web. The notion is that you can create a search in a single interface—the meta-tool then converts your string to the various syntax and command structures of the primary search engines and feeds them the search. It then collects the results, de-dupes them (removes duplicates), merges and purges the results, and presents a neat list of documents from across the Web. Sounds great.

And they are great—for very simple search terms like *resume AND engineer*. But meta-tools break down quickly, once you introduce complex Boolean expressions and field search commands (which you'll learn about in detail in Chapter 15, Find People Linked to Companies, Colleges, and Organizations). The problem is that some of the engines these meta-tools pass the search to will understand some of the advanced commands. Others will understand a different set, and some won't understand any. The results can turn into a potpourri of weird pages that have little to do with your search.

But wait—meta-tools are still great for simple searches. That means you can use them to quickly search across the Web for a single term like a name, e-mail address, and phone number.

Remember the PeerSearch technique? Here's a meta-search trick. Whether you're looking for auditors, executives, or engineers, put the names of your own best employees into a meta-tool (one at a time) and hit go. You're liable to bring back lists they had no idea they were even on—with more great people just like them.

Here are the top online meta-search tools:

- **Mamma:** Fast, clean, simple, and powerful. Searches across the Web, and for Usenet threads, pictures, MP3 files, and more. Go to: www.mamma.com.
- **Profusion:** Start your engines—and go. Profusion de-dupes, relevancy-ranks the links, and serves them up. Go to: www.profusion.com.
- **Dogpile:** Search the Web, Usenet, newswires, directories, and more. Instead of de-duped results, you'll see the full list from each engine, in order. This approach allows you to follow a link to the original search engine, to use advanced options or refine the search. Go to: www.dogpile.com.

People Search Tools

There's a new class of meta-tools designed specifically to find people. Some use pre-configured search strings to execute complex commands on the best search engines, others spider resumes, home pages, and contact data into their own databases. Here are the market leaders:

- **SearchStation:** Web-based ASP (application service provider) from AIRS that searches over 150 resume banks, the Web and Deep Web for resumes, then Flips and X-rays companies, colleges, organizations, ISPs, events, discussion groups, and other community destinations for passive candidates. Go to: www.airssearchstation.com.

- **Eliyon:** Natural language processing tool that sweeps through news articles, press releases, company Web sites, and SEC filings on the Net—and has a database with over 10 million contacts in it. Go to: www.eliyon.com.

- **Infogist:** Desktop application that searches free and paid resume banks and the Web, sweeps resumes and home pages back to the desktop, then sorts, ranks and stores them. Go to: www.infogist.com.

Let's Go Find Some Resumes

Okay, it's time to turn some of this theory into action. In the next two chapters, we'll be using search engines, keywords, and our wits to find resumes and home pages on the Web and in the shadowy Deep Web—then on to find passive candidates, wherever they gather to work or play.

13

Find Resumes
on the Web

etworking for jobs has been an Internet activity since the days of
Telnet and Gopher. In fact, some of the first news groups and
bulletin boards were used to post jobs and resumes. In the early
days of the World Wide Web, only hard-core techies in the government
and academic sectors posted there—but soon a few hardy adventurers in
the ranks of the recent college grads put a page up, and the numbers of
resumes on the Web began to grow.

For years, there were many perceived risks to having a resume
online. Some people were worried about personal security—others
thought that they might seem like desperate job seekers, or that their
employer would find out and think they were looking for a job. The safer
alternative was to use a resume bank, preferably one that offered some
level of confidentiality.

But in the late 1990s, Internet tools were suddenly easier to use, huge
new homesteading sites that offered free Web hosting exploded into
view, and trusted brands like AOL and Yahoo! began urging users to
express themselves on the Web. As a result, putting up a personal home
page became a popular pastime.

As personal home pages went up, so did resumes. In fact, home pages began to resemble resumes. As the market ignited, tens of millions of Web users added biographical information to their personal pages. Very quickly, the number of actual resumes and Web pages published by passive candidates rocketed past the number of active job seekers in commercial resume banks.

Today, there are far more resumes and resume-like documents hosted on the Web than in all the job boards combined. The stigma and fear associated with the early Web has disappeared, and people from every profession, industry and background are represented there today.

Most people consider publishing a biographical home page to be a more passive career activity than downloading a resume to a resume bank. So, many academics and executives who are still resistant to any kind of job board, instead publish a home page that effectively serves the same purpose—providing exposure and making them easier to find, for any headhunter with an interesting proposition.

In this chapter, we'll take a fast look at searching resume banks, and then head for the Web. Resume-hunting across the Web is all about search engines—so the rest of this chapter focuses on incorporating Boolean expressions, field search commands, and keywords into PowerSearch strings that take you to the right group of documents, and help you filter through them quickly.

Start with Your Resume Banks

Your active search plan should start with resume banks, particularly if your organization has made the investment to build its own, or is paying for access to job boards. You never know where your candidate may be hiding, and it's possible he or she is right at hand. Start with your in-house database, and then check any commercial boards that you have access to.

If you can afford it, think seriously about a subscription to Monster.com or the other big boards. Monster now has 20 million or more resumes on tap. That's a huge population, and it's likely to include some great people. Though it's a bad idea to restrict your search to job boards, the fact is there are a lot of candidates there. For many companies the sheer convenience of being able to search across that pool in one fell swoop outweighs the cost and competition.

You already know that there are high numbers of recent college grads and other career starters at the national career hubs. But today, as a result of the economic implosion over 2001 and 2002, a great many older, experienced contributors, managers, and even executives are there, too.

As you evaluate the big boards, take time to consider the niche boards, professional groups, and other communities who are aggregating targeted resumes by industry or skill. Again, the goal is to find the largest possible numbers of the specific candidates you need, at the lowest cost, and with a minimum of competition. It's worth looking through some niche boards to see which might fit that formula.

Go As Fast As You Can

Once you've selected the right resume banks, there's no reason to linger at the job boards. If your resumes are there, you'll want to harvest them as quickly as possible and move on.

If you are recruiting for a large organization, you may already have a dozen or more boards to monitor continuously. Corporations with aggressive hiring needs tend to use one or two of the majors, plus a wide variety of niche boards for hiring across the enterprise.

The business problem here is that it quickly becomes difficult to search to them all on a continuous basis. Like search engines, every board seems to have its own syntax and schema, and the process can quickly become a major time sink.

If you're spending too much time searching the same job boards, consider developing a set of software drivers and search formulas into a meta-interface that can drill through all your boards at once. This may sound daunting, but it is a relatively straightforward project for a good software engineer. If you don't have access to those resources, consider investing in turnkey tools like SearchStation or Infogist, which offer the drivers, search queries, and interface.

Searching across a dozen boards manually can take hours. By automating the process, you can search all your boards in minutes.

Old Resumes Are Better Than New Ones

Many recruiters are convinced that the "freshness" of a resume is a key indicator of the quality of a candidate. Actually, a resume that was downloaded to a job board yesterday is only better if you are competing with your peers to find the latest job seekers that come into the market. Really old resumes are what you're looking for if you want passive candidates.

For example, if a terrifically talented sales manager named Beth submitted her resume to CareerBuilder over a year ago, where is she now? That's right, she's working productively alongside a bunch of other passive candidates somewhere. Hello! Do you want to fight with all the other recruiters for that freshly out-of-work or currently disgruntled job seeker who submitted his or her resume today—or go find Beth and her friends?

Passive candidates are better—and there may be a whole bunch right in your own resume bank—or at Monster.com. Active job seekers go to job boards—but passive candidates went there a year ago, and are now passive again.

Resumes and Home Pages on the Web

Remember, home pages are resumes. In fact, they often resemble the European-style curriculum vitae (CV), which is a resume that includes family information, preferences and interests, and non-business-related activities. The CV paints a more robust picture of the person, not just the skills, education, and experience he or she brings to the table. In fact, CVs are better recruiting documents altogether, and home pages can be, too. It's important to include them in your thinking and search strings.

On their home pages, people also tend to link to the topics they're most interested in or that make them interesting to others. Their jobs, where they went to school, their career accomplishments, and friends (often people they met in college, at work, or in their professional lives) are key topics, and most everyone links to some assortment of these. Each of these links can lead us to more people—and should be considered an additional search term or destination to explore.

Many people publish only a resume page. Others attach a separate resume page to their personal home page. Some do neither, but publish other biographical data that can be very useful to recruiters. For example, if you're looking for a highly skilled optical communications expert, you may find a home page with only a glancing nod toward skills and experience, but links to a dozen detailed theses and research reports on SONET and wavelength division multiplexing (WDM)—authored by the page's owner. Guess what? This guy's a guru.

Let's say you do a search for travel agents using the phrase *"american express"*, and land on a home page for Elaine, with the sentence "I really enjoyed my time with American Express, because I made so many new friends." No other reference to her profession or to AMEX, and no resume attached—is Edith a travel agent or did she work in the credit card division? Well, let's say she also has links to pictures of herself in Aruba, Cancun, Hawaii, and Disney World—and to ASTA and ICTA, both travel industry associations. Is she a travel agent? You bet she is—call her.

Look for Clues While You Look for Resumes

As we begin a search, remember we're hunting across a vast tract of information, not in a dedicated resume bank. You're liable to run across all kinds of interesting signs and markers as you search. The trick is to recognize them—and follow the ones that lead to your candidates, or to people who know your candidates.

Let's say you're searching for a Microsoft Network Engineer. You run a search for resumes, and on the first page of results you find a speaker's list for a Microsoft Certified Network Solutions conference. One of the speakers is a fellow named Wayne, with the title "Senior Architect." There are 22 other folks on the list with titles like "Director of Network Engineering" and "Manager of Data Systems."

What can we deduce? First, Wayne is a senior contributor, because he's a speaker on a list with other senior contributors. Second, he's an expert with network solutions, especially the Microsoft variety, since that's what the conference is about. Third, he's probably not drawing house plans—he's a software or data architect who designs network systems. If you're looking for senior network engineers, chances are you've just found one. But if not, at least you've found a fellow that knows a lot of network engineers.

This may seem elementary, but many recruiters are working so hard to find the exact resume that they pass right by a lot of good candidates, and people who know good candidates. Don't leave your basic networking and phone skills at home—and don't hesitate to leave your resume search to chase down names and contacts as you find them.

For example, what can you do if you accidentally find Wayne and his buddies in your search results? You can jump over it entirely and go on to find more resumes, you can bookmark it so you can come back later—or you can try this:

1. Pick up the phone and call Wayne, or send him an e-mail asking for help.
2. Do the same for everybody else on the list; they all know a lot of network engineers, too.
3. Systematically PeerSearch every name on the list, looking for more lists full of senior network engineers.
4. PeelBack the URL to the conference folder and see if you can find any more speakers, sponsors, or attendees. PeerSearch every one of those, and contact them, too.
5. Now go back and look for more resumes.

When you pull off the road to make some phone calls, you create the possibility of many more new candidates—who may not even have a resume in a job board or on the Web. And you've not only made contact with them—if you ask courteously, most will help you by forwarding your opportunities to their friends.

By the way, resumes are full of clues, too. Before you pass by a resume that's not perfect, see if it's close. Is this person working in the right company, have similar skills or belong to the same professional organization as your candidate? Hey, call him or her up—your candidate might have been a college roommate, or may be sitting in the next cubicle.

Talking to people or creating relationships through e-mail are often faster, better ways to find your candidate than running serial searches all day long, looking for the elusive perfect resume. Okay? Let's head for the Web!

The Resume Hunting Grounds

R esumes are scattered all over the Internet, but tend to pool inside particular types of Web sites. The problem is, few of these communities are self-profiling as to skills, industry, or other useful recruiting characteristics—so you can't use them the same way you'd use a resume bank for dentists or airline pilots. But don't worry, there are plenty of ways to search across all of them and harvest the right resumes.

Here are the kinds of Web sites that host resumes and home pages:

- **Free resume banks:** There are not too many of these on the Web anymore, and the ones that remain are not very compelling, as a rule (see Chapter 11, Narrowcast to Targeted Candidates in Niche Job Boards, for tips and resources to help you find niche boards and resume banks).
- **National ISPs:** Many national Internet service providers offer free hosting for personal and small business home pages to attract clients.
- **Local ISPs:** The same applies for smaller regional and metro players. Though it is difficult to predict the types of resumes that might be there—at least an ISP in Dallas is pretty sure to contain Dallas area residents. This can be helpful for strictly local searches.
- **Virtual communities:** GeoCities, Tripod, and AOL home pages are all examples of homesteading sites that offer free hosting, in return for being able to advertise to the community. There are millions and millions of resumes and profiles in these sites.
- **News groups:** There are a series of job and resume news groups dedicated to collecting resumes.
- **Colleges:** Many colleges host resumes and home pages for their students, faculty, researchers, and alumni. Colleges can be self-profiling by department (you'll find engineers in the engineering department) and graduate focus (you'll find MBAs in the business school).

Here are Web sites where you probably won't find resumes hosted—but you will find resumes and home pages that are linked to them from other sites:

- **Companies:** There may be employee and staff home pages in there (which are a lot of fun to find)—and lots of other biographical information that is useful to recruiters. But you're not likely to find personal home pages or resumes. Where's the upside in a company providing disk space so its best people can advertise themselves to recruiters?

- **Organizations and user groups:** Many are building their own resume banks—be prepared to pay. Otherwise, it's not likely you'll find home pages or resumes inside their Web sites.
- **News, publications, and events:** Nope. Lots of great names, contacts, biographical, and profile information here, but no personal home pages or resumes.

Because there's no easy way to tell which sites actually do have resumes or home pages inside, or the kinds of candidates those resumes represent, the best way to search is across the entire Web at once. That way, you'll be building search strings that root out the right resumes regardless of whether they are inside a national ISP, local ISP, virtual community—or even in the unlikely event they're hosted inside a company or association Web site.

Fundamental Tools and Ideas

The Web is a very complex database, but there are many search techniques and methodologies that can take you deep inside, to find virtually anything you're looking for. Unfortunately, it would take a reference shelf lined with explanations, diagrams, and examples to explain it all—and a full-time librarian to keep it up to date.

The Web changes constantly—documents come and go; search engines lead the field, then fail; job boards ditto. The Web and Deep Web grow larger every day, different kinds of pages are suddenly indexed and appear, tools and sites come and go—new search techniques emerge, while others become less useful.

Bottom line, there are few absolute standards for searching the Web. The chapters ahead provide a snapshot of powerful, basic resources and methodologies available to recruiters today. The objective is to cut through the static and simplify the steps, not to teach the most contemporary techniques for advanced search.

The best way to gain a deeper understanding of Internet searches and to apply current principles to your own recruiting challenges—is through a more intensive training process, preferably in a hands-on environment.

That said, in the shifting sands of the Web, there are some fundamental tools and ideas that should serve you well, far into the future. Search engines, Boolean terms, field search commands, and keywords are the building blocks for searching the Web today. We will use them to create Web-wide search strings, then to attack specific destinations, one at a time. Here's how.

The Language of Search

B oolean Logic offers the fastest means of retrieving a given page from a text database. It offers a simple, elegant formula that matches keywords and phrases to text areas and specified fields on a Web page. Boolean concepts have been adopted as a fundamental search methodology by most search engines.

The logic formula is named for its originator, George Boole, an otherwise obscure nineteenth-century English mathematician. Boole was a guru in his day and was one of the first to explore binary logic, which became the foundation for digital circuit design, and subsequently, of the computers we know and love today.

Boolean logic expresses the relationship between a set of objects (in this case, words, phrases, and images). It is the language of the Web, because pages are primarily composed of these elements.

Boolean strings are the instruction set used to determine the search. They ask a simple yes or no question: Does this page conform to these variables? If so, the search engine retrieves the page—if not, the page is ignored. The question itself is called a Boolean expression—and is composed of three elements:

- **Operators:** True Boolean operators are three powerful commands that manipulate the true/false values in the search string. They are: AND, OR and NOT. Some search engines also recognize the term NEAR, though it is not a true Boolean operator.
- **Modifiers:** Symbols used to clarify operators—for example, a phrase is defined by quotation marks.

- **Keywords:** Words or phrases that *must* or *must not* appear on a page to be retrieved.

Boolean Operators and Modifiers

This chart presents a concise view of operators and modifiers used to construct search strings. Boolean operators and modifiers are the first important building blocks for your search string.

In addition to pure Boolean operators, there are related commands that have been adopted by one search engine or another. They are:

AND	All keywords connected by the AND operator must be present on the page. For example, **programmer AND java** will only return pages that contain both words—but not in any particular order.
OR	Any keywords connected by the OR operator must be present on the page. For example, **programmer OR java** will return pages with either or both words on them—again, in no particular order.
NOT	No keywords following the NOT operator can appear on the page. For example, **programmer NOT java** will return pages with the word programmer, but not those also containing the word Java.
" "	Defines an exact phrase. For example, **"java programmer"** will return pages with that title.
( )	Defines a related subset, as in an algebraic equation. For example, **(resume OR vitae) AND "java programmer"** will return Java programmer resumes or CVs. Parenthesis are a good idea for OR statements.
*	Retrieves all words with the same root. For example, **program*** will return pages with program, programs, programmer, programming, programmed, programmable, and programmatic.

- **Positional operators:** NEAR, ADJ, SAME, FBY are all ways to express the concept of words related by proximity. Of the search engines we'll be using, only AltaVista uses the NEAR operator, which it uses to capture terms that are within 10 words of each other.
- **Implied operators:** The plus (+) or minus (−) symbols can be used in place of the AND and NOT operators, in many search engines. This syntax is actually required by a few. These operators must be placed in front of the terms to be included or excluded.

Field Search: Location, Location, Location

Many search engines rank relevancy according to where a word or phrase appears on the page. For example, the words or phrase "Java Programmer" in the URL or title usually denotes the topic of the entire page—whereas the same phrase buried in a sentence in paragraph 7 may not mean much.

Let's apply this thinking to resumes. When a document contains the word "resume" in the URL or page title, there's a very good chance the page is actually a resume document. But if it only appears in paragraph 7, it may be in a sentence like: "Sarah's face was flushed, but she soon *resume*d her composure." Big difference.

So, as search engines index the pages retrieved by their spiders, they isolate words and phrases into distinct fields, according to where they're found on the page. Field search commands can target your search in powerful ways. The most common field search commands are:

- **URL:** Matches words in the URL. Because URLs are really file names, most page developers try to make them as intuitive as possible. That's why URLs with "resume" in them usually lead to resumes, and URLs with people words like "staff," "employee," and "team" often take you to folders and documents containing people.
- **Title:** Matches words in the page title. Again, most page titles are intuitive indicators of what's on the page itself. Think of "Bob's Home Page."
- **Host:** Matches words in documents stored inside a particular Web site. This is the AIRS X-ray command. When looking for resumes,

you'll use it to look inside colleges. Once we start going after people pages, you'll use it on every community Web site you can find.

- **Link:** Finds links to a particular Web site (actually a specific page in
  that Web site). This is the AIRS FlipSearch command. Now let's think
  about what kinds of documents might be linked to company home
  pages—how about resumes and home pages? Yep, and lots more.
- **Domain:** Restricts a search to a specific domain type (i.e.,
  .com/edu/org., etc.). This will come in handy when you want to
  search for resumes across *all* colleges at once.

Pick Your Search Engine

Boolean operators, modifiers, and field searches are standard concepts—but each engine uses its own syntax to execute them. The dif-
ferences can be subtle, but a single character out of place is enough to
botch the whole search. So, before you start to assemble search strings,
it's important to decide which search engine you're going to use.

The chart on the next page shows a summary of the command syntax and settings for each of the top four headhunting engines.

As you can see, each engine uses different words and settings to execute the various operators, modifiers, and field search commands. As we
build examples in this chapter and going forward, we will use standard
Boolean syntax and terms. Use the chart above to convert the strings for
each engine as you go.

Remember, every search engine offers more options—and there are
many more strategies and considerations than can be presented here. To
effectively learn to execute complex commands requires study, practice,
and advanced training.

The PowerSearch Process

It's time to put our operators, modifiers, field search commands and
keywords together and go hunt resumes. PowerSearch strings are complex Boolean expressions designed to filter through millions of documents fast—and surface the best resumes, in the fewest steps possible.

Here's a PowerSearch string that started with the three-word phrase,

Engine	Google	Alltheweb	AltaVista	Hotbot
Address	www.google.com	www.alltheweb.com	www.altavista.com	www.hotbot.com
Search Type	Simple Search	Advanced Search	Advanced Search	Advanced Search
Interface	Search Line	Drop Down Boxes	Boolean Search	Drop Down Boxes
AND	Defaults to AND	Choose "all the words"	AND	Choose "all the words"
OR	OR	Choose "any of the words"	OR	Choose "any of the words"
NOT	—	Choose "must not include"	AND NOT	Choose "must not contain"
Quotes	"_"	Choose "the exact phrase"	"_"	Choose "the exact phrase"
Parentheses	(_)	N/A	(_)	N/A
Wildcard	N/A	N/A	*	N/A
URL	inurl:	Choose "must include" and "in the url"	url:	N/A
Title	intitle:	Choose "must include" and "in the title"	title:	"Look for" choose "in the page title"
Host	site:	Domain Filters Section: "only include": <Web domain>	host:	Domain Section: <Web domain>
Link	link	Word Filters Section: choose "must include" and "in the links to the url"	link:	"Look for" choose "in the links to this url"
Domain	site:	Domain Filters Section: "only include": <domain extension>	domain:	Location/Domain Section: choose Domain and enter a type of domain

"total quality management." The first search returned 61,000 pages. By adding operators, modifiers and field search commands, the string narrowed the results to 93 pages—virtually all of which were resumes or home pages, and most were qualified prospects: *(title:resume OR url:resume OR title:cv OR url:cv) AND ("total quality management" OR tqm OR cmm OR cim OR "continuous improvement methodology") AND "project manager" AND ("quality assurance" OR "malcolm baldrige" OR "iso 9000")*

> ### *Best Practices:* More Field Search Commands
> There are a handful of secondary Field Search commands that recruiters can use for special-purpose situations. Here are a few; check the Help section of each search engine for more:
> - **Image:** This command returns graphics—it's best recruiting use is finding awards, icons, or emblems that go along with designations, for example, the Microsoft Certified Systems Engineer or SAP Partner logos.
> - **Anchor:** This command matches words in a link. So, if you are anchor-searching the word "resume," it will return pages with links that read: "Go here to view our resumes," or "Click to see my resume".
> - **Text:** This command returns only pages that have your keyword somewhere in the text. Often, sites will embed a string of keywords in the meta-tag (a behind-the-scenes identifier that helps search engines categorize the page), which don't appear on the page itself. This is a good modifier to try if you're stuck with this problem.
> - **Like:** This command finds pages that are alike, or specifically related to your target. As you can imagine, this can be a very useful recruiting step if you've found a mother lode of candidates who fit your search.

AND NOT *(submit OR apply OR opening)*.

Let's examine the logic behind building a string like this. Here is a step-by-step AIRS process for thinking your way from a standing start to your own PowerSearch string.

1. **Test the water:** Use a simple set of the most accurate keywords you can think of. These can be AND words, OR words, or a simple phrase. Your first objective is to make sure you're in the right ballpark
2. **Check your results:** Are you in the right place? Are you looking at search results that are relevant to your candidate's skills and industry? If yes, keep going. If no, try some different keywords.
3. **Count your results:** Are there thousands of pages? Hundreds? Dozens? A few? If your results are anywhere from several hundred

pages to millions, you're in a good place to start filtering. If you have fewer than a hundred pages, you may want to check those keywords again.

4. **Add your resume words:** We're looking for resumes hiding in the results. Words and phrases like "resume," "CV," "vitae," and "home page" will begin to surface them.

5. **Add your NOT resume words:** For every resume hiding on the Web, there are 10 job postings, and a couple of resume writing services lurking, with the same keywords. You have to wash those out with NOT words like "submit OR opening". As in, "please submit your resume" or "we have the following openings".

6. **Add common field searches:** If you're still working with an unwieldy batch of pages, use your resume words with title: and URL: field commands to refine the list.

7. **Add better keywords:** Put in cities, states, or area codes, if you're focusing in specific markets. Skills, functional titles, companies, organizations, degrees, and tools are all great keywords for refining your search.

8. **Try a different engine:** If you are just not getting the right results, move your string to another of the top engines—open it back up a few steps, if you need to, and start in again.

9. **Pull out the stops:** Okay, nothing works? First, go back and try another set of keywords. Then see if any of the more exotic field searches work. Still nothing? Go directly to step ten.

10. **Forget it:** Stop looking for resumes. Shake it off, take your keywords and go hunting for employee directories, staff lists, attendees, members, and other people pages hidden inside companies, colleges, organizations, news, events, and other destinations.

Don't worry if you haven't found just the right resume. Think about all the clues you can gather from the information you have retrieved so far. Are there people with the wrong resumes that work alongside the right candidate? Are there companies, organizations, and other destinations listed that you can X-ray and FlipSearch? We'll be moving past resumes to find hidden people in the chapters ahead.

Creating PowerSearch Strings

Okay, that's the process—now let's follow it with a hypothetical search. Let's say we're recruiting for a wireless telecom company and we need a senior software engineer to design CDMA networks in a facility near San Francisco, California. They need to live nearby, because there's no budget for relocation.

Here's how that PowerSearch might go:

1. First, let's test the water with our title and our "must have" skill, CDMA—hit search! *"software engineer" AND cdma.*

2. Okay, we're getting all kinds of related documents here. Job openings, white papers, articles about wireless networks—the works. Looks like a good place to start.

3. Hmmm—570 pages. There must be a few good resumes in there. Let's keep going and see what we can find.

4. Let's filter out some static and surface some people by adding our resume words: *(resume OR cv OR "home page") AND "software engineer" AND cdma.*

5. Well, that took it down to 340 results—but a lot of them look like job postings. Let's wash those out with our NOT resume words: *(resume OR cv OR "home page") AND "software engineer" AND cdma AND NOT (openings OR positions OR opportunities OR jobs OR submit OR staffing OR services).*

6. Great—down to 184, but still a lot of chaff in there. Let's pop the resumes out with some field searches in the URL and title: *(title:resume OR url:resume OR title:cv OR url:cv OR title:vitae OR url:vitae OR title:bio OR url:bio) AND "software engineer" AND cdma AND NOT (openings OR positions OR opportunities OR jobs OR submit OR staffing OR services).*

7. Okay, down to 89—lets zero in with some companies we'd love to steal a wireless software engineer from: *(title:resume OR url:resume OR title:cv OR url:cv OR title:vitae OR url:vitae OR title:bio OR url:bio) AND "software engineer" AND cdma AND (qualcomm OR ericsson OR sprint) AND NOT (openings OR positions OR opportunities OR jobs OR submit OR staffing OR services).*

8. And let's make sure we're only getting local candidates, with some Bay Area filters: *(title:resume OR url:resume OR title:cv OR url:cv OR*

*title:vitae OR url:vitae OR title:bio OR url:bio) AND "software engineer"
AND cdma AND (qualcomm OR ericsson OR sprint) **AND (California
OR ca) AND (415 OR 408 OR 925)** AND NOT (openings OR posi-
tions OR opportunities OR jobs OR submit OR staffing OR services).*

That should do it—hit search!

And ... Voila! 22 Software engineers, who are probably employed
today (or have worked in the past) at Qualcomm, Ericsson, or Sprint—who
work with CDMA technology, and live within 45 minutes of our office.

With some practice, this kind of search will take 10 minutes or so,
and move you past hundreds of thousands of pages to the precise subset of candidates that really fit your search. If it's not working, you'll know
within the first few refinements, and you can adjust with better keywords,
or take the search in a different direction.

Good researchers take a few keywords, jump on the Web and start
adding, subtracting, and substituting field commands and better keywords
until a data pattern emerges. Once there, it's like being on a highway, where
every result is relevant and almost every document leads to people.

The Keys to the Network

K eywords are the most powerful part of your string. In fact, all the
complicated commands and sophisticated techniques in the world
won't take you to the right candidates if you're using the wrong keywords.

As in the example above, the best way to work with PowerSearch
strings is in an iterative fashion. You add, change, and move through lay-
ers of keywords until—wham! You find your candidate. In the process
you'll test, add a few more, and test again—changing direction with new
words whenever you slow down or run aground.

Gathering keywords starts at the front end of your search, and continues all the way through. Here are the best kinds of keywords to gather:

- **People:** People tend to clump together with similar people on the
  Internet. Names, e-mail and land addresses, and phone numbers
  for people who are very similar to your target candidate make
  great search terms.
- **Jargon:** This is a powerful profiling tool. The candidates you're
  hunting probably speak in professional shorthand of some type—

Best Practices: PowerSearch Strings

Keep these additional tips in mind as you build PowerSearch strings:

- **First things first:** Use your strongest terms at the front end of your string—and start with two or three keywords, or a brief phrase.
- **Case matters:** Though not universal, it's safest to assume that Boolean operators should always be in capital letters, e.g., AND, OR, NOT, NEAR—and that keywords should be in lowercase letters, e.g., resume, java, programmer.
- **Space matters:** Always leave a space before and after a Boolean operator. But there's no space between a field search command and the next word, e.g., title:resume.
- **Dial carefully:** Just like a telephone, if you're one digit off you'll get a wrong number. PowerSearch strings are complex—watch for typos, take your time, and get it right before you hit go.
- **Check your Ps and Qs:** Parenthesis and quotes are very important. Make sure they're in the right places, and have open and closed partners.
- **Check your length:** One of the reasons search gurus love AltaVista is that it will execute a paragraph-length search string flawlessly. Google, on the other hand, has a severe keyword limit. Make sure you understand how many keywords are allowed and how they're counted before you build your strings.
- **Check your string:** Most search engines will display your search string at the top of the results page. Take one last, fast glance at it to make sure it's correct and that it's executed properly, before you start to pore over the links.
- **Get help:** If you're in trouble run straight for the Help pages. Most engines do a very good job of pointing the way. With so many variables (and new features to boot), something may well have changed since your last visit.

---

and they'll often use those insider terms and buzzwords in their resumes and the documents they share. For example, if you search on the term "consultant," you'll bring back lots and lots of pages.

But if you search on a set of acronyms like RMP (Risk Management Program), PSM (Process Safety Management), and PHA (Process Hazards Analysis), you're going to bring back only the consultants who specialize in process risk management. This is an especially effective approach for technical candidates, where there are acronyms and abbreviations for just about everything.

- **Skills:** Skills are critical, since most requisitions are specific about these requirements. The trick again, is to transform the common skills terms into the abbreviations or combinations of words that might appear on resumes or home pages.

- **Company names:** These are targeted as to industry—and are powerful keywords because no matter whom you talk to there, they may know your candidate.

- **Organization names and designations:** These are targeted keywords as well. The only folks who belong to the Arkansas Trial Lawyers Association are trial lawyers in Arkansas. Of course, certification and membership acronyms are great keywords, too.

- **Tools and proficiencies:** These also make good keywords. If you are looking for semiconductor design engineers, many will refer to Mentor Graphics—small business accountants may list QuickBooks or PeachTree. By the way, the tool sites have lots of great jargon, for more keywords.

- **Titles:** Titles can be good keywords, but you have to be careful. There are a hundred ways to say "salesperson"—there are even lots of ways to say "janitor." Look at your competitor's job openings and surf out to the big job boards to collect various ways to describe your target function.

- **Locations:** Geographic location is important; and so are the ways you search for them. City names are okay, but think of all the little suburbs surrounding the city itself. Do you really just want people from San Francisco? Or can they live 25 minutes away in Menlo Park, Mill Valley, or Berkeley? It's pretty hard to list every suburb on the map—so the most efficient way to cast your net over metro areas is to use strings of area codes. If you are looking across states and regions, remember to include both California and CA.

Here's how you gather them:

- **Think hard:** Try to visualize the perfect candidate's resume. What's on it? What specific words and phrases are there?
- **The job req:** "Must have" skills, degrees and other qualifications are generally listed in the req. Make a list, but be careful. Until you talk to the hiring manager, you don't really know what you're looking for.
- **The hiring manager:** At the end of the day, a successful hire is the one that best matches your manager's mental picture. Find out what the real hot buttons are—then drill down and get jargon, buzzwords, and other terms only this candidate will know.
- **Your best model:** Ask the hiring manager who best fits this person on your staff, and who might know him or her. They will have more jargon, maybe some companies and organizations—maybe even your candidate.
- **Old searches:** Have you looked for this candidate before? Have your co-workers? Go back to your files and theirs—see what you have on hand, and where you found the last candidate that fit this search. Are there references in there to call? How about everyone you networked with last time?
- **Old candidates:** Have you placed a candidate like this before? Her name and references are good keywords for this search. What skills, companies, organizations, and jargon are on her resume? By the way, that's your first phone call, to see whom she knows.
- **Job boards:** How are your competitors advertising for similar positions? What titles are they using? What acronyms and jargon are in the ads? By the way, your candidates may already be inside one of these companies—their names, addresses and e-mail domains are all good keywords, too.
- **Directories:** There are thousands of directories and vortals that list companies, colleges, organizations, and other kinds of communities.
- **On the Web:** Plug in the keywords you have and see what comes back. Don't search for resumes or people; just see what keywords are there. Remember—jargon, acronyms, tools, titles—you're looking for the language of your candidates, and how they describe their skills, experience, education, and proficiencies.
- **As you go:** If you're on the right road, as you search for resumes you'll be finding more relevant keywords with every click. Resumes that don't fit your specific search may be chock-full of

---

Best in Class: **Specialized Sites**

Here are three specialized sites that may help you gather keywords:

* **Webopedia:** Webopedia is an online technical terminology look-up that is very dynamic and gives the user detailed descriptions as well as links to other resources. Go to: www.webopedia.com
* **Acronym Finder:** This site will help you make sense out of the alphabet soup of acronyms. Type in the acronym you are trying to decipher and it will give you various versions of what that particular acronym stands for. Go to: www.acronymfinder.com
* **Dictionary.com:** This is an online dictionary. Type a word and it will give you the detailed definition for the word as well as other web resources. Go to: www.dictionary.com

---

good keywords—and you'll find lots of non-resume pages can help move you closer to your candidate. Take a few seconds to sweep any new terms into your search folder.

Resume Words and NOT Resume Words

There are three types of keywords in a resume PowerSearch string:

1. **Resume words:** These are words and phrases commonly found in the URL, titles, or text of resumes, home pages, and profiles.
2. **Your keywords:** These are your best guess at what words and phrases will match words and phrases in the best resumes and home pages.
3. **NOT resume words:** These are words and phrases used to filter pages that may contain resume words, but aren't resumes.

The chart on the next page shows sample words and categories for each type.

On to the Deep Web

Knowing how to find resumes in the Internet database is fundamental knowledge for recruiters and managers. A good search engine and well-constructed search string can take you to exactly the right candidate in a matter of minutes. The alternatives are settling for less, search-

Resume Words	Keyword Categories	Not Resume Words
Resume	People	Submit
CV	Jargon	Opening
Vitae	Skills	Recruiter
Homepage	Companies	Send
Bio	Colleges and degrees	Benefits
Qualifications	Organizations and designations	Requirements
Objective	Tools and proficiencies	EOE
Experience	Titles	Apply
Education	Locations	Services
References		
Work history		

ing forever, or paying a 30 percent search fee. In the long run, investing to acquire strong Web search skills will return huge dividends.

But it's time to leave the well-charted reaches of the Web for a while. In the next chapter we'll explore the places search engines fear to tread, as we go hunting for resumes in the Deep Web.

14

Find Resumes in the Deep Web

The Deep Web is a universe of documents linked to the Web, but not accessible via the consumer search engines. This region is estimated to range from 5 billion to as many as 50 billion documents—a breadth that dwarfs the 2 billion documents that have been indexed by search engines so far. No one really knows how vast it is, because there's no device today that can crawl its entirety and confirm its size.

Obviously, this is an enormous set of new documents to hunt through. In this chapter we'll understand what's there and why and how to get at it—and we'll provide some search strategies that will take you inside to harvest passive candidates.

The Invisible Web

The World Wide Web is composed of pages created in simple Hypertext Markup Language (HTML) and linked together in open, searchable directories inside Web sites. Spiders build their indexes by crawling through the links, from page to page.

But the vast repository of Deep Web documents are conventional pages with no Web links, or are stored in sites that are not readily accessible to search engines—and so are invisible to their spiders, and ultimately to their users.

These sites include documents behind firewalls, inside proprietary databases, in password-protected sites, archived pages, in tools like dictionaries, and inside many otherwise accessible Web sites.

For the average Web surfer, the most useful pages tend to be commercial, educational, or informational in nature, while the least useful tend to be personal home pages with pictures of Bobby-Jean's prom dress, or details on the family reunion. So, as search engines focus more on business pages and less on personal, the family picnic pages are increasingly left in the shadow. But for recruiters this is a problem, because that's precisely where our biographical data and resumes are—on personal pages. We want to see Bobby-Jean's dress and her family photos, because there's a good chance that Mom is a big executive with Bank of America—and her resume may be attached, too.

As more home pages are ignored by the leading search engines, and more documents are converted into data fields to be called up and reassembled on the fly, many of the best recruiting pages on the Web are being swept into the Deep Web. That means understanding and searching this region is becoming an ever-more-important recruiting focus.

Doorways to the Deep Web

There are two ways to find sites with Deep Web content. First, you can use a variety of Deep Web directories and search engines to find the home page.

The second way is to peel your way back to them, as you see evidence of a Deep Web domain in a URL indexed by a traditional search engine. Let's look at each in turn:

The Front Door: Searching Databases

Specialty directories and search engines can take you to the Deep Web. But because each database is proprietary, and often stored behind a passworded gateway, these resources can't take you to the individual pages inside.

Some database sites are generally accessible, some require registration or membership, and some are commercial resources that require a subscription fee. Here's a list of the best Deep Web directories and search engines:

- **CompletePlanet:** In January, 2002, search firm BrightPlanet announced a directory of over 100,000 databases and specialty search engines that provide access to over 4 billion documents. Go to: www.completeplanet.com.
- **InvisibleWeb.com:** This is a directory and search engine that can take you to over 10,000 Deep Web databases, and resources. Go to: www.invisibleweb.com.
- **Direct Search:** Gary Price, of Gary Price Library & Internet Research Consulting, is an authority on Deep Web resources. Price has assembled a collection of links on his Direct Search page. Go to: www.freepint.com/gary/direct.htm.
- **Fossick:** The WebSearch Alliance Directory is a collection of links to 3,000 specialty search engines and sites with on-site search capabilities, many of which drill-down to specialty information in Deep Web sites. Go to: www.fossick.com.

Internet Libraries can also be powerful gateways to Deep Web information. Here are a handful of best-in-class resources:

- **The Internet Public Library:** www.ilp.org.
- **Librarian's Index to the Internet:** www.lii.org.
- **Digital Librarian:** www.digital-librarian.com.
- **RefDesk.com:** www.refdesk.com.
- **LibrarySpot:** www.libraryspot.com.
- **Virtual Library:** www.virtuallibrary.com.

And here are a handful of specialty resources that can take you to people:

- **FTP Find:** Many companies use File Transfer Protocol (FTP) to move large data files around on the Internet or to store reams of data on FTP sites. You may find project teams, contact lists, and more. Go to: www.ftpfind.com.
- **Adobe PDFs:** There are many pages on the Internet stored in Adobe PDF format—including documents like phone lists and biographies. Go to: www.searchpdf.adobe.com.
- **Articles:** Many articles are in the Deep Web—and many contain

names and titles linked to business topics, technologies, and companies. Go to: www.findarticles.com.

- **IT and Engineering:** This is a comprehensive portal offering access to thousands of tech-related sites. It's a great resource for finding communities of software developers, programmers, systems experts and more. Go to: www.devsearcher.com.

Going Through the Side Door to Find Personal Home Pages and Resumes

Though you can find thousands of sites with Deep Web directories and search engines, the real pay dirt for recruiters are those home pages and resumes that are gradually slipping into the shadows.

Remember, these pages are falling out of the general indices, but not off the Internet. If we can figure out where they're stored, we can go directly to those sites and look inside. Let's see what's actually going on, to understand this more fully:

1. It can take a search engine spider weeks, even months, to crawl the entire Web and build a new index. That means a resume or home page published today may not appear for quite awhile. But if there's an on-site search capability, you can retrieve that page immediately by visiting the site itself.

2. A search engine may have spidered a Web site months ago, but subsequently decided that the information is not useful and so has put it into a longer spider cycle or skips it altogether now. As a result, the search engine index may contain only a fraction of the pages that now exist on the site.

In either case, there are clues that can alert you to hidden resumes and home pages nearby, and show you where to find them. As you're searching the Web, you'll often cut across the trail of a Deep Web site. Follow the tracks, and you'll end up at a hidden pool of untapped candidates. Wherever you find one resume or home page, there are liable to be lots more in the vicinity—but where?

The clues are in the URL. Here's an example of a resume URL that hints at a larger pool upstream:

http://members.tripod.com/~robertahollis/resume.html

Take a look at the root domain. Tripod is a site that provides free home page space to millions of users—and "members" is a people word, indicating there are lots of other member documents here. We happen to know Tripod is a well-known virtual community—but there are thousands of smaller, relatively obscure sites filled with home pages and resumes hidden in the depths of the Web.

Remember—no matter where you are, take a fast look at the URL of the home pages and resumes you find. Are they part of a subfolder that contains more candidates? In this case, we see the resume is in a community site—and we know there should be lots more resumes there. But a similar URL might take you to a folder full of staff home pages inside a company, or alumni home pages inside a college.

Best Practice: Tilde

The tilde (~) is the universal Web extension for names, resumes, and home pages. Whenever you see this symbol, followed by a name—you can be pretty sure there are more people inside the folder. Use the PeelBack technique to open it up and check.

Okay, back to our example. If we know about this site, and the document has been indexed (otherwise we couldn't have retrieved it with a search engine, right?)—then according to what we've said before, this can't be the Deep Web.

That is correct. This document is not in the Deep Web—but there's a good chance that a large portion of the Web site itself is. Why? Because we know that it is a community site composed almost entirely of personal home pages, and we also know that search engines are indexing fewer and fewer of these types of documents.

How do we prove it? Well, if the entire site (or a large portion of it) has been indexed, then most of the home pages and resumes will appear in an X-ray search. X-ray is the "host:" field command that will retrieve pages indexed on a specific Web site (see Chapter 13, Find Resumes on the Web, to review field search commands).

Let's see if the theory holds. We found Roberta using AltaVista, and when we open her resume, we see that she is a registered nurse from Dallas. First, let's see how many other RNs we can find by X-raying Tripod with AltaVista. The search string is: *host:tripod.com AND resume AND rn*

Hey great! We got 28 resumes back. Now, let's go to Tripod and try again, using their on-site search engine. The search is the same: *resume AND rn*

But this time we get 485 resumes back. That's a huge difference—in fact, it suggests that at Tripod today, 95 percent of registered nurses' resumes are hidden in the Deep Web.

Where the People Are

M ost of the resumes and home pages slipping into the Deep Web are hosted in virtual communities, or local and national ISP (Internet service provider) sites. ISPs (along with Online Service Providers like AOL) offer low-cost monthly access to the Internet. Because they serve so many people, they have become de facto Web communities.

Virtual communities offer free Web hosting for personal and small business home pages, free e-mail and other services, in return for the right to advertise to members and visitors. These sites aim right for the general consumer, by making it as easy as point, click—and hit Enter. There's your new home page. As a result, consumers have flocked to these sites in droves.

One of the first documents most people link to their home pages is their resume. In fact, many communities now offer resume-building templates as part of their tool set.

There are thousands of sites that offer free Web hosting. Alongside the many virtual communities hoping to build an audience are ISPs offering free Web space as an enticement to subscribe. Like many businesses on the Web, there are a handful of active, successful communities—and many more subsisting with only a smattering of activity. Similarly, there are a group of strong, local ISPs—but many more are barely scratching by, or are being rolled up by the national providers.

As a result, Web researchers will often turn up a resume and peel it back to the root domain, only to find a tired community or small local ISP, with few home pages and almost no traffic. Unless there's evidence that more of the kinds of candidates you're hunting may be in the site (as in the case of an IT recruiter who stumbles across a small community named softwaredevelopercity.com), it's probably best to keep moving.

If you think it's worth mining the site, go directly to the home page and see if they offer an on-site search option. If not, X-ray the site using a search string like this sample: *host:softwaredevelopercity.com AND resume AND "software engineer"*

With luck, you'll have a list of great results. But whether you do or not—remember to look for related resources, more keywords, and names to PeerSearch.

Virtual Communities

The best hunting grounds are the big communities and ISPs. These sites are really free resume banks—filled with passive candidates instead of job seekers. Most of the larger communities do offer their own search—these are simple sites, and you'll use simple terms to search them. In general, you can assume the standard Boolean Operators AND, OR, NOT will work in each.

The most prominent Virtual Communities are:

1. **GeoCities:** www.geocities.com.
2. **Angelfire:** www.angelfire.lycos.com.
3. **Tripod:** www.tripod.lycos.com.

Remember, wherever there is free Web hosting, there are liable to be pools of home pages and resumes. To find more virtual communities, try these resources:

- **AIRS Virtual Community Directory:** 80 tried-and-true virtual communities. Go to: www.airsdirectory.com/communities.
- **Click Here Free:** A large directory of free ISPs and of sites that offer free Web hosting. Go to: www.clickherefree.com.
- **FreeWebspace.net:** A gateway to free Web hosting options. Go to: www.freewebspace.net.

ISPs and Online Service Providers (OSPs)

Like the large virtual communities, ISPs and OSPs offer free home pages to build communities they can tap into—though they grow revenue through subscription fees, as well. There are large groups of home pages and resumes at each of the top three:

1. **AOL member home pages:** www.hometown.aol.com.
2. **MSN home pages:** www.msn.com.
3. **EarthLink home pages:** www.earthlink.net.

To find more Internet Service Providers in the U.S. and around the world, check out these resources:

- **ISPworld:** Otherwise known as BoardWatch, this is a comprehensive list of local and national providers, organized by area code. Go to: www.ispworld.com.
- **The List:** Another big, searchable list brought to you by Internet.com. Go to: http://thelist.internet.com.
- **AIRS ISP Directory:** A directory of ISPs that host home pages. There are over 900 national and local ISPs listed and linked, organized by state and area code. Go to: www.airsdirectory.com/directories/isps.

As the World Turns

Many online communities are struggling today, as companies like Yahoo! and Terra Lycos work to transform their advertising-only model into a portfolio of fee services. As a result, we may see many more personal pages falling into the Deep Web over the next several years.

Now it's time for us to head back to the main avenues of the Web, to find people hidden inside companies, colleges, and organizations.

15

Find People Linked to Companies, Colleges, and Organizations

Headhunters have always known that the best candidates come from your best competitors. Employment agreements and non-competes aside, there's a tremendous gratification in taking the best people from companies that are trying to take yours. As a result, all through the 1990s phones were ringing from cubicle to cubicle, as recruiters struggled to make contact and persuade people that it was time to make a change.

Today, things have settled down, but the staffing gurus agree the next wave is coming fast. This time around, fewer third-party recruiters will be in the advance wave. The best corporations have gotten over their decades-old aversion to direct sourcing—and are preparing their own staffs to get inside, rummage around, and find the right candidates in their competitors' companies.

New Internet techniques that allow companies' own researchers to access information via the Web, rather than trying to bluff their way past the receptionist, are important catalysts for this sea change. Corporate recruiters have always been squeamish (for good reason) about the tactics their third-party counterparts allegedly use to get inside and talk to the right people.

But there's no ethical tug-of-war when it comes to accessing information hosted on Web pages in the public domain and indexed by major search engines. These aren't secrets, and you don't have to lie to get at the information. You just have to understand where that information is, and how to get to it as quickly as you can.

Just as the Web transforms the process of finding people in the workplace, it also offers new ways to find seasoned professionals and the brightest graduating students inside university Web sites—and members of the best professional organizations where they gather to work and collaborate. If you know how to search these primary sites, you can leap past your competitors at the job boards and go straight to passive candidates inside their companies, colleges, and associations.

In this chapter, we'll introduce a five-step process for finding and mining these key Web sites, identify the kinds of people and documents you'll be looking for in each, and provide some basic search techniques to move those passive candidates off the Web and into your database.

Searching Destinations

Virtually every company, college, and organization has a Web site, and it is filled with documents that describe their mission, projects, and people. If these documents are hosted outside the firewall on a Web server linked to the Web, they are public documents. It's as if the company, college, or organization posted those pages on a billboard in Times Square, for all to see.

Of course, it doesn't seem that way to Web users or to the company, college, or organization that has published them. It's hard enough for most of us to just get on the Web and find anything, let alone navigate all the way to some company site, understand that there may be pages inside it with no visible links to the outside world, then figure out how to get in there and read them.

So, companies, colleges, and organizations that publish documents on the Web just aren't thinking about how recruiters (or other representatives of their competitors for that matter) might be able to use those pages, if they were to find them.

And find them we shall—because recruiting is about finding the best people, wherever they are, and convincing them to join your organization. It's a sales job, and that means we need customers. Bottom line, companies, colleges, and organizations are where the best customers hang out—and where the best recruiters find them.

Although each kind of site contains a different set of documents, the methodology of search, harvest and repeat, are the same across all destination sites. The process is:

1. **Find the right site:** We'll use directories, search engines, and vortals to pinpoint the right companies, colleges, and organizations.
2. **Go through the front door:** Most sites leave a lot of information lying around in plain sight. Rummaging around, following the links, and clicking through the site map can take you to great information and important clues—if you know what you're searching for.
3. **Go through the side door:** X-ray the site and see what kinds of documents are inside but may not be linked or not accessible to the casual surfer.
4. **Go through the back door:** FlipSearch the site and its key pages to see who and what are linked to them.
5. **Find one, find them all:** Use the clues you've gathered—names, e-mails, office addresses, more companies, colleges, organizations, other destinations, and new keywords—to drill farther into the Web and surface more passive candidates.

Finding the Right Domain

As we look at each type of destination site, we'll discuss ways to find them. But what if you already know (or find more) names of target companies, colleges, or organizations—but don't know how to find them on the Web? One way is to just search the name in Google—the name you are looking for will usually be among the first results.

As we've discussed, each Web site is registered with a unique domain name and URL. These domain names are stored in a public database, and a number of sites offer searchable access to them. However, the easiest way to find the domain of a company, college, organization, or other site you're searching for, is to just search the name in Google, where you're most likely to find it quickly.

It's time to take our search process to each type of site, understand what we should be able to find there, and then do some sample searches.

Companies

There are tens of millions of .com domains registered today. Not all are company Web sites, but by the rules of Internet registration, all are involved in commerce in some way.

Step one in searching companies is to find the right ones. This is a three-step process in itself:

- **Profile your candidate:** As you interview the hiring manager, members of your team, and review similar searches you've completed in the past, make an initial list of your target companies.

  Also, take the keywords in your requisition out to the major job boards and run some searches for jobs. The companies that are posting jobs for candidates like yours are likely to have similar candidates already working there.

- **Use the directories:** There are numerous sites that list and link to companies on the Web—and many sites have organized lists of employers. In general there are two kinds of lists to look for. First are public companies—these are listed by category, in hundreds of sites such as Hoover's and Edgar, as well as in financial sites like CBS BusinessWatch and Morningstar. Public companies are simple to find.

  Second are private companies. These are much more difficult to locate, because there are no free, central lists of the millions of private companies in the United States or worldwide. You can pay for this information or find it in vortals.

- **Harvest more as you go:** Look carefully at the pages you sort through in your search. If you're on the right path, you'll run into pages and pages that list more of the right companies, colleges, and organizations.

Finding the Right Companies

Comprehensive directories of public companies are listed all over the Web. Here are a handful of good resources:

- **Edgar Online:** Searchable window into the SEC database of companies and filings—as well as company profiles worldwide. Go to: www.edgar-online.com.

- **Corporate Information:** This site meta-searches, and aggregates data from public companies all over the Web. Go to: www.corporateinformation.com.
- **Hoover's:** Great vortal, with lots of free profiles and links to public companies. Go to: www.hoovers.com.

Private companies are tougher to find, because there's no central listing outside of large fee information services like Dun and Bradstreet. But here are several sites that do list a large number of private companies, as well as public:

1. **Business.com:** This is a large directory linking to businesses of every shape and size. Go to: www.business.com.
2. **AIRS Employer Directory:** Over 9,000 public and private companies listed. Links to home pages and executive and executive compensation resources. Go to: www.airsdirectory.com/directories/employers.
3. **Yahoo! Yellow Pages:** Extensive directory of links to companies of all kinds in every market. Go to: http://yp.yahoo.com.

Start-ups are very volatile and capital is expected to be scarce through the first half of this decade. If you want to reach people inside newer companies who may be looking to jump ship, the best places to find them are at venture capital sites that list their portfolio companies. Here are two directories that will take you to VCs:

1. **Net Profits:** Solid jump list to lots of venture capital firms. Go to: www.net-profits.org/vc.html.
2. **Vfinance.com:** A comprehensive vortal for the venture capital community, with a large resource directory. Go to: www.vfinance.com.

If you haven't found the companies you need, or want to drill down further, it's time to look for vertical portals that list companies in their target industries. Here is a search string that will take you to vortals in your own industry: *(title:resources OR title:bookmarks OR title:links OR url:resources OR url:bookmarks OR url:links) AND <your industry keyword>.*

***Best in Class:* More Companies**
- **Fortune 500:** www.fortune.com/lists/F500/index.html
- **Global 500:** www.fortune.com/lists/G500/index.html
- **Fastest-Growing Companies:** www.fortune.com/lists/ fastest/index.html
- **Best Companies for Minorities:** www.fortune.com/lists/ diversi-ty/index.html
- **Forbes 500:** www.forbes.com/2002/03/27/ forbes500.html
- **Forbes 500 Private Companies:** www.forbes.com/ private500/
- **Forbes 400 Best Big Companies:** www.forbes.com/ platinum400/
- **Forbes 200 Best Small Companies:** www.forbes.com/ 200best
- **Inc. 500 Private Companies:** www.inc.com/inc500/ index.html

Going Through the Front Door

Companies tend to leave lots of people information lying around in plain sight. There may be links to the executive team, to a host of press releases that name project managers and marketing folks, to a roster of salespeople in each region, and more. As you go, keep your eyes peeled for white papers, PDFs, research, and annual reports, too.

The best way to hunt through the pages is with a site map, if one is provided. If there is an on-site search engine, try some "people" words, and some titles, to see what pops up. Or, just spend some time going through promising links and looking around.

It's a good idea on this first visit, to browse through the job board and product sections for keywords. What do they call their technologies, products, and service lines? These are usually great keywords. What titles do they use? What positions are they advertising for, and what skills are required? Along with the company's name, these are the kinds of words candidates will use to describe themselves inside and outside on home pages and resumes.

Going Through the Side Door

Okay, it's time to X-ray the company to see what we've missed, or might be hidden from view. Remember, the X-ray command shows us every document the search engine has indexed in the company site. Because the site is commercial, and should generate more traffic than individual home pages, it is likely that the major engines have indexed quite a few of the documents inside.

Let's try an example modeled on a large, successful company we all know. Our target builds office and enterprise business equipment and software—let's call it Big Company—and we're hunting for engineers.

As with PowerSearch, you can build a good X-ray string incrementally, narrowing the focus as you drill deeper. To start, let's see how many documents AltaVista has indexed inside Big Company's Web site. Here's the first string: ***host:bigcompany.com.***

This search returns 12,600 documents in AltaVista. (To compare, the same search yields over 22,000 in Google.) There are all kinds of pages in our results—sales pages, product pages, career center pages, and much more.

But we're looking for people. Wouldn't it be great if Big Company had some staff directories, or project teams in there somewhere? Let's go find out—by adding "people" words in the title or URL to our string: ***host:bigcompany.com AND (title:people OR url:people OR title:staff OR url:staff OR title:team OR url:team).***

Well, we've gone from 12,600 documents down to 84. Lots of them look like articles or press releases. But there's one on the first page with our tilde (~) symbol, followed by what looks like a name: **http://www.people.bigcompany.com/market/chic/~nicholsbar/index.htm.**

Sure enough, it's Barbara Nichol's profile. Barbara is a marketing director in the Chicago office, and works on a line of software utilities. If we peel this URL back to the Chicago folder, we get to meet everyone else in the Chicago marketing group. Peel back one more folder, and there's an alphabetical list of sales and marketing staff all over the country.

Well, that's great—but we're looking for engineers. So, this time, let's add some specific titles to our search instead of general "people" words. We know the titles Big Company uses for its engineers, because we've surfed around and run some searches on their job board. Let's search for pages with the right titles in them—as long as they're not job openings. Here we go: ***host:bigcompany.com AND ("architect" OR "principal engi-***

neer" OR "software architect") AND NOT (submit OR eeo).

Wow, that takes us right down to 643 pages. But that's still a lot—so, let's add some of the jargon keywords we know our candidates work with, and that we've found on other parts of the Big Company site: *host:bigcompany.com AND ("architect" OR "principal engineer" OR "software architect") AND (n-tier OR "ssi model" OR "op architecture" OR d-protocols OR "design api") AND NOT (submit OR eeo).*

Okay, we're at 112 pages—let's sort through. In the first results, we find a page linking us to three engineers carrying on a discussion about their projects in an in-house forum. There are e-mail addresses for all three—and we grab them.

On results page two, we find a document describing a Special Interest Group (SIG) at IEEE (an organization for engineers). When we click on the link, it takes us to a page with the SIG officers—names, titles, companies, and e-mail. Virtually all appear to be similar engineers from companies related to our search. We harvest three more engineers. (By the way, it would be a good idea to peel back our SIG page URL, too—because it's obvious there are lots more Special Interest Groups in this directory at IEEE—but let's head back.)

At the bottom of page two, we find a document with a link to an engineering conference. Two clicks later we're at the speaker's list, which includes a guru from Big Company, along with similar gurus with titles like Director, Software Engineer, and Software Architect.

There's more in the following pages, but you get the picture. We're after people, with these searches—not resumes. And people connected to companies are not just in documents with "people" titles—but in meetings, forums, minutes, membership pages, and more. Wherever people collaborate, they tend to leave behind their names, often their e-mail addresses—and usually clues to their skills or interests.

This X-ray search has already yielded a dozen or more good contacts. There's a good chance that dozens more are hiding in those 112 pages—and there are probably links to hundreds more in nearby documents.

Going Through the Back Door

Who links themselves to companies? Employees, past employees, people who use the company's products or services to do their own job in another company (for example, a programmer with great Oracle skills may link herself to Oracle's home page, or to a technical page about her specialty)—as well as people who are generally interested in the company.

Why are they interested? Most likely, it's because they are in the same orbit. They may be customers, vendors, partners, or have a brother, sister, mom, or dad who works there. Any of these linkages and more can take you to your candidate or people who sit next to them at work—or to people who know the people who sit next to them at work.

Follow the links and you're tapped into the community of interest. Remember to look around as you go, and think about how the people you're finding may be related to the people you're looking for—and how to network your way from them to your candidate.

It's time to FlipSearch your company, looking for resumes, home pages, and other people documents—and more companies, keywords, and clues. Like our X-ray search, let's start by looking at everything that's linked, then narrow the results down to the right pages and people. Here's our first string: *link:bigcompany.com*.

Wow, there are over 120,000 documents linked back to Big Company. Let's see how many resumes are in there. Our string is: *link:bigcompany.com AND (title:resume OR url:resume OR title:cv OR url:cv) AND NOT (submit OR eeo)*.

We're down to 840 documents. Let's see how many software engineers, developers, or similar folks are in there. This time, we'll use more general terms, not just Big Company titles—because many of these folks, are working at other companies now. Our string is: *link:bigcompany.com AND ("software architect" OR "software engineer" OR "software developer") AND (title:resume OR url:resume OR title:cv OR url:cv) AND NOT (submit OR eeo)*.

Best in Class: "People" Search Words for Companies

• People	• Employees
• Staff	• Directory
• Team	• Bio/Biography
• Group	• Research
• Project	• Home pages
• Associates	• Titles

We've got 81 resumes with the right general keywords, linked to Big Company. You can start clicking through now, or refine your string further with jargon and more targeted keywords. With luck, one or two of the candidates you surface will be dead on—and others will be close.

Colleges, Universities, and Grad Schools

W ho will we find in college, university, and graduate school Web sites? Well, students for sure. But there are lots of seasoned professionals there too. In fact, you will be amazed to see how many experienced workers, managers, and executives have a resume or home page hosted on their college server—as an alumnus, speaker, part-time professor, member of the faculty, researcher, or industry contact.

Even more people have linked their resumes and home pages from the outside, into their college Web sites. Where we went to school is an integral part of how we communicate our value, our status—or like sports, it provides a neutral point of common interest for cocktail chatter, or to build a relationship. Schools are a required field on resumes, so you can count on thousands of past students linking to the home page—and thousands more home pages linking to their favorite department or professor.

Colleges are great at building and nurturing alumni communities as a way to keep their recent students (customers) connected, raise funds and make sure future classes are filled with more legacy students (customers). As a result, there may be alumni directories, profiles, biographies, and other "people" documents hosted on the college Web site too—and connected to it from all over the Web.

School Web sites are fertile hunting grounds, but most recruiters ignore them—because it stands to reason they're filled with students, which few recruiters have any interest in at all. So, knowing that they also host and link to many of the best, most experienced people in every industry is a competitive bonus for you.

Let's take a look at how to find them and then at how to search for them.

Finding the Right Schools

ooking for top MBAs? Check out Harvard Business School, Stanford, Wharton, and Amos Tuck. Cutting-edge engineers? Try Carnegie Mellon, MIT, or Cal Tech. Looking for software engineers that live in Phoenix? How about Arizona State?

Many graduate schools, and some four-year schools, are clearly self-profiling by the type of degrees they're known for, or by their reputation. But most offer a variety of majors, and help their students matriculate into many businesses, industries, and professions.

The best ways to search for specific kinds of candidates in a general student body are by department and location. In other words, good chemical engineers come from chemical engineering programs at a host of schools all over the United States and abroad. But if you're looking for workers to staff a petroleum facility in Oklahoma, it makes sense to look for engineering programs in nearby colleges first.

Here are several resources that provide the information you need to find the school, its location, and the types of degrees offered:

- **Peterson's:** An authoritative directory of colleges and programs, offering detailed profiles of every accredited two and four-year U.S. college and university. Includes details on over 35,000 graduate programs. Go to: www.petersons.com.
- **AIRS College Directory:** Links to 1,400 colleges and universities, searchable by state or degree program. Go to: www.airsdirectory. com/directories/colleges.
- **College Rankings:** Top US universities and liberal arts colleges—ranked nationally and by region. Go to: www.usnews.com/usnews/ edu/college/rankings/rankindex_brief.php.

Go Through the Front Door

ollege Web sites are designed to sell the campus to prospective students and their parents—so you're liable to find lots of admission requirements, photos, maps, and tours. But we're looking for people—and for links that can take us to them.

Remember, many colleges and universities often include several separate schools or have more than one campus. These may all have pages in subdomains of the main college server, or be scattered across Web sites with their own domain names and URLs. Make sure you are searching across the right schools for:

- **Programs and departments:** These links will often take you inside to meet professors, visiting academics, researchers, and more. Department pages are also good places to find links to projects that are annotated with names, or contain jargon that can be turned into keywords for your search.

- **Research papers:** Your target companies may be sponsoring research projects for companies in your industry, or professionals in your industry may be named as references or experts.

- **Alumni tools:** This is pay dirt for most recruiters—you might find a directory, an alumni newsletter with names, titles, and companies, or a list of officers, directors, and chapter heads. Remember, one of the primary functions of an alumni organization is to network and provide opportunities to its members—so don't be shy about calling these contacts to see if they can help you with your search.

- **Fraternities and sororities:** These organizations are filled with people who remain loyal throughout their professional careers. Look for "people pages" and links to the national Web site—where there are certainly more profiles, biographies, and ways to get in touch with members.

- **Student home pages:** These days, many students are older and more mature and bring business skills to college with them. You may find seasoned professionals who have returned to finish a degree, or grad school students who already have terrific business experience. If there's a link to profiles or home pages, go take a look.

But that's enough poking around for now. Let's see what's inside.

X-raying College Sites

Before you start an X-ray search, make sure you're in the right place. If there are multiple servers at your target college, make sure you're X-raying the right one. In other words, if you are looking for engineers,

> ### *Best in Class:* Finding Them in College
> **Greeks**
> If you belonged to a Greek society in college, try these sites:
> - **We Alumni:** www.wealumni.com
> - **Greek Pages:** www.greekpages.com
> - **Greek Alumni:** www.greekalumni.com
>
> **Student Home Pages**
> If you're looking for student home pages, try these sites:
> - **Personal Pages Worldwide:** www.utexas.edu/world/personal
> - **Personal Pages Direct:** www.student.com/feature/ppd
>
> **Alumni**
> If you're looking for college alumni, try these sites:
> - **Alumni.net:** www.alumni.net
> - **Planet Alumni:** www.planetalumni.com

and there are separate math and engineering departments with their own domains and servers, you'll want to X-ray them individually, rather than focus only on the main site.

Building an X-ray string for a college server uses our now-familiar command structure, but we'll be adding different keywords as we go. Colleges are different from companies, in that you will find lots of resumes and home pages hosted there—so we won't mess with people searches unless we have to. Let's start by searching Big College, a well-known campus on the West Coast with a strong technical and engineering focus: *host:bigcollege.edu.*

Okay, our first search brings back 98,000 pages. It looks like all kinds of information about classes, enrollment, schedules, and more. Let's see if there are any resumes in there. Here's the string: *host:bigcollege.edu AND (resume OR cv OR bio OR "home page").*

Man, over 10,500 results! Let's filter with some engineering job titles: *host:bigcollege.edu AND (resume OR cv OR bio OR "home page") AND ("software engineer" OR developer OR "software architect").*

Okay, that takes our results down to 134—and about 90 percent of those look like resumes. Let's click a few and see how many are students and how many are experienced professionals:

1. Graduated in 1988 and works for the Jet Propulsion Laboratory.
2. Graduated in 1992 and works for GE Medical Systems.
3. Graduated in 1989 and is now a software architect at Xerox Parc Labs.
4. Graduated in 1997 and is a partner in her own software firm in L.A.

See the pattern here? None of the first four on the page are students—in fact, a very small percentage of the entire result set appears to be. These are all accomplished, seasoned professionals—with resumes in their college Web site!

How many other recruiters are even thinking about looking for candidates here—let alone know how to do it? These are great candidates, and probably as passive as they come—chances are you won't find them in the job boards at all.

Flipping College Sites

L et's take a fast look at who is linked to Big College from the outside. We can use exactly the same search string, except we'll change the X-ray fields command (host:) to the FlipSearch field command (link:)—here we go: link:bigcollege.com **AND (resume OR cv OR bio OR "home page") AND ("software engineer" OR developer OR "software architect").**

That was a good search! The fourth result on the first page is an Alumni Directory from an affiliated college, with over 700 names, titles, companies, and e-mail addresses.

Ninety percent of the other 476 pages retrieved look like resumes—but are they students? Let's pop a few open:

1. Graduated 1992 and works for a software firm in the Silicon Valley.
2. Graduated 1994 and is a senior software engineer in Sacramento.
3. Graduated 1981 and works for United Air Lines.
4. Graduated 1998 and works at IBM Research.

Between X-raying and FlipSearching Big College, we have over 500 resumes for software engineers—the vast majority of whom are almost certainly passive candidates. We've also found at least one alumni directory with 700 more passive candidates—and chances are there are lots more where that one came from.

Best in Class: "People" Search Words for Colleges

- Students
- Faculty
- Staff
- Team
- People
- Degree
- Fraternity
- Sorority
- Position titles
- Company names

In the interest of brevity, we've jumped right over X-raying and Flipping colleges for people pages—but the commands are virtually identical to those we used to search companies. Try a few, and you'll find just as many (in fact, probably more) lists, directories, and other "people" documents inside, and linked to colleges.

Colleges, universities, and alumni sites are great places to find passive candidates. Go through the front door, side door, and back door—and you'll be tapping into untouched pools of terrific people.

Professional Organizations

There are thousands of professional and trade organizations on the Web—and they are natural communities that attract candidates with similar skills, professional backgrounds, industry knowledge, and experience levels.

Most provide a membership opportunity, networking and educational resources, and a certification, designation, or other emblem of proficiency. Members, particularly those who are certified or credentialed in some way, invariably name the organization or their designation in resumes, home pages, and sometimes in their signature lines.

As a bonus for recruiters, many also imbed the association's graphic logo or their designation emblem on their Web page. You can find these pages quickly by conducting an image search in Google. Simply search for your target organization in the text search engine—then click the Image tab above the search box. You'll be linked to all the pages on which your target logo appears.

Otherwise, the process, search commands and search techniques are very similar to those we've used for companies and colleges.

Finding the Right Organizations

There are many organization look-ups on the Web. The most comprehensive are:

- **Gateway to Associations:** A great site sponsored by the American society of Association Executives. Go to: www.asaenet.org.
- **Associations on the Net:** The Internet Public Library's collection of associations and organizations. Go to: www.ipl.org/ref/AON.

Go Through the Front Door

Organizations aren't likely to leave their membership rosters in plain sight—but they usually sprinkle a lot of useful information around for the public to poke through. This might include:

- **The Board:** Board members are typically the senior folks in an industry or profession. These are great contacts to touch base, and grow relationships with.
- **The Officers:** Big organizations have lots of Officers—national, regional, sometime local.
- **Chapters:** National organization sites often provide contact information and staff names for their local offices in various metro areas. If you're recruiting accountants in Denver, you may want to get to know the staff at the Colorado Society of CPAs (www.cocpa.org).
- **Conferences:** Lots of organizations sponsor conferences—and at conferences you can find speakers, attendees, white papers, vendors, and more.
- **Publications:** Newsletters, monthly pubs, articles, and press releases online can link you to member's names and their companies. Now, they are only a phone call away—or look them up on the Web to get their e-mail address.

Organizations are supposed to help their members—and passing along job opportunities are a good way to do that. If you're planning to recruit a batch of the same kinds of people, by all means make contact and introduce yourself to the organizations they belong to. You may just get plugged right in, and save yourself a lot of search time.

X-raying Organization Sites

U nless the organization has its own resume bank (which is becoming more and more common), you won't find resumes, home pages, or profiles in the site itself. It is a good idea to run a quick "people" search on the site to see what might surface, though. You just never know what's going to be right there inside a Web site.

Let's use a midize specialty engineering organization for our example. We'll call it Average Organization—and stay with our software engineering search. Here's the first X-ray: *host:averageorganization.org.*

This search brings back 7,900 pages in AltaVista (15,000 in Google). Now let's add the kinds of keywords that might be in the title or URL of pages that contain people: *host:averageorganization.org AND (members OR attendees OR committee OR minutes OR group OR officers OR board OR chapters OR speakers OR author).*

All right—we're looking at 203 pages in our results, many of which look like they have some leads for us. In the first 50, we find:

- A directory of Chapter home pages, with links to officers and committee heads.
- Minutes for a committee meeting held in September, with an attendee roll call. When we peel back to the next folder in the URL, we find minutes with different attendees for meetings in June and March—and another folder up is the committee home page with links to all meetings in 2001 and 2000.
- The national Board of Trustees and several national committee leaders, with full contact information.
- An entire page of links to research papers submitted by members. All papers have the author's name, title, company, and contact block, including e-mail.

Looks like there are people in there, all right. Now let's Flip it.

Flipping Organization Sites

J ust like colleges, organizations and certifications are natural line items for a resume. In fact, acronyms (as in CPA for Certified Public Accountant, or MCSE for Microsoft Certified Systems Engineer) are some of the most powerful keywords.

> ### Best in Class: "People" Search
> ### Words for Organizations
> - Attendees
> - Members
> - Minutes
> - Officers
> - Chapters
> - Agenda
> - Board of Directors
> - Directories
> - Staff
> - Speakers
> - People

Lets flip Average Organization now: ***Link:averageorganization.org***.

There are 16,900 pages linked back to Average Organization. Let's filter that down to just bring back resumes and home pages for the engineers we're hunting: *link:averageorganization.org AND (resume OR cv OR bio OR "home page") AND ("software engineer" OR developer OR "software architect")*.

Find One Find Them All

C ompanies, colleges, and organizations are filled with great passive candidates. But other Internet destinations will provide the same kind of harvest. These techniques work with Web forums, business news, trade publications, conferences and events, user groups, and more. Wherever people gather to work and play on the Net, you'll find links to names, contact information, and more clues.

Get to the right sites for your search—then go through the front door and nose around, X-ray through the side door to find hidden pages, and FlipSearch the site to find links. You should end up with a stack of data—and a strong competitive advantage.

16

Special Tactics for Recruiting Graduates, Senior Executives, and Diversity Candidates

S tudents and recent graduates, executives, and diversity candidates are three very distinct hiring pools with special characteristics, interests, and preferences. In general, the Internet tools and practices for attracting and finding these candidates are the same:

- A focus on employee referral and networking.
- A strong, attractive Web site.
- A compelling recruitment ad campaign and job postings in niche boards and communities.
- Active search for candidates hiding in targeted companies, colleges, organizations, and other destination Web sites.

But the recruiting tactics you'll use to capture and hire each of these specialized types of candidates are different. In this chapter, we'll take a look at these three populations, understand the general characteristics of each—and then explore best practices to help you configure your recruiting message, career center, ad campaigns, and search activities—to recruit the very best candidates in each pool.

Students and Recent Graduates

Today's students and grads have grown up on the Web. Job boards are an instinctive first place to visit for these job seekers—and they have no reservations about downloading their resumes to many at once. In general, they are also savvy Internet researchers, and will travel the Web often to the companies they've targeted in various industries.

For most major corporations, it's not only important to be able to reach into this population, but to sort through it quickly to surface the candidates with the most potential. Let's look first at how to make your site and ad campaigns attractive to the group in general, then at some ideas about finding and growing relationships with the best students, long before they graduate.

Best in Class: College Job Boards

- **BrassRing Campus:** www.brassringcampus.com
- **JobGusher:** www.jobgusher.com
- **College Central Network:** www.collegecentral.com
- **CollegeJobBoard.com:** www.collegejobboard.com
- **AfterCollege:** www.aftercollege.com
- **CollegeRecruiter:** www.collegerecruiter.com

Your College Career Folio

As you craft a college folio, keep in mind that your audience includes people who are seeking—or have recently completed—undergraduate, graduate (MBAs, MSEE, et al.), professional (MD, JD, et al.), and alternative programs such as tech school and executive education.

To attract the specific people you are seeking within this general population, your Web site must be welcoming and resonate with an appreciation for their concerns and career objectives. The style of your presentation must be congruent with the candidate's own worldview and vision of success.

Students and recent grads are generally young. The ones you'll want to hire are also smart, ambitious, and hardworking, and they bring specific skills or aptitudes to the table with them. So, aim your content at these top performers. The best career-starters are intelligent, well informed, and on top of the latest academic and professional jargon, so make sure your presentation is crisp and gives them the sense of a dynamic, market leading workplace.

At the same time, these are fresh, enthusiastic, and energetic people. They crave a mission, a way to really make a difference—and the best and brightest are attracted to organizations that can articulate a clear and attractive vision for positive change.

The best college folios are professional, fun, and exciting all at once. Through words and pictures, they promise hard work and challenge—leavened with a great team spirit and exciting opportunities for personal growth, new relationships, and enjoyment.

Here are some features to consider:

- **Easy access:** Your college folio should be prominently linked from all of the major pages in your career center, from college-level jobs that turn up in your job board search results and other related pages. This is a boutique just for the college crowd—make sure they see it and go inside.

- **Career paths:** Provide a candid picture of the types of opportunities your firm offers, and where those opportunities may lead in the future. Some companies chart the candidate's degree to a series of entry-level jobs that then branch out to higher-level positions in the chain. Others narrate growth opportunities in detail. The point is to paint a broad picture of a successful career—not just describe a job.

 Explaining your company's opportunities for personal and professional growth is central to the sale—it helps career-starters understand how their careers might bloom, and what they will learn along the way.

- **Links to key initiatives:** College students spend the majority of their Web time researching companies, not running job searches on job boards. Make sure you are linking them from your college folio to the most exciting initiatives you are working on—and to project teams that include people like them.

- **Mentoring opportunities:** Grads today realize their long-term success often relies on the quality of people they can tap for advice and who are committed to help them rise within an organization. Mentoring programs are a powerful attractant and can be used as a recruiting tool to engage the best students long before they enter the job market.

- **Pre-hire training:** Some companies now offer simple Web-based training programs for students and others who have an interest in their industries, markets, products, or technologies. Training builds relationships, and it offers you the opportunity to sort the best candidates to the top, as you go.
- **Hot jobs:** Advertise the most interesting jobs you have to offer this population—and describe exciting projects and skill-building opportunities, too.
- **Special benefits:** Does your company offer a Student Loan Reduction Program, home-buying assistance, or other benefits aimed at young professionals? And of course, a link to the benefits and compensation information in your main career center.
- **Stories from the trenches:** As with all special populations, students and grads like to hear first-hand accounts from their peers. Interviews, videos, or brief articles are all effective.
- **Assessment and matching:** Offer a simple exam that maps aptitudes, skills, and behaviors to the positions most likely to fit the candidate. This is a great way to communicate both cultural and skills-based competencies to candidates—and is a powerful screening tool for you.
- **Design counts:** In a recent WetFeet survey, college job seekers indicated that two of the three most important elements in a successful corporate Web site are related to design. The overall texture and professionalism of the site, ease-of-navigation, and simplicity of the resume submission process all weighed in as principal success factors.

WetFeet also reports that 24 percent of visitors decide *not* to pursue a company, simply based on its Web site. So your college folio, like the rest of your site, is a critical sales tool. If it's warm, candid, well organized, and attractive, you're in great shape. If it's cold and kind of twisted up—well, it is sending a message that the rest of your organization may be, too.

By the way, your relationship with the college career center is important, too. Help them understand your company and opportunities, and they can become key allies in your recruiting efforts. Here are some ways you can help them:

- Set aside part of your own college folio for downloadable brochures and other tools they can use to help sell your organization.

- Make sure your campus recruiting events and career fairs are calendared and up to date.
- Pay attention to internships and other cooperative education programs. These are valuable relationship-builders for your company, for the school, and for students. Make sure these programs are highly visible and attractively detailed in your college folio—and keep your counterparts at the colleges abreast of your current opportunities.

Best in Class: Corporate Examples

- **Boston Consulting Group:** www.bcg.com/careers/ bcg_on_campus/AreaSelection/area1.asp
- **Microsoft:** www.microsoft.com/college
- **Koch Industries:** www.kochcareers.com/college_recruiting/default.asp
- **Procter & Gamble:** www.pg.com/jobs/jobs_us/college_recruiting/index.jhtml
- **Fidelity:** http://jobs.fidelity.com/college/index.html
- **Federated Department Stores:** www.retailology.com/9 college/home.asp

---

Driving Grads to Your Jobs

Just as job seekers at Monster.com are more likely to click on a job from a name brand company like Microsoft or Coca-Cola, Web surfers are most likely to search for *Fortune* 500 or other companies with strong brand and market recognition.

Many major corporations are getting well over 50 percent of their daily Web traffic from job seekers. If your company is already one of these, you should have a ready supply of students and grads in the mix. If not, start by building relationships with the right on-campus career centers. Once you've built a pipeline to the colleges you've selected (whether by major, affiliation, or location)—then move your traffic campaign to the Web.

Career-starters are all over the big three job boards—and there are a variety of niche boards designed specifically for different kinds of college students and recent grads. As with general candidates—select one or two of the big boards, and a handful of college niches, and give the package a try.

As for driving students to your own career center, start with inexpensive ads in the offline college weeklies—then try low-cost banners and buttons on sites heavily traveled by the college crowd.

As of late 2002, comScore Networks report that 7.7 percent of Web users are sitting at college-based PCs. Music sites are hot, as are movies, sports, and gaming—in fact, here's a representative handful of Web sites where college traffic is abnormally high:

- **www.livejournal.com:** Interactive journaling.
- **www.audiogalaxy.com:** Peer-to-peer music file-sharing system.
- **www.billboard.com:** Billboard magazine is a leading source of music information.
- **www.mircx.com:** Access to IRC and other downloads.
- **www.imesh.com:** Another peer-to-peer file-sharing site.

As expected, these sites are aimed right at the tech-loving audiophiles in those dorm rooms. Sites like these are off the beaten track, and may be great places for targeted ads.

Active Search for the Best Students

We've already discussed the numbers of student, faculty, and alumni home pages in college servers all over the world. You know how to search across the entire universe of .edu domains with a PowerSearch string, how to X-ray college servers to find people inside—and to Flip college sites to find those who've linked themselves from outside.

But these are techniques that recruiters normally use to find experienced candidates—not students. Why? Simply because college recruiting has always been a separate discipline, one that has traditionally relied on campus visits, career fairs, and open houses to build a candidate base.

But doesn't it make more sense to search for the very best students and actively recruit them, well ahead of campus career day? In every school there is a top percentile of students that you can now identify and make contact and build relationships with. The sooner, the better.

The Web can take you inside, to the departments where the best students are working right now; it can introduce you to their professors and help you make contact via e-mail. Jostling with hundreds of other companies on career day just doesn't seem like the best way to hire the best grads. Instead, use the Web to take you directly to them—and help you become their sponsor, mentor, or friend.

Bottom line, begin a relationship early, so that neither one of you have to stand in line at career day. You've already selected your candidates—and they've already selected you, long before.

Senior Executives on the Web

E xecutives aren't traditionally noted for their practical tech skills. In fact, it's a good bet that a fair percentage of *Fortune* 500 chieftains had no idea how to open or send an e-mail before about 1998. And, because of many more pressing commitments, few have had the time to develop mature Web skills, even today.

But ironically, it's much easier to find executives on the Web than any other kind of candidate, including technical workers who spend every waking hour surfing and chatting online. That's because executives live their professional lives outside the firewall—they are "public" candidates.

Finding Public Candidates

N ot many companies, even today, find their key officers in a resume bank or job board. Not that there aren't a number of niche boards focused on executives—and not because they're not active. It's just that a successful executive is the most passive of passive candidates—and when they are ready for a change, they're much more liable to work it through their own personal network than start surfing for executive jobs.

The other side of that equation is equally compelling. There are many reasons why a company would hesitate to broadcast the fact that they need a new VP of Sales by posting a job for it. So, how can the Internet help?

Well, in two ways. First, it will help the executive find *you*. Second, it gives you the tools to headhunt execs the same way a search firm would—by finding clues, and networking your way towards them. Let's look at each model.

Best in Class: Executive Job Boards
- **ExecuNet:** www.execunet.com
- **6FigureJobs:** www.6figurejobs.com
- **Leaders Online:** www.leadersonline.com1
- **FutureStep:** www.futurestep.com
- **Chief Monster:** http://chief.monster.com
- **Netshare.com:** www.netshare.com
- **BigFiveTalent:** www.bigfivetalent.com

Attracting Executives

Executives are seasoned business professionals, and they presumably have a good sense of where they want to land next. At least they understand where their talents might take them—and know the market basket of industries, companies, and functions they fit best.

If you are a prominent company in an executive's target industry, chances are they'll visit, just to check you out. If you're not a known contender, then keep polishing your brand and networking with your partners, board, industry, community, and customers until you are. Execs are looking for opportunities and opportunities have a buzz around them— whether a fast-growing market space, a new technology, or an interesting firm.

A company doesn't have to be in the *Fortune* 500 to have a great brand story—it just has to have a key differentiator and a vision. Great execs can do the rest, and they know it. But your opportunity must be in their line of vision, and they're not looking at banner ads or job postings. They're listening to the buzz. Create enough and you'll always have a management team in the pipeline.

Your Executive-Friendly Web Site

Execs interested in your company are liable to head for your Web site, stay quite awhile looking around, but never even peek into your career center. They won't search for a job, won't linger on the benefits page, or care much about your culture. They are looking at your *business*.

Here are the sorts of things they'll be interested in:

- A strong description of your company, products, markets, and key differentiators.
- Intellectual property, research, and white papers.
- Annual reports and financial performance indicators.
- Your current executive team.
- A way to privately contact your own execs, including your CEO.

There's no need to think in terms of an executive career folio. But it's important to provide clear links to attractive, robust materials that describe your company, its leadership, and its vision.

It's also important to provide a way to make confidential contact with your senior management. The best way to do this is to provide a secure e-mail form, instead of publishing executive contact information. It must be clear that the e-mail goes directly to the exec, not to HR.

Active Search for Executives

E xecutive search starts with name generation—you're looking for your candidate, or anyone who may know your candidate. As soon as you have names, it's a good idea to snap off your browser and pick up your headset. Search is a one-to-one relationship-building process that requires you to make contact, develop trust, and gather intelligence, as you get closer to the right candidate.

For decades, executive search firms relied first on their own Rolodex of contacts, then on expensive commercial databases and name generation firms to fill in the blanks. Today, you can find virtually any public candidate on the Web. Executives are in plain sight—and here are some places you'll find them:

- **"Meet Our Team":** Most companies publish senior management bios on their Web site.
- **Company press releases:** Senior managers and executives are often quoted in press releases linked to the Web site. Sort through—you'll find all kinds of senior managers and executives in PR about new products, alliances, financial performance, expansion, and more.
- **Press release databases:** PR Newswire, BusinessWire, and other press release databases store huge numbers of documents filled

with executive names. Most offer a simple on-site search capability. A good string is: *<title> AND <industry>, or <title> AND <company name>.*

- **SEC filings:** The Securities and Exchange Commission (SEC) require key officers to be listed in public filings. You can search this database through a variety of gateways, including Edgar Online at www.edgar-online.com.
- **News:** Business, financial, technical, and trade news sites all store archives of articles filled with executive names. Find the sites most appropriate to your search, head out, and see what's there.
- **Events:** Execs are often recruited to speak at major industry conferences and summits.

Executive search requires advanced networking and relationship sales skills—and the best executive search professionals just need someone to call. There's no better way to keep a search professional on the phone, and no faster way to a successful placement, than by providing a pipeline of great public candidates to network with, one right after another.

Diversity Recruiting on the Web

D iversity recruiting is not only a political and social imperative, it is a fundamental process for offering opportunities and gaining market knowledge and perspectives across our landscape of cultures. As we address a global marketplace of rapidly emerging economies, and an ever-more-diverse domestic economy, market-leading companies understand how important it is to recruit and hire an equally diverse workforce.

Finding and attracting the best diversity candidates are not easy tasks. There is tremendous competition for those who have clearly excelled—while it is often difficult to surface those with similar potential through a traditional search process. Because of these dynamics, it is absolutely critical that your company embrace diversity as a core principle, not as a quota-driven task. A body of the best leaders and business thinkers in the world originated in diverse communities—our job is to find them on the Web.

Diversity recruiting focuses on populations of minority race, color, religion, gender, national origin, physical or mental handicap, age, or sexual orientation. Let's take a fast look at a handful of target populations:

- **African American:** Now, the second largest ethnic group in the United States, with a total population of 36.4 million, African Americans are participating and making important contributions in every field.
- **Hispanic American:** With a population of 35.3 million people, Hispanic Americans now comprise 12.5 percent of the total U.S. population, having grown 58 percent over the last decade. Mexican Americans are the largest ethnic group among U.S. Latinos, followed by Puerto Ricans.
- **Asian American:** As the third largest minority group with 10.2 million people, Asian-American representation is growing rapidly, particularly in fields like engineering, science, and research. The largest Asian-American group is Chinese, followed by Filipinos and Asian Indians.
- **Gay and Lesbian:** Estimates of the number of gays and lesbians vary from 3 percent to 10 percent of the U.S. population. About 20 percent of gay/lesbian households have children, compared to about 40 percent of heterosexuals.
- **Women:** Women now account for 46.6 percent of the U.S. workforce and hold almost half of the managerial and leadership positions of *Fortune* 500 companies.
- **Differently-abled:** Many firms have found disabled workers to be among their best, most reliable employees. Finding and hiring qualified differently-abled candidates can be as simple as contacting local support agencies, whose mission is to help source, screen and place their clients.

Diversity Job Boards

Surveys show that most diversity candidates stay close to the traditional job board highway. First, they visit one or more of the big three job boards, then they migrate to the most visible niche boards aimed at their skills, industry, or function.

But there is an additional tier of niche boards, aimed specifically at the general diversity marketplace or specific market segments. Of course, these boards are self-profiling, which gives you the advantage of knowing the diversity characteristics of the population beforehand. Here are some top examples:

General Diversity

- Hire Diversity: www.hirediversity.com
- Diversity Link: www.diversitylink.com
- Best Diversity Employers: www.bestdiversityemployers.com
- Diversity Job Market: www.diversityjobmarket.com
- Imdiversity: www.imdiversity.com
- Diversityforhire.com: www.diversityforhire.com
- Diversity Job Network: www.diversityjobnetwork.com
- Diversity: www.Diversity.com
- Corporate Diversity Search: www.corpdiversitysearch.com
- Minority Executive Search: www.minorityexecsearch.com

African American

- Black Voices: www.blackvoices.com
- Black Greek Network: www.blackgreeknetwork.com/jobs/
- The Black World Careers: www.tbwcareers.com

Hispanic American

- iHispano: www.iHispano.com
- Latin American's Professional Network: www.latpro.com
- Job Centro: www.jobcentro.com

Asian American

- Asia Jobs: www.asia-links.com/asia-jobs/
- Asia Net: www.Asia-Net.com
- Bilingual Jobs: www.bilingual-jobs.com

Gay and Lesbian

- ProGayJobs: www.progayjobs.com
- GayWork: www.gaywork.com
- Gay and Lesbian Professionals: www.glpnyc.com

Women

- Society of Women Engineers: www.resume-link.com/society/swewebportal.htm
- Career Women: www.careerwomen.com
- Women in Technology International: www.witi4hire.com

Disability
- **Able to Work:** www.abletowork.org
- **Destiny Group Recruitment Network:** www.davjobs.com
- **DisabledPerson:** www.disABLEDperson.com

Your Diversity Career Folio

In order to attract the best candidates, it's important to clearly demonstrate a sincere commitment to your diversity workforce—and to reflect that commitment in your diversity folio. Here are some best practices to consider:

- **Diversity commitment:** Share your company's vision for a diverse workplace—what it means, the benefits to all, and your commitment to success.
- **Profiles:** Show the diversity of your company at work, through photographs and accompanying descriptions—and incorporate profiles of people from your various diversity communities.
- **Outstanding achievers:** Celebrate the diversity workers, managers, and executives who have made outstanding contributions to your company or industry.
- **Track record:** Demonstrate your commitment through milestones achieved in your diversity programs, including minority hiring and advancements.
- **Leadership and support:** Show your involvement and contribution to affinity groups and professional organizations, as well as your support of community activities and acts of corporate citizenship.

Here are some best-in-class examples of diversity career centers:

- **Dell:** http://dellapp.us.dell.com/careers/diversity/index.asp
- **IBM:** www-3.ibm.com/employment/us/diverse/index.shtml
- **Federal Express:** www.fedex.com/us/careers/diversity/
- **Lucent Technologies:** www.lucent.com/work/culture.html
- **McDonald's:** www.mcdonalds.com/corporate/diversity/
- **Marriott:** www.marriott.com/corporateinfo/culture/diversity.asp

Weaving Diversity into Your Workplace

Time and time again, diversity candidates report that they can sense which companies are pursuing a sincere commitment to building a diverse workforce—and which are not. This sincerity, and the commitment underlying it, are absolutely critical to hiring the best candidates. Here are some thoughts and best practices on how to weave diversity into the fabric of your organization:

- Emphasize competence-based credentials rather than past experience. Encourage the placement of interns and co-op students who are members of diverse groups. Establish formal relationships with schools that have great diversity in their student body. This measure will ensure that you are always cultivating talent for your future talent pool.
- Make sure that all levels of management have received diversity training, or they may not be in a position to give a fair evaluation during the hiring process. Cultivate organizational partnerships with groups catering to the needs and interests of people of color, women, and the disabled. When using an interview panel, make sure that it is culturally diverse to minimize potential bias.
- Be sure that the qualifications established for a given position are really ones needed to do the job, and are not ones based on historical assumptions. Understand your own beliefs and attitudes about the positions that you are filling and the populations that you are targeting. Be aware of how this could affect both the way you write job descriptions, as well as how you screen and interview.
- Incorporate non-traditional networking channels to produce a diverse applicant pool. A strong, diverse, informal network is a critical part of any successful diversity recruitment effort. Encourage seniors, people of color, women, and people with disabilities in your organization to assist in providing names of possible recruits.

Active Search for the Best Diversity Candidates

Professional organizations are often founded to assist people with specific skills, from specific communities, such as the Cuban American CPA Association, an organization of accounting professionals in Miami—or the Asian American Journalists Association. Because these groups are self-profiling, they are the best places to start an active search.

First, to find the organization—we'll build a string that searches for descriptive cultural and skill keywords, across all organizations (the .org domain): *domain:.org AND (hispanic OR latino) AND (engineer OR programmer OR software)*.

Pay dirt! In our first result set, we see a link to the Society of Hispanic Professional Engineers at www.shpe.org.

Let's X-ray the site. Remember our organization "people" words? We're looking for documents containing the words "members", "officers", "speakers", and others that imply people's names will be there, too. Here goes: *host:shpe.org AND (agenda OR speakers OR officers OR directors OR chapters OR minutes OR members)*.

Well, we get 5,500 results—and on the first page is a link entitled *SHPE, Inc.—NBOD Meeting Minutes*. Does NBOD stand for National Board of Directors? Let's click and see.

Why, yes it does—and we're now on a page that links to the minutes of each monthly board meeting held in 2001 and 2002. Each meeting page contains a list of the directors and guests. We'll harvest about 30 names in less than five minutes.

Now, let's do a resume PowerSearch to see how many engineers mention this site on their resumes out there. Our string is: *"society of hispanic professional engineers" AND (title:resume OR url:resume OR title:cv OR title:bio)*.

We get back 300 results—most of which look like resumes. Let's click one—and we find Armando Bertin, an engineer with a well-known software company in Sunnyvale, California.

Even better, Armando's resume gives us links to three powerful new places to search:

1. **The Stevens Technical University School Chapter of the SHPE:** Filled with more engineers just like Armando. Go to: http://attila. stevens-tech.edu/shpe.

2. **The Latin Business Association:** Which links us to more business professionals in the Hispanic community. Go to: www.lbausa.com.
3. **La Unidad Latina, Lambda Upsilon Lamba Fraternity:** A fraternal service organization aimed at uniting men in service to the Latino community. Go to: www.launidadlatina.org.

Okay, let's take stock. We found one organization, the SHPE on the first results page—and we've already harvested hundreds of new contacts. And if we go back and look through the rest of those results, then Flip the site, then PeerSearch our names, there's a pretty good likelihood we'll find hundreds more.

So, it's clear from this snippet of a simple search that there are diversity candidates all over the Web—yet diversity remains one of the most prohibitively competitive markets in recruitment today. How can that be?

Well, a good guess is that too many recruiters and employers are fighting each other over the obvious candidates at job boards, or sorting through a flood of resumes from job seekers—while the best, truly passive candidates work quietly away out on the Net.

Best in Class: Affirmative Action/EEO on the Web
- **American Association for Affirmative Action:** www.affirmative action.org
- **American Civil Liberties Union:** www.aclu.org
- **Center for Equal Opportunity:** www.ceousa.org
- **Civil Rights:** www.civilrights.org
- **Equal Employment Opportunity Commission:** www.eeoc.gov

Appendix

Directory of Web-Based Recruiting Tools

Part One. First Steps in the Search

Employee Referral

Team Rewards: www.careerrewards.com
ERM Referral-Trac: www.ereferralmarketing.com

Corporate Alumni

AIRS: www.airscareerportal.com
Corporate Alumni: www.corporatealumni.com
SelectMinds: www.selectminds.com
Aptium: www.aptium.com

Part Two. Your Recruiting Web Site

Web Design

Jacob Nielsen: www.useit.com
About Web Design: www.webdesign.about.com
Internet.com: www.internet.com
Web Monkey: www.hotwired.lycos.com/webmonkey

Salaries

Salary.com: www.salary.com
Salary Expert: www.salaryexpert.com
World at Work: www.worldatwork.org

Benefits

Benefit News: www.benefitnews.com
Benefits Alerts: www.benefitsalerts.com
Employee Benefit Research Institute: www.ebri.org

Stock Options

MyOptionValue.com: www.myoptionvalue.com
National Center for Employee Ownership: www.nceo.org
Foundation for Enterprise Development: http://fed.org

Incentives and Rewards

National Association of Employee Recognition: www.recognition.org
Corporate Rewards: www.corporaterewards.com
Bravanta: www.bravanta.com

Turnkey Job Boards

RecruitmentBox: www.recruitmentbox.com
SearchEase: www.jobboardsoftware.com
Jobbex: www.jobbex.com

Resume Indexing Tools

DtSearch: www.dtsearch.com
AltaVista Desktop Search: www.altavista.com

Register Your Site

Google: www.google.com
AltaVista: www.altavista.com
AlltheWeb: www.alltheweb.com
Inktomi: www.inktomi.com
Overture: www.overture.com
Teoma: www.teoma.com
Open Directory Project: www.dmoz.org

Submission Services

Submit It!: www.submitit.com
AutoSubmit: www.autosubmit.com

Promotion

Web Site Promotion Directory: www.websitepromotiondirectory.com
Self-Promotion.com: www.selfpromotion.com

Banner Networks

DoubleClick: www.doubeclick.com
24/7 Real Media: www.247realmedia.com
Link Exchange: www.bcentral.com

Build Forums

Web Crossing: www.webcrossing.com
Vbulletin: www.vbulletin.com

Build Mail Lists

Yahoo! Groups: www.groups.yahoo.com
Topica: www.topica.com
List Builder: www.bcentral.com
Messagemedia: www.messagemedia.com
L-Soft: www.lsoft.com

Monitor Your Web Traffic

WebTrends: www.webtrends.com
Accesswatch: www.accesswatch.com

Part Three. Advertise Your Job Openings

e-Recruitment Ad Agencies

Bernard Hodes Group: www.hodes.com
TMP Worldwide: www.tmpworldwide.com
Shaker Advertising: www.shaker.com
Davis Advertising: www.davisadv.com

Job Ad Distributors

IIRC: www.iirc.com
Hodes iQ Post: www.hodesiq.com
Recruit USA: www.recruitusa.com
WhotoChoose: www.whotochoose.com
GoJobs: www.gojobs.com

Top Consumer Portals

America Online: www.aol.com
Microsoft Network: www.msn.com
Yahoo!: www.yahoo.com
About.com: www.about.com
Lycos: www.lycos.com

Big Three Job Boards

Monster.com: www.monster.com
Yahoo! HotJobs: www.hotjobs.com
CareerBuilder: www.careerbuilder.com

Niche Job Boards

AIRS Job Board Directory: www.airsdirectory.com
Riley Guide: www.rileyguide.com
Career X-Roads: www.careerxroads.com
Weddle's Web Guides: www.weddles.com

Part Four. Active Search for Passive Candidates

Best Headhunting Search Engines

Google: www.google.com
AlltheWeb: www.alltheweb.com
AltaVista: www.altavista.com
Hotbot: www.hotbot.com

Meta-Search Engines

Mamma: www.mamma.com
Profusion: www.profusion.com
Dogpile: www.dogpile.com

People Search Tools

SearchStation: www.airssearchstation.com
Eliyon: www.eliyon.com
Infogist: www.infogist.com

Deep Web Directories

CompletePlanet: www.completeplanet.com
InvisibleWeb.com: www.invisibleweb.com
Direct Search: www.freepint.com/gary/direct.htm
Fossick: www.fossick.com

Targeted Deep Search

FTP Find: www.ftpfind.com
Adobe PDFs: www.searchpdf.adobe.com
Articles: www.findarticles.com
IT and Engineering: www.devsearcher.com

Internet Libraries

The Internet Public Library: www.ilp.org
Librarian's Index to the Internet: www.lii.org
Digital Librarian: www.digital-librarian.com
RefDesk.com: www.refdesk.com
LibrarySpot: www.libraryspot.com
Virtual Library: www.virtuallibrary.com

Domain Resources

Accredited Registrars: www.internic.net/regist.html
Verisign: www.netsole.com

Keywords

Webopedia: www.webopedia.com
Acronym Finder: www.acronymfinder.com
Dictionary.com: www.dictionary.com

Home Pages

GeoCities: www.geocities.com
Tripod: www.tripod.lycos.com
Angelfire: www.angelfire.lycos.com/
AOL Homepages: http://hometown.aol.com

MSN Homepages: www.msn.com
Earthlink Homepages: www.earthlink.net

Find Virtual Communities

AIRS Virtual Community Directory: www.airsdirectory.com/communities
Click Here Free: www.clickherefree.com
FreeWebspace.net: www.freewebspace.net

Find Internet Service Providers

AIRS ISP Directory: www.airsdirectory.com/isps
ISPworld: www.ispworld.com
The List: http://thelist.internet.com

Find Public Companies

Edgar Online: www.edgar-online.com
Corporate Information: www.corporateinformation.com
Hoover's: www.hoovers.com

Find Private Companies

AIRS Employer Directory: www.airsdirectory.com/directories/employers
Business.com: www.business.com
Yahoo! Yellow Pages: http://yp.yahoo.com

Find Start-ups

Net Profits: www.net-profits.org/vc.html
Vfinance.com: www.vfinance.com

Find Hot Companies

Fortune 500: www.fortune.com/lists/F500/index.html
Global 500: www.fortune.com/lists/G500/index.html
Fastest-Growing Companies: www.fortune.com/lists/fastest/index.html
Best Companies for Minorities: www.fortune.com/lists/diversity/
    index.html
Forbes 500: www.forbes.com/2002/03/27/forbes500.html
Forbes 500 Private Companies: www.forbes.com/private500/
Forbes 400 Best Big Companies: www.forbes.com/platinum400/
Forbes 200 Best Small Companies: www.forbes.com/200best
Inc. 500 Private Companies: www.inc.com/inc500/index.html

Find Colleges

AIRS College Directory: www.airsdirectory.com/directories/colleges
Peterson's: www.petersons.com
College Rankings: www.usnews.com/usnews/edu/college/rankings/
rankindex_brief.php

Find Students

Personal Pages Worldwide: www.utexas.edu/world/personal
Personal Pages Direct: www.student.com/feature/ppd

Find Fraternities and Sororities

We Alumni: www.wealumni.com
Greek Pages: www.greekpages.com
Greek Alumni: www.greekalumni.com

Find College Alumni

Alumni.net: www.alumni.net
Gradschools.com: www.gradschools.com

Find Organizations

American Society of Association Executives: www.asaenet.org
Associations Central: www.associationcentral.com
Google Directory: www.google.com Drill down to Society >
Organizations > Directory

Find Web Forums

Yahoo! Groups: http://groups.yahoo.com/
Topica: www.topica.com
Cool List: www.coollist.com
Delphi Forums: www.delphiforums.com

Find User Groups

American Personal Computer User Groups: http://cdb.apcug.org/
loclist.asp
Google Directory Listings: www.google.com Drill down to Computers >
Organizations > User Groups

Find PR

PR Newswire: www.prnewswire.com
Internet News Bureau: www.internetnewsbureau.com
PRWeb: www.prweb.com

Find Local News

Newspaper Directory: http://newslink.org/metnews.html
Business Journal Directory: www.bizjournals.com
NewsCentral: www.all-links.com/newscentral/

Find Business News

Business Wire: www.businesswire.com
News Index: www.newsindex.com
Reuters: www.reuters.com
Business in Depth: www.businessindepth.com

Find Tech News

CNET News.com: www.news.com.com
NewsHub Technology News: www.newshub.com/tech/
Tech Web: www.techweb.com

Find Financial News

Bloomberg: www.bloomberg.com
CNN's Financial Network: www.cnnfn.com
CBS MarketWatch: www.marketwatch.com

Find Trade Publications

Trade Publications Search Engine: www.newsdirectory.com

Find Events

American Library Association Events and Conferences: www.ala.org/
    events/
Business Wire's Tradeshownews.com: www.businesswire.com/
    tradeshow/
Trade Show News Network: www.tsnn.com

Industry Resources

Recruitment Research

WetFeet: www.wetfeet.com
iLogos: www.ilogos.com
Watson Wyatt: www.watsonwyatt.com
Talent Market Group: www.talentmarketgroup.com

Recruitment Analysts

Forrester Research: www.forrester.com
Robinson Humphrey: www.robinsonhumphrey.com
Sun Trust: www.suntrust.com
IDC: www.idc.com
Baird: www.rwbaird.com

Recruitment Forums

AIRS Forums: www.airsdirectory.com/forums
Electronic Recruitment Exchange: www.erexchange.com

HR Organizations

Society for Human Resource Management (SHRM): www.shrm.org
Employment Management Association (EMA): www.shrm.org/ema
The International Association for Human Resource Information
    Management (IHRM): www.ihrim.org

Recruiting Organizations

The Association of Executive Search Consultants (AESC): www.aesc.org
National Association of Personnel Services (NAPS): www.napsweb.org

Recruiting and HR Portals

AIRS Directory: www.airsdirectory.com
Electronic Recruiting Exchange: www.erexchange.com
HR.com: www.4.hr.com
About Human Resources: http://humanresources.about.com

Index

About the Author

Michael Foster is founder and CEO of AIRS, a global leader in recruitment training and a provider of recruitment software tools and media services. Mr. Foster also serves as a director of Hanover Capital Management, Inc. and is a director and advisor to a number of firms in the software and information industries. A native of the San Francisco Bay Area, Mr. Foster now lives with his family in the Connecticut River Valley of Vermont.

About AIRS

AIRS has trained over 30,000 search firms and market-leading corporations, including a majority of the *Fortune* 500, to find people on the Web. In the process, AIRS techniques like FlipSearch, X-ray, and PeelBack have entered the common recruiting vernacular. AIRS Certified Internet Recruiter (CIR) designation is recognized worldwide, and has become a hiring prerequisite for recruiters in many organizations.

Today, AIRS provides human capital solutions for recruitment, career development, and transition, via self-service corporate portals filled with information and e-learning options. AIRS award-winning Search-Station ASP is licensed to over 5,000 recruitment desktops and is the fastest-selling candidate-hunting application in the market today. AIRS Media Services operates airsdirectory.com, the largest recruitment portal on the Web, and AIRS News, which provides breaking industry coverage and information to over 50,000 recruiters daily.

Praise for AIRS

FLIPPING. PEELING. X-RAYING. Sounds like what chefs and radiologists do, right? These are also some of the ingenious tricks executive headhunters use in the age of digital resumes and electronic job searches. ... AIRS ... is one of a few firms at the forefront of the burgeoning specialty of Internet recruitment training. —*The Wall Street Journal*

Among the best-known consulting firms in that new industry is ... AIRS ..., whose seminars have attracted thousands of professional third-party recruiters and in-house human resources managers. —*Inc. Magazine*